VINTA
KATHMANDU

Ranjit Rae is a former Indian ambassador to Nepal. He also headed the Northern Division in the Ministry of External Affairs, dealing with India's Himalayan neighbours, Nepal and Bhutan, from 2002 to 2006. Since retirement, Rae has been involved in travelling, trekking and trying to make sense of the developments in Nepal.

This is his first book.

PRAISE FOR THE BOOK

'*Kathmandu Dilemma* reflects Ranjit Rae's deep and extended engagement in India's relations with Nepal, and is unmatched in its meticulous and careful research into the wellsprings of a truly unique relationship between two neighbouring states. The book provides the geopolitical context in which the relationship has been unfolding, including the rising footprint of China throughout India's periphery. The author has explored the many assets India enjoys in consolidating and expanding what is indisputably one of India's most important and significant relationships. There are valuable policy prescriptions which are clearly spelt out, reflecting Ranjit Rae's profound understanding of what drives Nepal's attitudes towards India, both the elements of anxiety as well as affinity. This book will remain an indispensable reference on Nepal and India–Nepal relations for years to come'—Shyam Saran, former foreign secretary, and former chairman, National Security Advisory Board

'Ambassador Ranjit Rae's portrayal of India–Nepal relations from the Indian perspective is meticulous, nuanced and insightful. It presents a sharp scrutiny of contemporary and controversial issues in this complex and unique relationship. Will be found valuable not only by scholars and analysts but also by teachers, leaders and policymakers'—S.D. Muni, professor emeritus, School of International Studies, Jawaharlal Nehru University, and former ambassador and special envoy, Government of India

'In *Kathmandu Dilemma*, Ranjit Rae breaks down the paradox of India's very intimate yet troubled relationship with Nepal. Combining a genuine affection for Nepal and an extensive diplomatic experience in dealing with its government and people, Rae makes sense of Kathmandu's deep discomfort with the overpowering Indian embrace and outlines steps that could help Delhi reconstruct the relationship based on sovereign equality and mutual benefit'—C. Raja Mohan, director, Institute of South Asian Studies, National University of Singapore

'A rare nuanced take that provides a template for Delhi to win back friends in the country, and for Kathmandu to get over its insecurities about Indian ambitions'—Wire

'An insider's view'—*The Hindu BusinessLine*

'Forthright'—*Tribune*

'Rae gives an insider's view of the developments [in India–Nepal ties], and [explains] how some misunderstandings blew up beyond proportion'—*Week*

KATHMANDU DILEMMA
RESETTING INDIA-NEPAL TIES

RANJIT RAE

VINTAGE
An imprint of Penguin Random House

VINTAGE

USA | Canada | UK | Ireland | Australia
New Zealand | India | South Africa | China

Vintage is part of the Penguin Random House group of companies
whose addresses can be found at global.penguinrandomhouse.com

Published by Penguin Random House India Pvt. Ltd
4th Floor, Capital Tower 1, MG Road,
Gurugram 122 002, Haryana, India

First published in Vintage by Penguin Random House India 2021

Copyright © Ranjit Rae 2021

ISBN 9780143460152

Typeset in Adobe Caslon Pro by Manipal Technologies Limited, Manipal

www.penguin.co.in

For Devika, Devayani, Ananya and John

Contents

Preface

This is not an academic or scholarly work. Rather, it is based on the experience and assessment of someone who is deeply committed to the India–Nepal friendship and has had a ringside view of some of the major developments in Nepal's contemporary history—events such as the peace process that brought the Maoist insurgency to an end, and those leading up to the promulgation of the new Constitution and what followed thereafter. I have looked at the civilizational underpinnings of the relationship, the economic dimension and issues, such as the boundary and the Friendship Treaty of 1950, that bedevil it.

The great earthquake of 2015 was a black-swan event, and it demonstrated the capability of India to be a first responder in the neighbourhood in times of crisis. Of course, the COVID-19 pandemic has somewhat dented this image. The evolving geopolitics and its impact on Nepal, particularly in terms of the role of China, are examined in this book. I am circumspect on security and intelligence cooperation, mainly because this is a sensitive matter outside the public domain, though I do refer to the excellent military-to-military engagement and the role of the Gorkhas. I conclude with some thoughts on a long-term strategy for Nepal.

Needless to say, I view developments from an Indian perspective. There are always many ways of looking at and understanding events; at a fundamental level, this is a subjective matter. Some of my Nepalese friends, in their published works, have viewed these developments through a very different prism. This book does not claim to be an authoritative commentary on a relationship that is deep, intense and wide-ranging, a relationship nonpareil. It is one view on some contemporary issues.

Unfortunately, I have never kept a diary. This book is therefore largely based on recollections, and luckily my memory did not fail me. Many former colleagues have helped me in this venture. Vinay Kumar, in almost every conversation, egged me on to write about my experiences in Nepal. Abhay Thakur, Munu Mahawar and L. Savithri jogged my memory to recollect events from days gone by. Piyush Srivastava was a pillar of strength during the earthquake of 2015, as was Colonel (now Brigadier) M.R.S. Mann. Anju Ranjan held the fort in Birganj and reminded me of many facets of the cross-border relationship. The compendium of documents on India–Nepal and Nepal–China relations, painstakingly collated by Avtar Singh Bhasin, is a critical source for scholars and others interested in Nepal. My gratitude to him.

Shyam Saran is a mentor, friend and now a trekking buddy, and I have always turned to him for advice. I have benefited from conversations with former ambassadors Shiv Shankar Mukherjee and Rakesh Sood. V.P. Haran, my batchmate, Amitabh (Tony) Mathur and Madan Pyasi, partners during the difficult days of the Maoist insurgency, have helped put things in perspective. Constantino Xavier and Sandeep Bharadwaj have contributed to a better understanding of complex subjects on the development partnership between the two countries through their writings.

I am particularly grateful to Nihar Nayak for his help on the chapter on the boundary dispute and the 1950 Treaty of Friendship. My gratitude, too, to General Sir Sam Cowan, for his magnificent studies on all matters Nepalese and especially for his historical perspective on the India–Nepal boundary; and to Nrip Singh Napalchyal, for introducing me to the society and culture of the Rung/Bhotia people of Uttarakhand. Discussions with Vijay Gokhale on the China–Nepal relationship have been very useful. Rahul Barua and Nalini Gyawali, through their innumerable links in Nepal, have kept me up to date. I wish to thank my friends Nikhil Seth, Hamid Ali Rao, Sharat Misra, Deepa Wadhwa and Amit Pande for their encouragement. Prashant Jha has been a sounding board on every subject related to Nepal and many more. My thanks to Shubhajit Roy, who thought that I was the most suitable person to write on Nepal.

In Nepal, I owe a debt of gratitude to many friends. To Lok Raj Baral, Krishna Hatchetu and Vijay Kant Karna, for sharing with me their deep knowledge about their country; to Kamal Dev Bhattarai, Vijay Pandey and Anil Giri, for their advice and interesting conversations. Amresh Kumar Singh, with his encyclopedic memory, has provided a lot of information and food for thought. Thanks to Dipendra Jha for his help, and to Ambika Prasad Joshi, for assisting me in identifying several references from the public domain, especially those in Nepali, a language that I can broadly understand and read but, alas, do not speak. I have benefited from interactions with a large number of politicians in Nepal, too many to name, over the years. Many have become personal friends.

I'd like to thank Devayani Chandra, for her help in preparing the graphic of the new map of Nepal in Chapter 5. Indira Vaish and Nisha Agrawal read through the draft manuscript and provided valuable comments.

I would like to thank Gaurav Gupta for the cover design. The clouds depict the state of the relationship; the chortens and the mountain pass, transitions; and lurking behind the Himalayas is the big northern neighbour.

My gratitude to Elizabeth Kuruvilla of Penguin Random House, editor par excellence, who responded to all my queries, concerns and anxieties with patient encouragement. I have known her, virtually, since June 2020, when I received a cold call requesting me to do a book on Nepal. I told her that I was daunted by what appeared to me an insurmountable task. In the Indian Foreign Service, we are trained to send dispatches from missions abroad and write notes on file; nevertheless, the thought of putting down 60,000 words into a book, coherently, seemed impossible at the time. Elizabeth was very persuasive. She said that I was well suited to write the book; that the task was not as difficult as it seemed. I simply needed to prepare a concept, divide the book into chapters and think of each chapter as a long essay of 7000–8000 words. Things would fall in place. She also told me that the book could be part memoir. This made it easier, and things eventually did fall in place.

I am grateful to my family, to Ritu and Amit and Vivek for being there.

The book's faults, and there may be several, dear reader, are my sole responsibility, and I beg forgiveness in advance.

1

Why Don't They Like Us? Identity, Nationalism and Mutual Perceptions

It was a few weeks after the devastating earthquake hit Nepal in April 2015. Measuring 7.8 on the Richter scale, this was the most severe shock that Nepal had experienced since the great earthquake of 1934. India responded swiftly, and our first military aircraft carrying rescue and relief material and personnel landed in Kathmandu within six hours of the quake. Over the next few weeks, scores of Indian soldiers and military engineers, members of the National Disaster Response Force, medical doctors, aircraft and helicopter pilots toiled in difficult conditions in far-flung inhospitable mountain terrain, providing help and succour to those in need. The people of India opened their hearts and their wallets as thousands of trucks carrying food, water and medicines crossed the India–Nepal border and snaked up the mountain roads to the fourteen most affected districts. Overall, India's immediate rescue and relief assistance was valued at Rs 450 crore (US$65 million), the largest provided by any country. In addition, a sum of US$1 billion was pledged for reconstruction efforts.[1]

Despite this massive support the Nepalese remained suspicious of India's intentions. Kathmandu was rife with rumours fanned both by the regular and social media: The Indian Army was helping stranded Indians rather than the Nepalese;[2] the Indians had taken over the Tribhuvan International Airport; India was supplying sub-standard relief material not fit for human consumption.[3] There was a reluctance on the part of the Nepalese authorities to publicly acknowledge India's contribution. At the pledging conference in Geneva, the Nepalese Permanent Representative, in his intervention, did not refer to India's assistance. Whenever any reference was made, it was always clubbed with the assistance by China, even though the two were not comparable in terms of magnitude of support or the swiftness with which the help was rendered. Social media had gone viral with the hashtag #IndianMediaGoBack and #BackOffIndianMedia.

On one of my trips to Delhi after the earthquake, I met Prime Minister Narendra Modi at his Lok Kalyan Marg residence. The first question that he asked me was: 'Why don't they like us?' We have done so much for Nepal and this is how they respond, or words to that effect. This chapter is an attempt to respond to the question.

I start with some personal recollections that will provide a flavour of the nature and complexity of the India-Nepal relationship.

As was my wont, I used to meet the top Nepali leaders from all political parties informally on a regular basis. I was meeting Madhav Kumar Nepal, a senior leader of the Communist Party of Nepal (Unified Marxist-Leninist), or CPN (UML), at his modest home in Koteshwor early in my tenure as an ambassador. We were feasting on the delicious Malda mangoes, similar in taste to the *langra* variety from Banaras, and speaking to each other in Hindi. Madhav Nepal looked at me and asked why India talks about *bhai bhai ka rishta* (fraternal relations) between the two countries. In such a relationship, there is always an elder brother and a younger one. Nepal did not want to be the younger brother. It only wanted to be friends with India, equal partner, no more, no less. Perhaps he had in mind remarks made by the late Sushma Swaraj, the then external affairs minister, who was fond of saying that India was not a Big Brother, India was an elder brother that looked after its younger kin! She was genuine in her affection for Nepal, but the Nepalese found this patronizing.

A football match was taking place at the Dasharath Stadium in Kathmandu. Nepalese are crazy about football, though cricket too is growing in popularity among the youth. This was a face-off between India and Afghanistan in September 2013. And India was at the receiving end of the crowd with catcalls and boos and shouts of *Dhoti*, a term which the Indian footballers would have been perplexed about. *Dhoti*, the dress of the Indian plains for men, is a generic term of abuse for the Madhesi community from the Terai, who are culturally and ethnically different from the Pahadis. The Madhesis are more akin to the people of UP and Bihar. The default position in the valley if there is any contest between India and a third country team, even if it is Pakistan, is to support that team!

Early in my tenure, I was travelling in the Flag Car to Hanuman Dhoka in the heart of Kathmandu. Somewhere near New Road, we saw a gathering of youth wearing tee-shirts emblazoned with the slogan, 'Buddha was born in Nepal'. This is a historical fact; Buddha was born in Lumbini, which is now in Nepal. My personal security officer became nervous as we neared the demonstration. He said that we should immediately turn back, otherwise the situation could turn nasty. We returned. I kept wondering why there was a need for Nepal to reiterate through a public demonstration the fact that Buddha was born in Nepal. Why has this become a touchy subject in Nepal? If any Indian were to say that India is the land of the Buddha or that Buddha was born in India, there are protests in Nepal.

An innocent comment by External Affairs Minister S. Jaishankar at a Confederation of Indian Industry-sponsored webinar in August 2020 that the Buddha was one of the two greatest Indians ever, led to a storm of protests in Nepal. Buddha was not Indian, the Nepalese asserted. Intellectuals, former bureaucrats, and even a former PM said that this was a mischievous remark. The Ministry of Foreign Affairs of Nepal released an official statement:[4] 'It is a well-established and undeniable fact . . . that Gautam Buddha was born in Lumbini, Nepal.' It added that Lumbini was also the fountain of Buddhism, whatever this means. Reference was made to PM Modi's speech to the Nepalese Constituent Assembly in 2014, where he affirmed that the apostle of peace in the world, the Buddha, was born in Nepal. The Ministry of External Affairs of India calmed the situation by saying that there was no doubt that Gautam Buddha was born in Nepal and that the EAM was referring to the shared Buddhist heritage of both India and Nepal. Nepal deeply cherishes the fact that the Buddha was born in Nepal; this is linked to its national identity. It vigorously opposes what it sees as attempts by India to expropriate this heritage.

Another recent incident clearly reflects Nepal's desire to assert its own cultural identity as distinct from India. Prime Minister K.P. Sharma Oli commented last year on the birth anniversary of Bhanubhakta,[5] the great Nepalese poet who translated the Ramayana into Nepali, that India had twisted historical and cultural facts to create a fake Ayodhya in India, and that the real Ayodhya was near Birganj in Nepal. 'We did not give Sita who was born in Janakpur to an Indian prince but Sita was married to Ram of Ayodhya, not the one in India.'[6] His logic was that a prince from a place so far away as Ayodhya in India, could not have come to Janakpur as there were no means of communication and transport in those days. Though he was criticized for this comment by several leaders in Nepal, including from within his party, Oli's statement represents an extreme nationalistic view wherein he is denying the ancient cultural and historical links that tie Nepal with India. In a similar vein, on the International Day of Yoga,

21 June 2021, Oli asserted that yoga originated in Nepal and not in India[7]. Incidentally, Oli's ancestors, Kumai Brahmins, would in all likelihood have migrated from the Kali Kumaon region of Uttarakhand!

What I have narrated are some anecdotes from the Kathmandu valley that reflect the mindset of the valley, home to the ruling elite of Nepal. The Valley dominates the politics of Nepal. Indeed, in the old days, it was the valley that was known as Nepal. This mindset is more prevalent in the leftist and communist forces, less so among the democratic forces such as the Nepali Congress, and not at all among the Terai-based parties. But this sentiment is growing among the Nepali youth and is something that India needs to be sensitive to.

Ours is perhaps the most intimate and hence complex relationship that exists between any two neighbouring countries. Everything that binds us—religion, culture, traditions, language, ties of kinship—also creates tension. Even the famous religious *sankalp* or pledge that every Hindu takes before a *puja*, refers to Nepal as being part of *Bharatkhand*! If everything in Nepal is similar to that in India, then what is it that makes Nepal a unique nation-state? Nepalese sometimes resent cultural commonalities, especially when referred to by Indians; harping on these can become counterproductive.

What is Nepal's own sense of its identity? How is it different from India? Given the asymmetry in size and in population, the fact that Nepal is surrounded on three sides by India, engenders a siege mentality and a desire to break away. The Nepalese also dislike and resent their utter dependence on India. Therefore, they try and fight geography! Two unique markers that Nepal has claimed for its own national identity are being the birthplace of the Buddha and home to the highest peak in the world, Mount Everest. Unfortunately for Nepal, both these markers are shared, the former in terms of the common Buddhist heritage with India, and the latter with China.

The treatment meted out to the Hindi language also goes to the heart of Nepali identity. Even though Indian soap operas and serials as well as movies are very popular in Nepal, and most Nepalese understand Hindi and speak it, and it is the lingua franca of the Nepalese Terai, the language has no official status in Nepal.[8] Till recently, it could not be spoken in the Nepalese Parliament despite the fact that almost all Nepali leaders cutting across the political divide are fluent in Hindi. Indeed, they are far more comfortable conversing with Indian politicians and diplomats in Hindi rather than English. Three Nepalese prime ministers and scores of other politicians, judges and senior bureaucrats have studied at Banaras Hindu University and are fluent in the language, but would be loath to speak it in public. A former Vice President of Nepal, Parmanand Jha, a Madhesi from the Terai, decided to take his oath of office in July 2008 in Hindi. This was later declared to be void by the Nepalese Supreme Court. Despite the court decision, Jha refused to take the oath in Nepali. It is only after the interim Constitution was amended to allow for the oath to be taken in the mother tongue that Jha was again sworn in as Vice President in February 2010. This time he took his oath in Maithili, his mother tongue, and Nepali.

Sometimes small issues assume crisis proportions. A false rumour was spread in Nepal in 2001 that actor Hrithik Roshan had issued a statement saying that he hated Nepalis. This led to days of rioting in Kathmandu with four people killed in street violence directed against the Madhesi community. Roshan's films were banned and there was fear that if the situation was not brought under control, the Indian community could be targeted. Ultimately, a video was circulated wherein the actor denied ever having made the statement. In 1998, actor Madhuri Dixit, on arriving in Nepal, reportedly made a statement that Nepal was once a part of India, provoking huge protests. Indian films and television shows suggesting that the Buddha was born in India have also resulted in demonstrations in Nepal.

Of course, the Nepalese are a proud people and particularly so of their martial prowess and military valour. Nepalese leaders, including former prime minister Oli, often say that they had fought long and hard battles and shed blood to unify the country. Prithvi Narayan Shah, the founder of the Shah dynasty that ended after over 200 years with King Gyanendra, militarily subdued the rulers of the territories surrounding Gorkha, where he belonged. This included the Malla kingdoms of the Kathmandu Valley, which were defended by soldiers from Tirhut in the Terai. The Shah Empire extended to Kangra, then a small kingdom in Punjab in the west, included Garhwal and Kumaon and stretched all the way to Sikkim and Darjeeling in the east. This 'Greater Nepal' existed for some 25 years before it clashed with the British East India Company in the famous Anglo–Nepalese wars of 1814 and 1815 and lost its possessions to the west of the Mahakali River and east of the Mechi River. At one time, Nepal had also fought wars with Tibet. The descendants of the Shahs and the Ranas that subsequently ruled Nepal under a treaty relationship with the British, saw themselves as conquerors and victors and hence the natural ruling elite of Nepal. Even the British were greatly impressed with the courage and bravery of the Gorkha soldiers during the Anglo-Nepal wars. They used Nepalese forces to suppress the First War of Indian Independence in 1857 and to this day, the Nepalese Rana refer to the Loot of Lucknow that added significantly to their coffers. Rana forces under Jung Bahadur Kunwar (subsequently Rana) were given several days to pillage this rich city.

Even as Nepal is justifiably proud of the fact that it has never been colonized unlike India, formal public statements of its contemporary leaders are always full of terms such as national sovereignty, national pride and glory, respect, honour, equality, we will never bend, etc.—statements that are normally not heard in old established nations that have existed for over 200 years as independent entities. Indeed, in a famous speech to the

Constituent Assembly of Nepal in August 2014, Prime Minister
Narendra Modi affirmed India's respect for Nepal's sovereignty
to thunderous applause and thumping of desks from the leaders
and members present. Why does Nepal constantly talk about
preserving and protecting its sovereignty? Why does it need
an affirmation of its sovereignty from its neighbours? In other
cases, a foreign leader saying that he respected another country's
sovereignty would be seen as gratuitous. But not in Nepal. There is
somehow a certain anxiety of someone casting an evil eye on Nepal
and for it to be forever alert. The *divyaupadesh* (Divine Counsel) of
Prithvi Narayan Shah referred to Nepal as a yam/gourd between
two hard rocks! Unsaid, but clearly in the mind, the yam could be
squished! In the immediate years after India's independence and
the victory of the Communist Party in China in 1949, it was the
fear of China's machinations in Tibet that motivated the Rana
oligarchy to enter into a treaty relationship with independent
India. Today, with the ascendance of the communists in Nepal,
India is the rock to be worried about!

Those who have taken one of the Indian air carriers from
Kathmandu would have wondered at the origin of the second
security check that takes place before one ascends the aircraft. Just
before you board the plane, you climb two steps onto a movable
trolley where your hand baggage is checked and you are frisked
once again. Only then do you get into the aircraft. Following the
hijack of IC 814 from Kathmandu, which eventually headed to
Kandahar in 1999, India was keen to strengthen aircraft security
at Kathmandu airport. We wanted our security personnel to do
the frisking and security check of passengers. The Nepalese were
outraged. How could they permit Indian security personnel on
sovereign Nepalese territory? It is then that a compromise was
worked out. Indian security personnel would not stand on sacred
Nepalese soil, but a foot above it and do their job! Such are the
sensitivities that sometimes have to be taken into account in
dealing with each other!

Nationalism in Nepal is defined largely in terms of the *pahadi* or hill sentiment. The narrative is that the country was militarily unified by the Shah Kings and nurtured and protected by the hill Brahmins and Chhetris, the ruling elite of Nepal. The latter still dominate the army and security forces whereas the former dominate politics and administration. Even the *Muluki Ain* or national code established a hierarchical pecking order with the Brahmins and Chhetris at the top. Indeed, in days gone by, no Brahmin could be given a death sentence; at most he could be exiled. The Pahadi elite are the rulers, the others are the ruled! Other communities, including the Madhesis, which form a third of the population with the Janjatis forming another third, are expected to accept this. A high official close to an ambitious senior Madhesi leader of the Nepali Congress, once told me that he advised the latter, as he tried to advance his political career, never to forget the fact that Nepal is a Pahadi country.

Apart from geography and cultural factors, modern Nepalese nationalism is very much a product of the mindset of the monarchy and the historical experience of Nepal, particularly under King Mahendra. Unlike his father before him, who was a prisoner of the Rana autocracy and who collaborated with the political parties and India to usher in a phase of multiparty democracy, short lived and flawed as it was, King Mahendra was no democrat. And neither did he have any hesitation in usurping all power and ruling as no king had done since the advent of the Ranas. Mahendra became the first executive monarch in the last century. He abolished multiparty democracy in 1960 and brought in a new Constitution that ushered in a party-less Panchayat system, a kind of guided democracy similar to the one brought in by Marshal Ayub Khan in Pakistan. Nehru responded by criticizing this action, calling it 'a complete reversal of democracy and the democratic process'. He went on to say that he viewed such a development with 'considerable regret', and also referred to the incident as a 'coup'.[9]

Political parties, particularly the Nepali Congress led by its visionary leader B.P. Koirala (BPK), were extremely critical of the move. One faction led by Subarna Shumsher Rana began a brief military struggle; another led by BPK went into exile in India. The Nepali Congress, established in Banaras in 1947, had a deep and abiding link with India. Its founding leaders had participated in the Indian freedom struggle and cut their democratic teeth in India. Deeply influenced by the winds of political change in India, they were keen to bring about a similar transformation in Nepal. They were friendly with Nehru as well as politicians of the Socialist wing of the Indian National Congress, such as Jai Prakash Narayan and Ram Manohar Lohia. The abolition of multiparty democracy by King Mahendra was a bitter blow to the Nepali Congress. It was natural for the Government of India and particularly Pandit Nehru to side with the democratic forces and criticize the autocratic monarch for this move.

King Mahendra responded to India's criticism in various ways. First, he sought to consolidate his position in Nepal by rallying the traditional elite around the slogan of hill nationalism. Nepal's mantra would henceforth be, *Euta Bhasha, euta Bhesh, euta Raja, euta Desh*. One language, one dress, one king, one country. He sought to thrust homogeneity upon what was a very diverse society of different ethnic groups, religions, customs and traditions and language. In a country equally divided among the hill Bahun-Chhetri elite, the Madhesis of the Terai and the Janjatis, Mahendra tried to impose the upper caste hill culture on all, leading to resentment and discrimination. Nepal is still grappling with the ramifications of this policy. This othering of the Madhesis that did not speak Nepali as a mother tongue, did not wear the *daura saruwal* and *Dhaka topi* was further exacerbated with the promotion of a policy encouraging down migration from the hills. Following the elimination of malaria in the Terai in the 1950s, a huge swathe of Chure forest in the Himalayan foothills in the Terai was cleared to construct the East West Highway running from the Mechi to the Mahakali rivers. New towns were built all along the highway. These were settled by people that migrated from the inhospitable and difficult mountain areas, thereby altering the demographics of the Terai. As a result, today, the traditional district headquarters connected by the Hulaki (Postal) Raj Marg close to the Indian border are populated by Madhesis, whereas in the northern Terai, along the East West Highway, the population is largely Pahadi.

Second, the monarchy projected those Nepalese political parties protesting the king's takeover as *Bharatiya dalal* or Indian agents. In order to neutralize their domestic support in Nepal, the Palace began encouraging leftist and communist forces of various hues. The general secretary of the Communist Party, Keshar Jung Raymajhi, joined the Panchayat system. Mahendra portrayed India's criticism, not as against the action by the king against democracy, but as anti-Nepal, as a threat by India to Nepal and tried to encourage and rally the communist parties on this basis. This is the genesis of the anti-India nationalism that we see in Nepal to this day. The royalists and the communists, even though they had opposing views on various issues, came together on the plank of anti-Indian nationalism, to save Nepal from India! The schooling of left party cadres to this day includes a heavy dose of *Bharatiya Vistarwad* or Indian expansionism, which has now entered their DNA.

A third step taken by the king was to seek the support of forces in opposition to the government in India. In particular, Mahendra tried to tap into the Hindu sentiment. Tulsi Giri, the first prime minister under the Panchayat system, a brilliant politician who had earlier been a private secretary to B.P. Koirala as well as a member of the Rashtriya Swayamsevak Sangh or RSS, told me during my stint in Nepal that it was his idea to make Nepal a Hindu state. It is during this time that a stronger relationship developed between Hindu organizations in India and the Palace and the royalists. Mahendra's successor, Birendra, was declared to be a *Vishwa Hindu Samrat*, Emperor of all Hindus worldwide, by

the Vishwa Hindu Mahasangh, an affiliate of the Vishwa Hindu
Parishad, whose then leader Ashok Singhal was also an honoured
visitor of the king in Nepal. Most people in India are unaware that
Nepal became a Hindu state only under the Constitution of 1962
given by Mahendra to Nepal! And as an *avatar* of Vishnu, the
king became the divine ruler. This is how the monarchy became
deeply intertwined with the concept of Nepal as a Hindu Rashtra.
You could not have one without the other! More on this when
we discuss the debates around the new republican Constitution
of 2015.

And finally, King Mahendra played what is known as Nepal's
China card.[10] Given the problems he was facing with India, King
Mahendra built bridges with China. Not only did he develop
the Kathmandu–Kodari road that linked the valley to Tibet—
the friendship highway—but he also settled the Nepal-China
boundary in 1961. Maoist literature became freely available in the
bookstores of Kathmandu. In 1969, under Prime Minister Kirti
Nidhi Bista, known to be close to China, Nepal also asked India
to withdraw its troops from all seventeen forward checkposts
along the Nepal-Tibet border that had been established at Sardar
Patel's instance in 1951. China became the third factor in the
bilateral relationship that Nepal has since used to 'balance' India's
overarching presence.

Another factor that created fear in the minds of the Nepalese
vis-à-vis India was the merger of Sikkim into India by Indira
Gandhi,[11] which some viewed as an annexation. In Nepal,
these moves were greeted with fear about India and led to the
proposal for Nepal as a Zone of Peace, equidistant between India
and China. The policy garnered international support, but was
eventually allowed to fade away in view of India's opposition and
changing circumstances in Nepal that ultimately dismantled the
Panchayat system. Most recently, similar fears were raised during
the Constitutional debates in 2015 following the annexation of
the Crimea by Russia. Unstated and perhaps only whispered in

domestic political circles, there remains a fear in the minds of some Nepalese leaders about the intentions of India in the Terai, given what are perceived to be the dual loyalties of the Madhesi population. This perception perhaps may even go back to the days of the Anglo–Nepal Wars of 1814 and 1815. Indeed, Point 7 of the Memorandum of Approval for the Raja of Nipal relating to the Sugauli Treaty of 8 December 1816 states that 'the Rajah of Nipal agrees to refrain from prosecuting any inhabitants of the Terai, after its revertance to his rule, on account of having favored the cause of the British Govt during the war . . .'

There is a similar uneasy relationship with the Nepalese Gorkhas that serve in the Indian Army and after retirement, return to their motherland and survive on generous Indian pensions. These pensioners have the same rights as their brethren in India. In Nepal, they form a part of the well-to-do set in towns and villages where they have settled. Driving through Pokhara, you can see rows of houses belonging to the ex-servicemen—the fanciest bungalows belong to retirees from the British Army and the less posh ones, that are nevertheless far more impressive than the other houses, belong to Indian Army pensioners. There are over 1,25,000[12] such pensioners living in Nepal. Having retired from the Indian army after approximately twenty years of service, they are still in the prime of their lives (they are recruited at ages nineteen or twenty) and can contribute significantly to the development of their home country. Just prior to the elections following the adoption of the Constitution, I had suggested to Khil Raj Regmi, the chairman of the Interim Council of Ministers, that instead of recruiting fresh people and then training them for election security duty, the trained and disciplined pensioners from the Indian Army could be used. He listened to me but did not reply. In the event, he did not act on my suggestion. The main reason, I suspect, is that the Nepalese feel that the pensioners have divided loyalties and cannot be used for sensitive purposes such as election duty.

My own sense is that the strong anti-India nationalist sentiment is also due to the historical fact of India having been associated with most of the political changes in Nepal. Whether it was the anti-Rana agitation when India supported King Tribhuvan and a cohabitation agreement between the Ranas and political parties embedded in the Delhi Pact of 1950 or the support to the democratic forces in the years leading up to the Jan Andolan of 1989–90 that led to the dismantling of the Panchayat regime, India has sided with popular aspirations for political change and greater democracy in Nepal. In this process, India has riled the ruling elites of the day, namely the Ranas and the royalists, who have projected India's policy stance as a threat to the sovereignty and integrity of Nepal. More recently, India played a facilitating role in the resolution of the Maoist insurgency that lasted for ten long years and culminated, largely due to the missteps of the king, in the transformation of Nepal from a monarchy to a Republic! Here again, the ruling establishment in Nepal constantly fed the notion that India was in cahoots with the Maoists and had not only provided them shelter in India but also moral and material support! Similarly, India played a role in facilitating a settlement between the Madhesi parties that were agitating for a more inclusive and equitable society and the government in 2008. At the time, Kathmandu was rife with rumours that India had instigated the agitation, that India was supporting the armed Madhesi groups in the Terai, and so on.

In contemporary times, we see this most graphically in the rise of the Oli regime. Nepali politicians such as Oli have fanned and then mobilized this anti-India sentiment to further their own political ends. Indeed, Oli whipped up the anti-India sentiment[13] following the imposition of the so-called blockade in 2015 by projecting himself as the tallest nationalist leader who could stand up to India's 'bullying tactics' and gained a large majority in the Parliament. His government again tried the same tactic[14] on the boundary issue between India and Nepal and published a new map of Nepal by assimilating the territories of Kalapani, Lipulekh and Limpiyadhura and providing it parliamentary cover through an amendment to the Constitution! This stands in sharp contrast to the manner in which the Oli government handled the recent media reports of encroachment of Nepali territory by the Chinese. The Nepalese Foreign Ministry promptly issued a statement[15] denying any such encroachment and pulled up the local official in Humla District who had made this claim. Of course, the matter refused to die down and there were demands for a more thorough investigation into these reports.

Some politicians take pains in not being seen to be close to India. Narayan Kaji Shreshtha, a senior Maoist leader, was known to be close to China. On one occasion he called through his secretary and sought a lunch meeting with me at his residence. I agreed, since this was the first time that we were meeting. Some months later, I received another such request from him. I invited him to India House. I conveyed to his secretary that I would like to repay his hospitality. Again, I was given an excuse and told that it would be better if I could visit Shreshta's residence, which I did. During the earthquake, he sent word through his secretary that he wanted us to help by sending some relief material to his constituency. I readily agreed and said that we could have a nice handover ceremony. Knowing his politics, I knew that he would not agree. Eventually, given the dire need of the people, we did send some relief material to him. As the foreign minister in an earlier government, Narayan Kaji Shreshta had also introduced what he called a code of conduct for foreign diplomats. He wanted the Foreign Ministry to arrange for all meetings of ambassadors with Nepalese political leaders. In addition, an official would be present at such meetings. This was clearly intended to prevent free and frank conversations and to keep tabs both on ambassadors and political leaders. Clearly, this was more in keeping with a totalitarian state rather than a democracy. None of the ambassadors paid any heed to the code, neither did the political leaders. Incidentally, Narayan Kaji Shreshta himself always met me alone. These are some of the ways that politicians live up to their public image. As far as I was concerned, I took these in my stride. Public perceptions can be at great variance with reality.

There is another incident that is revealing of the Nepalese psychology. On one of my tours to Hetauda, I decided to take the Tribhuvan Rajpath, the first road built by the Indian Corps of Engineers in the 1950s connecting the Kathmandu Valley to the plains. At several places, I saw that marble slabs had been erected commemorating various stages in the construction process; at one location there was a small memorial to workers who had died during construction. Most of the commemorative plaques were defaced or had otherwise worn out. The same story repeats itself at the airports in Nepal that were built by India. I raised this matter with the minister in charge and said that India would be willing to pay the cost for replacing the slabs, but there was no interest.

Like many other countries in South Asia, the management of Nepal's pluralism has been a contentious issue. The ruling hill Bahun Chhetri elite is still to come to terms with the great ethnic diversity of the country, the growing political awareness and aspirations among the Madhesi and Janjati communities and desire for a share in political power and economic resources of the country. The Madhesis in particular look different, speak different languages—Maithili, Bhojpuri, Awadhi, Vajji and Hindi—and are more akin to their brethren across the border in Uttar Pradesh and Bihar. The Madhesis tend to be conflated with India and Indians, are suspected of having dual loyalties and resentment against one merges with the other. More recently, during the picketing of the border checkposts by the Madhesis in 2015 to demonstrate their anger against some features of the new Constitution, the Nepalese leadership and media projected this as an India-instigated and -sponsored blockade. #BackoffIndia became viral in Nepal.

The rise of social media is another factor that has contributed significantly to the rise of anti-India sentiment in Nepal. The number of users in Nepal of social messaging sites has mushroomed. Nearly half the population of Nepal uses smart phones to access the Internet. The Facebook and Twitter pages of the Indian embassy in Kathmandu, when I was posted there, received a surfeit of hate messages from trolls in the Valley.

In my conversations with Nepalese friends and political leaders, I have often queried about this anti-India sentiment and inquired about its genesis. I have received several answers. Pashupati Shumsher Jung Bahadur Rana, the grandson of the last Rana prime minister of Nepal, told me that this began during Sir C.P.N. Singh's time as ambassador,[16] when he began to sit in on Cabinet meetings in Kathmandu. Nepali political leaders nurse a grudge about the frontline representation of India in Kathmandu, namely, the embassy and its officials. There is a perception that some Indian ambassadors have behaved as viceroys—arrogant, patronizing and occasionally dismissive of Nepal's pride as a sovereign country. First secretaries in the Indian embassy have been known to browbeat senior Nepalese functionaries. Nepali politicians complain that the Indian political class have subcontracted the business of managing relations to the bureaucracy and the intelligence services. Unlike in the past, when Nepali leaders such as Matrika Prasad Koirala and Bisheshwar Prasad Koirala and even Girija Prasad Koirala had strong personal links with Indian political leaders, partly due to the fact that some had been in exile in India, today such links are the exception. There is little personal engagement between politicians on the two sides. Nepali politicians resent what they feel is micromanagement by Indian diplomats and intelligence agencies in the internal affairs of Nepal. This, however, is not always due to Indian initiative.

Let me narrate two incidents from my own experience. A new Inspector-General of Police for Nepal had to be selected since the incumbent was retiring. The home minister asked me for my views about the candidates. I checked with my colleagues since it was important to have an IGP who was cooperative with his Indian counterparts and received the advice that the senior-most candidate on the list was the most suited. I conveyed to the home minister my opinion that it would be appropriate to follow the criteria of seniority and merit. On the next occasion, when another new IGP was to be selected, there was a list of four. Each of the four candidates visited me at India House conveying their keenness to strengthen cooperation with their Indian counterparts. I had not invited them to visit me. This time there was an unseemly altercation between the home minister and his party chair who were backing separate candidates. The party chair's candidate was appointed IGP, but the appointment was quashed by the Supreme Court and another candidate became IGP of Nepal. The home minister's candidate subsequently quit and joined the CPN (UML) and became a Member of Parliament!

I have quoted the above incidents to convey that India was not micromanaging on its own. Perhaps it was seen to be a neutral objective player on such matters where we had the best interests of India–Nepal cooperation in mind. Of course, in politics, if you take a particular view that benefits one side, the other turns against you and alleges that India is playing a partisan game.

Lest the reader get an impression that the anti-India sentiment is widely prevalent, my own travels throughout the country reveal that this is not the case. In the Terai, the culture of the Madhesis is more akin to their brethren in UP and Bihar and there is a natural admiration and appreciation of India and Indians. In the far west of the country, which till the last century was linked to Kathmandu only through India and is more than twelve hours away from the valley by road, ties with India are robust. With a new four-lane motorable bridge over the Mahakali/Sarada River, just below the present Sarada Barrage, the time it will take for a traveller from Dhangadi in Nepal to New Delhi would be reduced to seven or eight hours! There is also a very cordial relationship between the Indian and Nepalese communities that live along the banks of the Mahakali River. For many residents of far western Nepal, the closest markets are across the Mahakali at Jhulaghat and Pithoragarh in Kumaon, Uttarakhand. Many Nepali pensioners of the Indian Army collect their pensions from the Army Office in Pithoragarh. The tradition of cross-border marriages is still strong. Of course, the controversy over the cartographic aggression by Nepal of Indian territory in Dharchula sub-division and the propaganda by some Nepali local FM stations has the potential of disturbing the cordial and friendly cross-border relations. Similarly, in eastern Nepal, particularly in the Ilam–Darjeeling area, relations between the communities on either side of the border are friendly. Sikkim, which is largely Nepalese today, also has cordial relations with its brethren in Nepal.

Having seen Nepal's perception of India, we now turn to how Indians see Nepal. Indians have a romantic notion of a beautiful mountainous country, a Hindu country that loves India and Indians. The temples at Pashupatinath and Muktinath are great attractions for those religiously inclined. Some Indians travel through Nepal to Mount Kailash and Lake Manasarovar, earlier via the Kathmandu–Kodari road and after the earthquake of 2015 disrupted this route, through Nepalganj and Humla–Simikot. For my generation, the famous film *Hare Rama Hare Krishna* starring Dev Anand had made Nepal famous, not only for its natural beauty, but also as a popular hippie destination in the 1970s! For those connected with the army, there is great affection and admiration for the Gorkha regiments. To this day, India recruits over a thousand Gorkhali soldiers from Nepal for its own army. Indeed, they are the glory of the Indian Infantry and have fought with great valour in defence of our motherland. Field Marshal Sam Manekshaw, himself a Gorkha officer, had famously said: 'If someone says that he is not afraid to die, he is either a liar or a Gorkhali!'

But I am amazed by the number of people that I have met in Delhi, well-educated and well-travelled, who have never been to Nepal, which is just an hour and fifteen minutes away by plane. For many Indians, their perceptions about the Nepalese people stem from their interaction largely with the migrant labour that is employed as security guards or household help or are otherwise engaged in menial tasks such as lifting heavy loads in the high altitudes of Uttarakhand. The following incident in the early 2000s demonstrates this graphically. The deputy speaker of Nepal, Chitralekha Yadav, was paying an official visit to India. She had an appointment with a senior official of Parliament who welcomed her and said that the closest aides of his leader are Nepalese. It subsequently turned out that these aides were employed as personal staff. I can still recall Mrs Yadav squirming in her seat. This was a well-intentioned remark that reflected little understanding of the complexities of the India-Nepal relationship. Sadly, for some Indians, their perceptions about the Nepalese are that they are loyal and trusted attendants and *chowkidars*!

Few Indians know about the great aesthetic traditions, the arts, crafts, fine arts, sculpture, woodwork and architecture of Nepal, especially of the Newar community. Six of the seven world heritage sites in the Kathmandu Valley (counted as one by UNESCO) relate to the Newar culture. The great architect Arniko, a Newar, developed the pagoda style of architecture that spread to China and the countries of East Asia as far away as Japan and Korea. Almost all Buddhist temples in these countries are built in this style. Hardly any Indians are aware of the beautiful kingdom of Mustang that retains its authentic Tibetan culture to this day. This ignorance about Nepal, and the fact that the only Nepalis most Indians meet work in low-paid menial jobs, creates a caricature of the Nepali character—loyal, obedient, hardworking, trustworthy, happy-go-lucky—that the educated people of Nepal resent. They find India's attitude patronizing and insensitive and far removed from the nuanced truth about Nepal.

Indians are also ignorant about the diversity of Nepal. Not many Indians know about the Madhesi community or that they are the original inhabitants of the Terai; or the fact that what used to be united communities got divided between the two countries following the Sugauli Treaty of 1816. Most Indians think Madhesis are migrants from India because of the way they look, their names, languages and attire. Politicians in India are known to greet political leaders from the Terai with names like Yadav or Mahato or Thakur, with the question: *'Accha to aap Nepal kab gaye India se?'* (So when did you migrate to Nepal from India?), much to the dismay and anguish of the visitors. Even Sushma Swaraj, who knew Nepal well, once tweeted about PM Modi's diaspora rallies and included a reference to Janakpur, in the Nepalese Terai, assuming that the people of Janakpur belonged to the Indian diaspora! The tweet was quickly deleted, and an apology issued after Nepal took offence.

More recently, following the incorporation of Kalapani, Lipulekh and Limpiyadhura into a new map by Nepal, and the strong criticism in the Indian media, which has given Nepal the kind of treatment that is normally reserved for Pakistan, a strong negative perception has been generated among the Indian populace about Nepal. Stories in mainstream Indian media attributing Nepalese actions to Chinese machinations, and yellow journalism suggesting that former prime minister Oli had been honey-trapped by the Chinese ambassador in Nepal, have vitiated the atmosphere further. In turn, this has caused widespread resentment in Nepal and even led to the temporary suspension of some Indian news media outlets in that country.

There is also a sizeable expatriate Nepali community living in India and an Indian community in Nepal. While there is no confirmed census, the number of Nepalese living in India varies from 4 million to 6 million people. Some of these people come to India for seasonal work and return home. The numbers increased substantially during the Maoist insurgency, when a large number of Nepalese men tried to escape recruitment into the Maoist army by moving to India through the open border. The expatriate Nepali community is quite active politically and each of the major political parties in Nepal has a branch in India. Indeed, during the Maoist insurgency, some of the leaders had taken shelter in various Indian cities with the help of Nepali expatriates. By and large, the Nepalese community in India is peaceful and law abiding, though there have been some cases of murder and robbery in Indian cities, after which the alleged culprits escape to Nepal. And in the absence of an updated extradition treaty, bringing such persons to justice becomes difficult.

The Indian community in Nepal is small compared to the Nepalese expatriates in India, though there is no detailed census. It is difficult to keep track, partly because of document-free travel between the two countries. Most Indians are engaged in petty businesses and are largely from Bihar and other neighbouring states, though in the past there were many teachers from as far away as Kerala! The Indian community is indistinguishable from the Madhesis and sometimes become the target of Pahadi anger when things go wrong between Nepal and India.

Anti-Indian nationalism in Nepal remains a fact of life and is ever present as an important factor in the relationship between the two countries, as we shall see in the subsequent chapters.

2

Violent Change: The Maoist Insurgency

As joint secretary beginning August 2002, I travelled regularly to Nepal for meetings with my counterparts. It was a surreal experience. Kathmandu was a city under siege. Even while landing at Tribhuvan International Airport—formerly known by the evocative name of Gauchar, since it used to be a grazing ground for cattle in days gone by—one could see the extent of new construction taking place all over the city, as people displaced from their traditional villages moved to the safety of Kathmandu to protect themselves and their children from the Maoist onslaught. Roadblocks managed by security forces behind sandbags were ubiquitous. It reminded me of Delhi during the days when the movement for Khalistan was active.

Our Deputy Chief of Mission, my batchmate Virupakshan Pranatharthiharan (since many northerners found it difficult to pronounce his name, he shortened it to V.P. Haran and became known to all as Haran, which in Hindi means to kidnap), once took us for dinner to a Nepalese restaurant. It was a large open-air place with a few private tables, with a Newar cultural performance taking place on the central stage. We were the only guests. The performance ended very early since the artistes were keen to go home, and so did our dinner. It was unsafe, even in Kathmandu, to travel after dark. On another occasion, I recall staying at the sprawling Hyatt Hotel near the airport; the hotel was empty save for a handful of guests. We were told that the Maoists had active members among the hotel staff and that most hotels and other commercial enterprises were paying protection money to the Maoists. The tentacles of the Maoists had reached the heart of the capital city.

Even as Kathmandu was terrified, the situation in the hill districts of Nepal was dire. Hill villages had emptied and young men in particular, who were vulnerable to forcible recruitment by the Maoists, had fled their homes for cities. Tens of thousands also moved to India, especially from western Nepal, where the insurgency had begun and was very active. The open border with India turned out to be a boon for such migrants, who would otherwise have become refugees. Indeed, during COVID-19 times, we again saw long queues of Nepalese workers at various border checkposts, patiently waiting to be admitted into India as they sought work and sustenance for their families.

Politicians, too, were largely stuck in Kathmandu. Those from the Terai could still visit their constituencies, but those representing the hill districts were loath to go to their hometowns and villages. For the Nepali Congress, it was even more difficult. Prime Minister Girija Prasad Koirala had been instrumental in mobilizing police action against the Maoists. His party cadres were a special target.

The Maoists had begun their people's war from a small village in Rolpa district, Thawang, in 1996. When it ended in 2006, after ten long years of violence and strife, it had spread throughout the country and left more than 17,000 Nepalese dead. What were the goals of the insurgent movement, what did it achieve, how did the Maoists join the democratic mainstream? And what was India's role?

The original demands of the Maoists were for a radical transformation of the Nepali state. They sought a constitution enacted by elected representatives for a new people's democratic system, the abolition of all royal privileges and the declaration of Nepal as a secular nation. Of the forty demands[1] presented in 1996, several related to India and included the abolition of all unequal treaties, including the 1950 Treaty of Peace and Friendship as well as the Mahakali Treaty, regulation of the open India-Nepal border and a ban on recruitment of Gorkhas into the Indian Army. In addition, Maoists wanted to ban 'vulgar Hindi films' that were presumably corrupting the innocent Nepali people and to stop domination of foreign labour and capital in Nepal. India was referred to as an expansionist and imperialist power.

At first, no one, not even the Government of Nepal, took these demands seriously and they were ignored. Even the insurgency that began around the same time was considered a law-and-order problem, a low-intensity conflict to be resolved by the police. It had not yet captured global attention. It is only after a series of attacks beginning with Jajarkot in June 2000 and Dunai in September 2000, which killed several police personnel and civilians, that the insurgency became a serious internal security threat and began capturing global attention. Over the course of the next few years, the Maoist insurgency gained considerable momentum, with major attacks on police and army personnel at various places, including in Rukum in April 2001, Dang in November 2001, Accham in February 2002, Sindhuli and Arghakhanchi in September 2002, Jumla and Gorkha in November 2002 and several others. The inspector general of the Armed Police Force (APF) Krishna Mohan Shreshta was killed in Kathmandu in January 2003.

International public opinion against terrorism also changed dramatically after the 9/11 terrorist attacks in New York on the World Trade Center in 2001. In late 2001, even before the Nepalese government had done so, External Affairs Minister Jaswant Singh referred to the Nepalese Maoists as terrorists. In March 2002, following the visit of Prime Minister Sher Bahadur

Deuba to India, the insurgency found mention in the joint statement between India and Nepal issued on 23 March 2002.[2]

My association with Nepal began when I joined the Ministry of External Affairs (MEA) as joint secretary (North) in 2002 August, during the tenure of the Vajpayee government. I was returning from a stint with the UN Peacekeeping Mission in Kosovo, UNMIK, and the Department of Peace Keeping Operations at UN Headquarters in New York and so was somewhat familiar with conflict situations and their aftermath. Kanwal Sibal was foreign secretary and he decided that I should replace Meera Shankar, who had been promoted and was moving on as Additional Secretary, Counter Terrorism. I was delighted that I had been posted to Northern Division, which dealt with our smaller Himalayan neighbours, relationships that were inordinately complex but where even a mere joint secretary could influence policy making and its implementation and make a tangible difference. Brajesh Mishra was the powerful national security adviser (NSA) and principal secretary to the PM at the time. Our incumbent ambassador in Kathmandu, I.P. Singh, had succumbed to cancer and the position was vacant. Shyam Saran, our ambassador in Jakarta, had been selected for the post and was under considerable pressure from the Ministry to join early. He assumed his post in Kathmandu in October just as the Maoist insurgency was surging to its peak.

At the time, the clear and unambiguous policy of the Vajpayee government was to support multiparty democracy and constitutional monarchy as the twin pillars of stability in Nepal. Nepal was already in turmoil following the patricide of King Birendra and most of the royal family in 2001. It was our considered view, which was shared by other countries such as the US and the UK, that the insurgency should be crushed. This could be achieved if the Palace and the parties worked together with the support of the international community. Our entire effort was devoted towards this goal. India was in constant touch with King

Gyanendra both through our ambassador as well as through the direct back channel between Principal Secretary Brajesh Mishra and the king's confidante and business partner Prabhakar S.J.B. Rana. I was privy to some of the back-channel conversations. Prabhakar Rana would normally stay at ITC Maurya Sheraton in Delhi. Mishra would ask me to be at the hotel at the appointed time. I was told to cover the conversation and then leave, following which the two principals would meet over dinner. In this manner, the Ministry of External Affairs was kept fully in the loop by the Prime Minister's Office.

India had deep reservations about the ultimate goal of the Maoists—a one-party people's republic—and we found abhorrent the violence that they were wreaking on society. We were familiar with the havoc that the Naxal uprising, which had begun from Siliguri on the border with Nepal and Bhutan, had caused in West Bengal. We were also grappling with our own home-grown left-wing extremist groups (LWEs) in Andhra Pradesh and Bihar, groups that had found fertile ground in tribal areas. Later, in 2006, Prime Minister Manmohan Singh was to refer to left-wing extremism in India as the single-most important security threat facing the country. Though some attempts at peace talks had been made with these groups—the legendary S.R. Sankaran of the Indian Administrative Service was a go-between—not much progress was made. Our assessment was that these groups had been transformed into criminal enterprises with no political agenda and needed to be crushed. The Greyhounds, a specially trained branch of the Andhra Police, had successfully dealt with the LWEs in Andhra Pradesh, and the strategy was sought to be replicated elsewhere.

Our greatest worry about the Maoists in Nepal was that they would link up with the LWEs in India. If successful in capturing state power in Nepal, it was felt that they would provide a safe haven to terrorists of all hues, including LWEs from India. That was a time when dark notions of a Red Corridor or Compact

Revolutionary Zone (CRZ) running from Andhra Pradesh all the way to North Bihar and Nepal were in the news. According to intelligence reports, IED (improvised explosive device) technology had already been transferred to Indian LWEs from the LTTE (Liberation Tigers of Tamil Eelam), a terrorist group in Sri Lanka, and thence to the Nepalese Maoists.

The prevailing view in the Government of India was that the Maoists needed to be degraded and destroyed militarily. Accordingly, the capabilities of the Royal Nepalese Army (RNA) required to be enhanced and strengthened. A joint secretary-level mechanism coordinated by the Ministry of External Affairs was established to sell military material on a 70:30 grant:payment basis. (Effectively, this was a full grant since the 30 per cent was seldom paid.)

At the political level, there was considerable turmoil in Nepal. After the patricide of June 2001, a new King, Gyanendra, had taken over power. Unlike his brother Birendra who was revered, Gyanendra was seen more as a businessman, worldly wise. A cloud of suspicion also hung over him and the circumstances in which he became the king; though no evidence was ever brought forward, there was an undercurrent of belief in Nepal that Gyanendra's son, Paras, may have somehow been involved. The manner in which the crime scene was cleaned up, the building where the killings took place destroyed and the bodies cremated post haste without any post-mortems made it impossible for any enquiry to come up with the true facts of the case. What was evident to the people was that Birendra's family was killed whereas Gyanendra's survived and the line of succession to the throne was dramatically altered by this single act.[3]

Nepal's democratic politics was also in a state of considerable flux. The ambitions of political leaders and interpersonal animosities complicated efforts for a coordinated move to protest royal machinations and the gradual erosion of democratic functioning. G.P. Koirala (GPK), who as the prime minister had wanted to launch a strong military attack against the Maoists, was hamstrung, given the king's refusal to allow the RNA to be deployed against the Maoists. In fact, Koirala resigned on this issue in 2001 and was succeeded by his party rival Sher Bahadur Deuba. At the time, the RNA was loyal to, and took orders directly from, the King and not the elected government of the day. It is because of the king's refusal that the idea of creating an armed police force under the civilian government was conceived. The APF was set up in late 2001 with considerable support both in terms of material and training from India. It is another matter that, over the years, the relationship of the APF with India has weakened and China has made inroads by constructing the APF Academy in Nepal. Our commitment to construct a similar academy for the police in Panauti has been stuck in red tape for several years, even though the foundation stone was laid jointly by prime ministers Narendra Modi and Sushil Koirala in 2014.

Due to a dispute between Deuba and GPK on whether the national emergency should be extended or not—Deuba was for and GPK against—Deuba was expelled from the Nepali Congress (NC) in May 2002. Fearing a trust vote, Deuba then dissolved the Parliament and established his own party, the Nepali Congress (Democratic). Thereafter, he was unable to hold elections within the stipulated six months due to the insurgency, creating a huge constitutional crisis. Sensing an opportunity, the king then sacked Deuba for incompetence and took over executive power in October 2002, ruling through appointed PMs—Lokendra Bahadur Chand first (October 2002 to June 2003), then Surya Bahadur Thapa (June 2003 to June 2004) and Deuba again (till January 2005)—with no parliamentary accountability.

Surya Bahadur Thapa's brief tenure was very productive for India-Nepal relations. Several development projects conceived by Shyam Saran, who was the ambassador, including the quick impact Small Development Projects (SDP), Hulaki (Postal) Roads project in the Terai and the integrated checkposts (ICPs), received the concurrence of the Nepalese authorities at this time.

The joint secretary-level group on military supplies and training was also established during this period.

I recall several visits to Kathmandu and meetings with Prime Minister Thapa. He would invariably meet with ambassador Shyam Saran first thing in the morning, around 7 a.m. The ambassador would ask me to accompany him if I was in town. Thapa would meet us alone. After a discussion on the military and political situation, he would turn to bilateral issues and hand over a copy of the list of equipment needed by the army. In the two years since it was established, the group approved a sizeable amount of military assistance to Nepal, including supply of India-made INSAS rifles.

Later, as ambassador, I got to know Thapa well. I made it a point to meet him regularly at his residence to exchange views on the political scene and process of constitution making. Thapa was an old world gentleman. He would always receive me formally attired in his *daura saruwal* and *Dhaka topi*, unlike some of the other leaders of the time who were more casual. We would meet in his small study on the first floor of his residence. At the end of each meeting, he would want to escort me downstairs to my car, but I always persuaded him not to do so.

Thapa was the elder statesman of Nepal, a towering personality with an experience of Nepali politics over several decades. A competent administrator and perceptive observer, his views were deeply valued by Indian leaders cutting across the political spectrum. He had been PM in the early sixties when his counterpart was Lal Bahadur Shastri. He had personally interacted with Mao Zedong on his official visit to China. I found that there was a huge convergence between his thinking and our overall assessment of the situation. Once I asked him how it was to work with King Gyanendra. Thapa was dismissive and said that Gyanendra was not like his brother at all.

Meanwhile, King Gyanendra, not satisfied with ruling through appointed prime ministers, engineered a royal coup on 1 February 2005 by sacking PM Deuba (who had replaced Thapa as prime minister), arresting senior political leaders and taking over all executive power as Head of the Council of Ministers,[4] with two deputies, Tulsi Giri and Kirti Nidhi Bista. This was a repeat of King Mahendra's actions in 1960 when he had dismissed the B.P. Koirala government, to the extent that he appointed the same individuals that his father had appointed more than four decades ago!

Given our clear policy for the political parties and the king to work unitedly to combat the Maoist insurgency, we were dismayed by the king's actions. The MEA spokesperson referred to the coup and arrest of senior political leaders as 'a serious setback to the cause of democracy in Nepal' that 'cannot but be a cause of grave concern to India'. Reiterating the twin pillar theory, India stressed the 'imperative to evolve a broad national consensus, particularly between the monarchy and political parties, to deal with the political and economic challenges facing the country'. The statement also included a warning that 'the latest developments in Nepal bring the monarchy and the mainstream political parties in direct confrontation with each other. This can only benefit the forces that not only wish to undermine democracy but the institution of monarchy as well.'[5] However, as we shall see later, no heed was paid to Indian concerns.

After the royal coup, India broadly viewed the struggle in Nepal as a three-cornered contest for power between the king, the political parties and the Maoists. Our sense was that any two parties that got together would have the upper hand. The king had rejected the idea of working jointly with political parties to combat the Maoists. We were also aware that there were a series of conversations taking place or that had taken place with the Maoists on various occasions since the insurgency began: between the king and the Maoists; between the CPN (UML) and the Maoists; and between the NC and the Maoists. Several rounds of peace talks between the government of the day and the Maoists did not lead to any productive results. The royal dismissal of Deuba set in train a series of developments that shook the foundations of the Shah dynasty and eventually led to its demise.

In retrospect, it is clear that both the king and the Maoists wanted to radically transform the political landscape of Nepal; both saw a common enemy in the democratic forces and wanted to use the other side for tactical gains, to marginalize the political parties. After the dismissal of the Deuba government in November 2002, when the king was ruling through appointed prime ministers, efforts to reach out to the Maoists were made by Narayan Singh Pun, the then Minister for Physical Planning, arousing suspicion among the political parties.[6] Ultimately, the efforts did not succeed, and the period of ceasefire and talks were used by the Maoists to regroup and strengthen themselves. The Maoists too had no love lost for the parties, because it was the governments of Koirala and Deuba that had unleashed the full might of the state against them; further a dominant Maoist sentiment at the time was that the political parties were beholden to India, that India was the principal enemy; accordingly, they were not averse to reaching a modus vivendi with the king. An alternative view in communist thought was that the monarchy was the principal enemy and 'argued for collaboration with the democratic parties, and India if necessary, to restore democracy as the first step to socialism and communism'.[7] Following the royal coup of 1 February 2005, it is the latter view that prevailed.

Over a period of time, India had started becoming suspicious of the intentions of the king. Unlike his brother Birendra, he did not want to be a constitutional monarch but an executive king like his father. My own assessment is that the king was toying with the idea of taking over absolute power as early as 2003, a few months after he dismissed the first Deuba government. During a visit to India in March 2003, at a meeting with Principal Secretary Brajesh Mishra, he raised the idea of establishing a Peace Council, with himself as its head, to govern the country. Mishra dismissed the idea out of hand and cautioned the king from doing anything that would alienate the political parties further. Our official policy was to support both constitutional monarchy and multiparty democracy. There was an established balance, and we did not want this to be altered in favour of one or the other. The king did not raise the matter in any of his other meetings. Evidently, he had paid heed to Mishra's warning, but not for long.

Political parties were also beginning to grow wary of the king and his desire for absolute power. This was anathema to parties that had fought for and secured, with the full backing of the Nepalese people, multiparty democracy after three decades of autocratic Panchayat rule. Meanwhile, in India, the Vajpayee government was replaced by a Congress government under Dr Manmohan Singh in mid-2004. To be fair to the king, he had scheduled a visit to India beginning 23 December 2004. Unfortunately for him, former prime minister P.V. Narasimha Rao passed away on that day. Foreign Secretary Shyam Saran conveyed to our C'DA Haran that the visit needed to be deferred in view of national mourning. Haran then got back to say that the king was almost on his way to the airport. His private secretary had strongly urged that the visit should not be postponed, but the format could be changed: that the king could begin his visit not in Delhi but somewhere else in India and then arrive in Delhi at a later date. None of these alternatives was found to be convenient to us and the visit was postponed.

One can only speculate that the king was coming to Delhi to sound out the government on what he was planning. In retrospect, my sense is that it was fortuitous for us that the visit did not take place as scheduled. I am not sure that anything that we could have said would have changed the king's mind and he may well have returned to Kathmandu, announced his coup and given an impression to his people that India had been consulted.

Immediately after the coup was announced in February 2005, India took decisive steps. In addition to issuing a strong statement condemning the king's actions, we announced that

PM Manmohan Singh would not attend the SAARC Summit scheduled to begin in Dhaka in a few days (we did not want the PM to provide legitimacy to the king's action by sharing a common platform with him; the summit was postponed). Separately, we were in regular touch with the US and the UK and both countries were critical of the king's steps to throttle democracy. Some weeks later, all military aid was suspended. This was a big setback to the king and the RNA.

The royal coup alienated democratic forces from the monarchy and provided a strong impetus for the formation of a joint front between the mainstream political parties and the Maoists. This eventually resulted in the famous twelve-point agreement of November 2005 in Delhi, an agreement that was owned and drawn up by the Nepalese political actors themselves, but one which had the support of the Indian establishment.

Even as senior leaders were arrested after the royal takeover, some second-rung political leaders fled to exile in India and established contact with us. Those were heady days with political parties planning strategy to combat the king's usurpation of political power. G.P. Koirala's key aides, namely, Krishna Prasad Sitaula and his nephew Shekhar Koirala, were involved in conversations with the Maoists and were instrumental in arranging for a meeting of principals during GPK's visit to India in June 2005. He had been released from prison in April prior to King Gyanendra's visit to Indonesia for the commemorative Asian Relations Conference that month, which was also being attended by Prime Minister Manmohan Singh.

Unlike other senior leaders of Nepal, GPK's favourite place to stay in New Delhi was the low-key Ambassador Hotel near Khan Market. I asked him once why he wanted to stay there and not at one of the posher hotels in Delhi. He said that he liked the south Indian breakfast at Dasaprakash, a popular place for idli, dosa, sambhar, vada at the hotel, since closed, alas. Though I did not know GPK well, Sitaula and Shekhar Koirala became good friends. We would engage in long conversations about the situation in Nepal and options available to political parties. The gist of our discussions was that parties should continue negotiations with the Maoists, try and arrive at an understanding and reveal it at the appropriate time. This was perhaps the only way to prevent the king from abolishing multiparty democracy altogether. A budding politician, actively involved in facilitating the stay of Nepalese politicians who had fled to India was Dr Amresh Kumar Singh, a young PhD student at Jawaharlal Nehru University (JNU) with an abiding interest in politics. He introduced me to a large number of Nepalese politicians as well as students in JNU, some of whom went on to occupy important positions in Nepal and with whom I was able to renew my acquaintance when I was posted as ambassador. These include Ram Baran Yadav, Krishna Prasad Sitaula, Shekhar Koirala, Rajendra Mahato, Mahant Thakur, Anil Jha, Rajan Bhattarai, Hridayesh Tripathi and Upendra Yadav, to name only a few.

The royal coup also threw up huge differences within different branches of the Government of India (GOI) on the evolving situation in Nepal. Key institutions involved in formulating Nepal policy were the Ministry of External Affairs, the national security adviser and the PMO, the Ministry of Defence and the army and our external and internal intelligence, RAW and IB. For the then NSA, M.K. Narayanan, an expert on left-wing extremism in India, the only option was to militarily crush the Maoists. This was also the IB and Home Ministry line. Our army chief, Gen. J.J. Singh, too was of the strong opinion that we should continue to extend support to the RNA, the king's actions notwithstanding. Singh was keen on strengthening the fraternal relationship between the Indian and Nepalese armies and unhappy at the suspension of military assistance. I remember a discussion where it was pointed out that despite the considerable material and training support that we had provided to the RNA, the best that they could achieve was a military stalemate. The RNA could not destroy the Maoists. The

Maoists, on the other hand, were finding it difficult to advance from rural areas to the urban centres. Meanwhile the king was using the situation to enhance his own powers. The MEA and RAW, both headed by officers who had served in Nepal (Shyam Saran and Hormis Tharakan), felt that the only viable option was a political settlement. There was a clear divide between the views of the MEA and RAW on the one side and the IB and the army on the other.

Our political leadership was also divided. Some leaders felt that the priority for India should be to eliminate the Maoists. Multiparty democracy in Nepal was a lesser priority at this juncture. If the king was usurping political power to strengthen himself in the fight against terrorism, we should not be worried and support him. EAM Natwar Singh was sympathetic to the king and organized a bilateral meeting for PM Manmohan Singh with King Gyanendra along the sidelines of the commemorative Bandung Conference in Indonesia in April 2005, just a few weeks after the coup. Another meeting was arranged at the postponed SAARC summit in Dhaka in November 2005, to the dismay of some of the officials. The latter meeting took place at a time when the king was making strenuous efforts to have China admitted as a full member of SAARC and there were reports of import of military material by Nepal from China.

Within the UPA-I coalition, the communists and socialists were keen to support the mainstream democratic parties in Nepal in their struggle against the monarchy, which they felt was trying to marginalize their role. Though the use of violence by the Maoists was abhorrent to most leaders, there may have been sympathy for some of their more progressive objectives for societal change. Further, one of the senior Maoist leaders, Baburam Bhattarai, had friends in leftist circles in India. He was an alumnus of JNU in Delhi, which was also the alma mater of Prakash Karat and Sitaram Yechury of the CPI (M), D.P. Tripathi of the NCP and Digvijay Singh of the Janata

Dal. Following King Gyanendra's coup, a group, Friends of Nepal, was set up under the chairmanship of the CPI (M) patriarch Harkishan Singh Surjeet and had representatives from several political parties. Tripathi, Karat and Yechury played important roles. Most of them were progressives and were dismayed that the king was trying to turn the clock back on democracy. This group had influence on the government, which depended on their support in Parliament. Around mid-2005, there were also some meetings between Maoist leaders and CPI (M) politicians, initially Sitaram Yechury followed by General Secretary Prakash Karat.[8]

It is also possible that the king was receiving mixed messages from India given the many channels of communication between India and Nepal. While the bureaucracy had generally taken a tough line, some elements of the political leadership were more indulgent towards the king. Senior political leaders cutting across party lines that had strong connections with the Nepalese royal family may also have wanted to give the benefit of doubt to the king. With a new government in Delhi and due to India's strong support to the global war against terrorism and the projection of the Maoists as an existential threat to Nepal, the king may have thought that India would protest the royal takeover but not take any further substantive action against Nepal. This was a cardinal mistake. And he underestimated the institutional continuity provided to our Nepal policy in the person of Shyam Saran, who had moved from Kathmandu as foreign secretary of India with the Nepal portfolio at the top of his agenda.

Meanwhile, Nepal was rife with all sorts of allegations: India was running with the hares and hunting with the hounds; it was supporting RNA and the king as well as the APF, but also providing shelter to Maoists in India; India wanted to keep Nepal in a state of 'controlled instability'; despite concrete evidence, India was not apprehending the Maoists; India wanted Nepal to become a republic! Providing an insider's account of the people's war, Hisila Yami, a senior Maoist leader during the insurgency, has debunked claims that the Maoists were supported by the Government of India in a recently published memoir.[9]

Our IB had told us that Nepalese intelligence about the whereabouts of Maoist leaders in India was poor. Where we received good intelligence, we did arrest people, viz., Matrika Yadav, Bam Dev Chettri, Suresh Ale Magar, C.P. Gajurel (August 2003) and Mohan Vaidya (March 2004). The reality was that at one time, we did not even have photographs of all the leaders of the Maoist politburo or even of Prachanda. There was a mystique about him, and people doubted whether he was a real person at all. When I joined the MEA as joint secretary in late 2002, I was given a dossier of key Maoist leaders, with photographs of only a few.

Contrary to the prevailing belief in Nepal that India was in cahoots with the Maoists, our facilitation of a rapprochement between Nepalese political parties and the Maoists was directly linked to the measures taken by the king to usurp political power. As S.D. Muni has recounted,[10] the Maoists had made overtures in writing to the Vajpayee government sometime during mid-2002. Despite these efforts there was no change in our overall approach to the Maoists, as demonstrated by the arrest of top Maoist functionaries in 2003 and 2004. Serious official level conversations began only after the royal coup of February 2005. It is in the context of the king's overreach, the military stalemate and the incipient discussions between political parties and the Maoists that India too decided to hold some conversations with Maoist leaders. The first meeting at the senior official level took place between Foreign Secretary Shyam Saran and Baburam Bhattarai, Hisila Yami and K.B. Mahara in Delhi in 2005, some months after the February coup. Shyam Saran's clear message to the Maoists was the following: they would never be allowed to take over by force. The only option for them was to give up arms, join the democratic mainstream and contest elections. A follow-up meeting, this time with Maoist supremo Prachanda, took place in Siliguri in mid-2006.

There are two interesting anecdotes about the arrest of Mohan 'Kiran' Vaidya and C.P. Gajurel 'Gaurav'. My colleague V.P. Haran, who was DCM in Kathmandu between 2003 and 2005, narrated this incident about Vaidya. A businessman in Biratnagar was receiving phone calls from India for extorting money. He called the First Secretary dealing with commercial issues in the embassy, Nagma Mallick, and complained about these calls from an Indian number. Ambassador Saran thereafter forwarded the number to Delhi for enquiries. It is only then that Vaidya, a very senior Maoist leader, one-time mentor of Prachanda, was nabbed by our internal intelligence in Siliguri.

C.P. Gajurel was trying to travel on a fake British passport from Chennai in 2003 and was nabbed at the airport. The immigration officer felt there was something not quite right about the passenger who claimed to be a white British doctor. Siddharth Varadarajan wrote as follows in *The Hindu* of 30 January 2007:

Unluckily for Mr. Gajurel, the wife of a British diplomat happened to walk past after seeing off her husband and the immigration official sought her opinion.

The Maoist leader thought it best to act friendly in order to get her on to his side. 'It turned out that the British woman's uncle worked at the same hospital where I said I worked. I said the hospital was big and that I didn't know him but if she wanted to send a message I would be happy to convey it,' said Mr Gajurel. 'She then asked me where I lived in London and how I commuted to the hospital. She also asked me about the tube fare and other details, which I couldn't answer. So I changed tactics and said angrily, "who are you to question me?"'

The diplomat's wife promptly told the immigration official she thought the passport was forged and Mr Gajurel was arrested on the spot.

He remained in Chennai jail for over three years. Much later, when he came to see me at India House in Kathmandu, referring to his days in Chennai, I jokingly said that by now he must be well accustomed to eating idli and sambhar. He was not amused!

A good initiative taken by Shyam Saran as foreign secretary was to organize an informal lunch meeting with the key bureaucrats involved in important foreign policy matters, generally the neighbourhood. Participants usually included the home and defence secretaries, the chiefs of RAW and sometimes IB, the DGMO or his deputy, if required, and the concerned joint secretary in MEA. There would be a freewheeling discussion on the subject of the day, and this was a useful way of exchanging views and sharing information. My predecessor Meera Shankar had started a similar practice at the joint secretary level and I continued this with vigour. Not only did it help in inter-organization coordination but enabled all officers to be on the same page and not work at cross-purposes.

Close cooperation between India and other countries, mainly the US and the UK, were critical to developing a coordinated international approach to the problems in Nepal. The US, in particular, was reluctant to back the political process of engaging the Maoists and continued to treat them as a terrorist grouping. The positions and assessments of the UK and India were more closely aligned, since we had a better appreciation of the ground situation and the military stalemate. Throughout this period of turmoil in Nepal, India kept up a vigorous interaction with both the US and the UK, explaining to them the logic of our policy. Unlike in the past, when we were opposed to other countries intervening in our neighbourhood, on this occasion, we followed a policy of regular exchanges at various levels. This generated considerable mutual trust and understanding as well as support for the Indian view and strategy. It also ensured that other countries did not do anything in Nepal that could have been misunderstood by us or caused us difficulties. Indeed, it is largely due to this approach that despite the desire of the Royal Nepalese Army to procure the sophisticated weaponry, M16s from the US and FN Minimi guns from Belgium, we successfully persuaded western interlocutors to desist from doing so on the grounds that these weapons could find their way to the Maoists and cause problems for India given the open border; that it was best for India to take care of requirements of the Nepalese security forces.

The year 2005 emerged as a critical year in the evolving contemporary history of Nepal. From the royal coup of 1 February to the twelve-point agreement between political parties and the Maoists in November, these became ten months that would bring about revolutionary changes in Nepal. My own assessment is that it was the missteps by the king that are principally responsible for the manner in which the situation developed. Others, namely, the Maoists, the political parties as well as India and the rest of the international community and the people of Nepal were in a reactive mode. The king, who had the reputation of being a shrewd businessman, overplayed his hand. He refused to heed sane advice and patch up with the political parties. He was confident that when it came down to brass tacks, the Royal Nepal Army would back him. Even this did not happen in the face of huge demonstrations by the Nepalese people in April 2006. When he was willing to compromise, it was too late and the situation became irretrievable. Gyanendra will go down in history as the monarch who presided over the demise of his kingdom.

Shyam Saran, supported by Hormis Tharakan, was the true architect of India's Nepal policy and persuaded PM Manmohan Singh that dialogue between the political parties and the Maoists was the best way to resolve the brutal insurgency in Nepal. Since he had been the ambassador, he was the most knowledgeable person in the Government of India on the situation in Nepal.

Even after the conclusion of the famous twelve-point agreement between political parties and the Maoists in New Delhi in November 2005, India was still wedded to the twin pillar theory of political parties and the monarchy working together. The agreement did not refer to a republic; it merely sought an end to autocratic monarchy and the election of a Constituent Assembly. Its biggest achievement was the laying down of arms by the Maoists and their entry into the democratic mainstream. The agreement also warned the monarchy that the democratic forces and the Maoists would launch a huge movement to achieve full democracy and end autocratic monarchy. The movement was launched in April 2006 with hundreds of thousands of protesters on the streets of Kathmandu urging the king to give up power, affirm that sovereignty vested in the people and restore Parliament. It was a unique movement that demonstrated the strength of popular and non-violent protest against brutal state power. India had sent Dr Karan Singh to persuade the king to give up executive power and rule as a ceremonial monarch. Following the visit, despite an announcement by the king that he would restore power to the parties, which was prematurely welcomed by India, the protesters remained dissatisfied, since their demand for restoration of the house and sovereignty of the people had not been met. Sensing the popular sentiment and dismayed at the criticism of India's stance in Nepal, India displayed nimble diplomacy, threw in its lot with people's aspirations and gave up the twin-pillar mantra. Once the army decided that it would not fight its own people, the king realized that his time was up; he restored the Parliament, agreed that sovereignty vested in the people and gave way to a government under the leadership of Girija Prasad Koirala.[11] Thereafter, the historic Comprehensive Peace Agreement was signed between the Government of Nepal and the Maoists in November 2006 that brought curtains down on the insurgency and set Nepal on the path of a Federal Democratic Republic.

I had meanwhile left for Hungary as ambassador in February 2006.

3

People's Aspirations: The New Constitution

Writing a new constitution was never going to be an easy task in a country as diverse as Nepal. From the high Himalayas to the Terai plains, with the population evenly divided between the hill Bahun and Chhetris, the ruling elite, the hill Janjatis that include the Rais, Limbus, Gurungs, Magars, Sherpa and Tamang and the Madhesis of the Terai plains, the food bowl of Nepal, the task before the newly elected members was to craft a foundational document that would meet the hopes and aspirations of thirty million Nepalese citizens. This was a society that was undergoing seminal transformations; what in other societies was achieved over decades, even centuries, largely in a sequential manner, Nepal was trying to achieve all at once with this new Constitution. The country was transiting from a monarchy to a republic, a unitary to a federal state, from a Hindu to a secular nation, and from a rigidly hierarchical society with a skewed distribution of economic and political power to a more inclusive, equitable society.

Change in Nepal has seldom been peaceful. Unlike in India, where the enlightened founding fathers of our republic chose to introduce affirmative action for the scheduled castes and tribes and later reorganized the states on the basis of linguistic identity, those at the top of the power structure in Nepal, the Ranas, the kings and subsequently the conservative ruling political elite, were loath to share power or economic resources; they viewed this principally as a zero-sum game. It is the have-nots in Nepal that have had to fight through *andolans* and street agitations, and in the case of the Maoists, a violent insurgency, to achieve their goals of a more inclusive Nepal.

In the early decades following India's independence, the struggle in Nepal was for political emancipation and multiparty democracy, initially against the Rana autocracy and thereafter against the party-less Panchayat system. These struggles were followed by demands for an even more radical transformation of Nepal. The Maoists began an armed insurgency for a federal republican Nepal and exploited the discontent among the economically and socially marginalized sections of society by giving strength to the politics of identity and inclusion. They set up autonomous ethnic zones in areas under their control and sowed the seeds for identity-based federalism and a more equitable state, demands that were subsequently taken up dramatically by the Madhesis of the plains.

The Madhesis and Janjati communities that represent two-thirds of the population of Nepal deeply resent what they perceive to be an unequal state with political power and economic resources controlled by the small hill caste elite of Bahuns and Chhetris. Janjatis were attracted to the idea of federal provinces based on ethnic identities that the Maoists had promised. In fact, this, together with acute poverty, was an important factor for Janjati communities, especially the Magars in the hills and the Tharus in the plains, to support the Maoist insurgency.

The Madhesis resented the Nepalese cultural nationalism introduced by King Mahendra in the 1960s based on hill symbols of dress and language that they viewed as exclusionary. They were concerned at the changing demography of the Terai that was now home to a large number of settlers from the hill districts, a policy that was encouraged during the Mahendra years. Indeed, the elimination of malaria in the Terai in the 1950s, the construction of the East-West highway in 1970 cutting through a swathe of the Chure forest in the Terai and the development of a large number of new towns along the highway resulted in huge down-migration from the hills. Over time, not only did the demography of the Terai change significantly, the centre of gravity of economic activity gradually began to shift northwards, away from the traditional district towns and roads of the Terai. Whereas in the 1950s, the Terai districts were among the most developed parts of Nepal, today they are the most backward in Nepal.

Over the decades, several Madhesi organizations, including Vedananda Jha's Nepal Terai Congress and Gajendra Narayan Singh's Sadbhavana Party, had been advocating for Madhesi demands with limited success. It is only after the advent of multiparty democracy in the 1990s and later, after the Maoist insurgency, that a critical mass had developed for achieving these goals. Even as the people of Nepal were celebrating the end of the Maoist insurgency with the signing of the Comprehensive Peace Agreement (CPA) in November 2006, there was trouble brewing in the plains. The Madhesis of the Terai were rising up to demand their rights.

A key element of the CPA was the formulation of an interim Constitution that would incorporate the many provisions of the CPA and provide the framework for participation of the Maoists in the interim Parliament till such time that a new Constitution was adopted by an elected Constituent Assembly. It was also expected that the key demands for identity-based federal provinces and proportional inclusion in state structures on the basis of population size, would be included in the interim Constitution. Though the interim Constitution of 15 January 2007 incorporated several elements of the CPA and stripped the monarchy of all its powers (it was formally abolished after a resolution of the first Constituent Assembly in May 2008), it did not contain the demands for federalism and inclusion, even though the CPA had

called for an end to the centralized and unitary state system of
Nepal. It is the absence of these two key demands that was the
proximate cause for the Madhesi Andolans of 2007 and 2008.

There is an interesting anecdote narrated to me by Krishna
Prasad Sitaula, home minister of Nepal at the time. It fell
upon him to carry the decision of the Constituent Assembly to
Narayanhiti Palace to formally inform the king that Nepal had
become a Republic. Sitaula told me that the ex-king was calm and
composed and ready to depart from the palace for his new home
in Nagarjuna. He made only two requests: that he be provided
adequate security by the army and that his mother, Queen Ratna,
who was very old, be permitted to live in her house in the sprawling
palace complex. Both requests were granted. Thus ended the two-
century-old monarchy of Nepal.

The Madhesi uprisings represented an assertion of identity
and a quest for equality and inclusion in state structures. They were
a reflection of the historical and deeply felt grievances of an entire
community that they were not treated as equal Nepali citizens.
Federalism was viewed as an instrument for inclusion, self-
governance and protection of their distinct cultural and linguistic
identity. The dramatic burning of the interim Constitution by
Upendra Yadav at the Maitighar Mandala in Kathmandu in
January 2007, Nepal's hallowed spot for public protests, a stone's
throw from the Singha Durbar, the seat of the government, set
in motion a series of events that eventually led to the signing in
February 2008 of the eight-point agreement between the United
Madhesi Democratic Front, a coalition of Madhesi parties, and
the Government of Nepal headed by Prime Minister Girija Prasad
Koirala, in the presence of the leader of the CPN (UML) Madhav
Kumar Nepal and Maoist Chairman Prachanda; this agreement was
facilitated by the then Indian ambassador in Nepal, Shiv Shankar
Mukherjee.[1] Following the agreement, the interim Constitution
was amended to include a provision for an 'autonomous Madhesh
Pradesh' in the Terai and for proportional inclusion in the organs

of the state. This agreement smoothened the way for the holding of elections to the first Constituent Assembly of Nepal.

Since the 1950s, there was a deeply held desire of the people of Nepal to write their own Constitution. It was a promise made by King Tribhuvan after he overthrew the Rana yoke, a promise that had remained unfulfilled for long decades. It was this desire that was expected to be fulfilled when the first Constituent Assembly was elected in 2008. All previous Constitutions were given to Nepal by the king, six of them between the 1950s and early 2000s. In all, national sovereignty vested in the monarch and not the people. The new Constitution would be a people's Constitution, where they would be sovereign. All sections of Nepal's diverse society—Bahun Chhetris, Madhesis and Janjatis, each representing a third of the population—wanted their aspirations to be accommodated in the new Constitution. They desired that the solemn agreements that brought the Maoists into the democratic mainstream and ended the Madhesi uprisings should be reflected in the new Constitution. Unfortunately, though it had achieved considerable progress on many issues, the first Constituent Assembly (CA) could not reach agreement on several key aspects of the Nepali state, particularly the vexed federal question and proportional representation as well as the form of government. The Maoists were insisting on a directly elected Presidential system, which was not acceptable to the NC and the CPN (UML). The CA was ultimately dissolved in May 2012 without promulgating a new Constitution, thereby creating a constitutional impasse.

I arrived in Nepal in September 2013, just prior to the conduct of elections for CA II. In the intervening period after my stint as JS (North), major developments had taken place in Nepal: the Comprehensive Peace Agreement, the interim Constitution, the DDR (demobilization, disarmament and reintegration) of Maoist soldiers under UN auspices, the Madhesi Andolans, the conduct of elections to the first Constituent Assembly (the

Assembly also functioned as the Parliament) with the surprisingly good performance of the Maoists who went on to form a government under Prachanda, the failure of the Assembly to draft a Constitution and its dissolution leading to a constitutional crisis. I arrived to a strange kind of government known as the Interim Council of Ministers headed by the sitting Chief Justice Khil Raj Regmi! It was a technocratic government with erstwhile secretaries elevated to the position of ministers. Run competently by Madhav Prasad Ghimire who held key portfolios of Home and Foreign Affairs under the guidance of Chief Justice Regmi, its only task was to conduct CA elections and hand over power to an elected government. The inspiration for this model came from the Bangladesh experience (since discontinued in that country), where in order to ensure that polls were free and fair, the sitting elected government gave way to an interim government headed by the Chief Justice, which conducted the polls. Ghimire, one of the finest bureaucrat politicians that I had the opportunity to work with closely and count as a friend, died tragically in a road accident in September 2016.[2]

The atmosphere in Nepal even as late as October 2013, a month prior to elections, was uncertain and confused. There were many doubts on whether elections would take place at all. At a meeting with editors of the leading newspapers of Nepal at India House just a week prior to the elections, I was surprised at the kind of scepticism expressed, including about the participation of the Maoists in the elections. My clear brief at the time was to do everything necessary to ensure that the interim government organized free and fair elections and thus provide an outlet for the many political problems facing the country. In the event, India played an important and supportive role by providing considerable moral and logistical support[3] to the interim government and the Election Commission. We also worked with the international community through meetings of resident ambassadors convened by the UN Resident Coordinator at UN House in Kupondole, and issued several statements conveying our strong support and backing for the elections.

The elections resulted in a defeat of pro-change forces, namely, Maoists and Madhesis. Status-quoist parties, the Nepali Congress and the CPN (UML), did extremely well. As a result, the composition of the new house altered dramatically. The NC, which was the second largest group in the first CA, became the single largest party with 196 seats followed by the CPN (UML), a close second with 175 seats. With 371 seats, the two parties were just short of a two-thirds majority in the 601-member house. The Maoists, the largest group in the first CA, came a poor third with eighty seats, way behind the CPN (UML). Madhesis too performed poorly and their representation fell sharply from eighty-two seats in CA I to less than fifty.[4] Many senior Madhesi leaders, including Mahant Thakur and Rajendra Mahato, did not find a place in the new Legislature-Parliament.

Maoists initially refused to accept the results and complained about rigging by security forces. In course of time, they realized that no one was buying this line and that the elections had been well organized by the interim government and were free and fair. They finally accepted the results after a face-saving agreement that a committee would be set up to look into their allegations.

Being the largest party, it was evident that the NC would lead the government. Their initial efforts to form a consensus government only drew support from the CPN (UML), with the Maoists, the pro-monarchy Rashtriya Prajatantra Party (RPP) and Madhesi parties opting to sit in the opposition. The Maoists and Madhesis were licking their wounds after the electoral defeat. The NC and CPN (UML) decided to join forces and form a grand coalition. They forged an agreement to adopt the Constitution within one year, with a rotation of prime ministers between the two parties thereafter. Both the NC and CPN (UML) shared similar views on the questions of federalism and inclusion. In addition, this coalition would be close to the magic number of 401, the two-thirds majority required to adopt the Constitution. While they would try and forge a consensus, they wanted to ensure that failing a consensus, they were not faced with the impasse in CA 1, which had to be dissolved without promulgating a Constitution. They wanted to rule out any possibility of another failure. Though both parties had been traditional rivals, they had joined together to bring the Maoists into the democratic mainstream and also cooperated in the Jan Andolan or people's movement of April 2006 that brought down the monarchy. I recall the late Sushma Swaraj expressing her scepticism to me about the rotational power-sharing agreement. She was prescient, as we shall see later. Sushil Koirala of the Nepali Congress was sworn in as prime minister in February 2014.

Fluent in English, Sushil Koirala (SK) was one leader that I had not met during my earlier stint as JS (North) in the MEA. I met him for the first time when he was President of the Nepali Congress upon joining my post as ambassador. An elderly, somewhat frail-looking man and soft-spoken, he was not in the best of health. A chain smoker, he had given up this habit after being diagnosed with tongue cancer, from which he recovered fully but was now suffering from lung cancer. He was a close associate of the late Biseshwar Prasad Koirala (BPK), the father of Nepalese democracy, was with him in exile in Banaras and helped in looking after BPK's family. Sushil Koirala was distantly related to BPK from his mother's side and unlike the main Koirala family that originated from Biratnagar, SK was from Nepalganj in the western Terai. SK had a reputation for honesty and his only possessions declared in his affidavit while contesting elections were three mobile phones. He did not own any house and lived in rented accommodation paid for by the party and subsequently in a property owned by Shashank Koirala, BPK's youngest son, a professional eye surgeon from BHU and the heir to BPK's political legacy.

Shashank was SK's favourite among the Koirala siblings that included Girija Prasad Koirala's daughter, Sujata, and nephew, Shekhar, all of whom are active in the Nepali Congress. Never having held public office and hence not tainted by allegations of corruption, nor having entered into any controversies, Shashank is the most popular of the siblings in the rank and file of the party. Shekhar had been a medical doctor and Vice Chancellor of the BP Koirala Institute for Health Sciences (BPKIHS), Dharan, an impressive medical college and teaching hospital that India had helped set up along the lines of the All India Institute for Medical Sciences in Delhi. He was close to the late Girija Prasad Koirala and was one of the mediators appointed by GPK for the secret dialogue with the Maoists. Sujata Koirala occasionally accompanied GPK on his visits to Delhi and gained in influence after the death of Nona Koirala, Shekhar's mother and GPK's companion for long years. She was appointed Deputy PM and Foreign Minister in the coalition government of Prime Minister Madhav Kumar Nepal in 2009 at GPK's instance though her tenure was clouded by allegations of corruption and controversy about a passport deal!

Sushil Koirala's rival in the Nepali Congress was Sher Bahadur Deuba. Neither could stand the other and the party was divided into two opposing camps. Deuba had been prime minister on several occasions. He took over as President of the Nepali Congress after SK's death. Deuba belonged to far western Nepal. He told me once that the district that he came from, Dadeldhura, had strong links with Pithoragarh, that there were more Deubas on the Indian side than in Nepal. His wife, Arzu, a charming lady belonging to the Rana elite, is a major influence on Deuba. She is a political leader in her own right and also runs some NGOs. She kept a beautiful home and entertained in style, unlike other Nepalese politicians. Unlike Deuba, who was a man of few words and conversation generally ran out very fast, Arzu was chatty and articulate. An astute leader, Deuba was sworn in as prime minister for the fifth time in July 2021.

Meanwhile, the Constituent Assembly got down to business and appointed several key committees, including three that were headed by political leaders with stature and well known to us, namely, Baburam Bhattarai (Maoist) for the Constitutional Political Dialogue and Consensus Committee, Krishna Prasad Sitaula (Congress) for the Constitution Drafting Committee and Bishnu Paudel (CPN [UML]) for the Constitutional Records Study and Determination Committee, all Brahmins. Bishnu Paudel's committee was tasked with examining the records of the first Constituent Assembly and forwarding agreed issues to the Drafting Committee for finalization. Issues on which differences persisted were sent to Baburam Bhattarai's committee for resolution. Debates on the form of government were resolved since the Maoists agreed, albeit with a note of dissent, to accept a multiparty parliamentary democracy with an executive prime minister and a symbolic presidency. The problems of first-past-the-post system were resolved by developing a hybrid system that also included proportional representation, a practice with which Nepal was familiar. However, the proportional representation (PR) system in the absence of fixed lists gave considerable power to party presidents to change the inter se ranking within PR lists after the vote! The contentious issues were 'federalism' and 'inclusion', with major differences between the NC and CPN (UML) on the one hand and Maoists and Madhesis on the other.

Of course, the question of drafting the Constitution was inextricably tied up with the political ambitions of leaders and the usual troubles of power sharing and distribution of portfolios in any coalition government. With the prime ministership going to the Nepali Congress, the CPN (UML) insisted on getting the home portfolio for their senior leader in Parliament, Bam Dev Gautam. The other senior leaders of the party had already been prime ministers and were presumably unwilling to join in a lesser capacity. Koirala was adamant that he would not give the home portfolio to Bam Dev, a leader with a formidable reputation; in 1997, when he was home minister, he had masterminded his party's victory in the municipal level polls.[5] The stalemate continued for some time. Koirala had also offered to appoint Bidya Devi Bhandari, a close ally of Oli, to this post. At a meeting with me in the Everest Hotel, Oli and Bam Dev Gautam were both at a loss on what to do in the face of the intransigence displayed by Sushil Koirala. I suggested that they should wait it out, since SK did not want to unnecessarily delay his cabinet formation. He had been sworn in alone as prime minister and some weeks had already passed without a swearing-in of the full cabinet. Eventually, Sushil Koirala relented and accepted Bam Dev Gautam as home minister.

At that stage, I had struck a very good equation both with Oli and Bam Dev Gautam. Oli had only just been elected leader of the CPN (UML) parliamentary party in February 2014. He would go on to win the elections to the party presidency, defeating rival Madhav Kumar Nepal by a slender margin later that year. Oli had never been PM in the past. At that time known to be our friend, Oli proved to be very helpful in getting approvals for the Project Development Agreements for the Upper Karnali and Arun III hydro-power projects after PM Modi's visits to Nepal in August 2014. Bam Dev Gautam went on to play an important role during the earthquake relief operations in 2015.

After the CA II elections and the formation of the Sushil Koirala government, I received word from New Delhi that PM Manmohan Singh was keen to visit Nepal. He had not done so in his entire tenure of ten years, largely due to the prolonged political instability in the country. The difficulty faced by us in the Ministry of External Affairs was that he was heading an outgoing government; elections had already been announced in India, and it was our view that it would be more appropriate for a visit to take place after the elections. It was finally decided to wait till the outcome of the general elections in May 2014.

Even before any visit from India could take place, the newly elected BJP government under PM Modi played a masterstroke by inviting all SAARC leaders to the swearing-in ceremony in New Delhi in May 2014. PM Sushil Koirala accepted the invitation and joined his SAARC colleagues in Delhi for what was his first interaction with PM Modi. Modi's foreign policy priority was the neighbourhood, and he was keen to invest it with substance. His first visit abroad appropriately enough was to Bhutan. His second foreign tour was to Nepal between 3–4 August, a mere two months after his government had taken over. Chandra Mohan Yadav, the son of the Nepalese President Ram Baran Yadav and a junior Nepali Congress MP, had met Modi in Delhi through his own connections and suggested to him that a visit to the Pashupatinath temple on the first Shravan Somvar (Monday in August) would be auspicious. I recall getting a call from Foreign Secretary Sujatha Singh telling me to firm up the visit, brush up my Hindu mythology and be prepared for questions that I may have to field.

I received a first taste of this when I went to brief the prime minister prior to his visit. The Prime Minister's Office (PMO) in South Block was still getting used to a new PM. Private Secretary (PS) Sanjeev Singla had just been appointed a day before and was trying to find his feet. I was waiting in his room with other senior officials from the PMO when I was told that the PM wanted to see me alone. I was ushered into his office, rather small compared to offices of the home minister and finance minister that I had visited in North Block. He was seated at his desk and asked me to sit across the table. He spent almost an hour listening to my assessment of the situation in Nepal and then called in his PS to note down a few recommendations for his speech at the Constituent Assembly, the principal one being to express strong support for a federal, democratic and republican Nepal. (President Ram Baran Yadav had called me, coincidentally when I was discussing the visit with Foreign Secretary Sujatha Singh at her office in South Block, and urged that PM must publicly endorse Nepal's desire to become a federal democratic republic; I had passed on the phone to the FS after suggesting that he convey this directly to her, which he did.) At the end of our conversation, though it was more of a monologue on my side, PM Modi asked me a question. 'How many Shakti Peeths are there in Nepal?' I was stumped and at a loss for answer. I said, 'Sir, I am sorry, but I don't know.' He nodded his head, and the meeting was over. My sense was that he was testing me; he obviously knew the answer. I hope I passed the test with my honest response! The first thing that I did after returning to Kathmandu was to find the exact number and names of the Shakti Peeths and send it to the PM's office.

Modi's visit to Nepal was a spectacular success. Not only did he wow the politicians but also the Nepali public at large. His address at the Constituent Assembly on 3 August 2014[6]—Modi was the first foreign leader to be so honoured—was superb. In a long and stirring ovation, he struck all the right notes. Modi said that Assembly members were not just drafting constitutional provisions, they were writing a foundational document like the Vedic *sanhitas*, they should do it with the minds of *Rishis*, sages and wise men, and create a document that would last a hundred years. The Constitution would inspire the hopes and dreams of the Nepalese people. He showered praise on the Maoists for entering the democratic mainstream and for moving from war and violence to the philosophy of the Buddha of non-violence and peace (*Yudh se Budh*) like the great Emperor Asoka had done centuries ago. He praised them for shedding weapons and moving to scriptures/law (*Shastra se Shashtra*), for jettisoning the bullet in favour of the ballot. He spoke of the great message from these developments that resonated not only in Nepal but throughout the world. Modi said that the Nepalese constitution should be like a vase full of flowers and every Nepali should feel that the fragrance of his/her flower is contained therein. (*Har Nepali ko lage ki yeh ek aisa guldasta hai jismein mere ek phool ki bhi mahak hai.*) India, he said, respected and supported the wishes of the people for a federal democratic republic. Every sentence of Modi's speech was greeted by loud and prolonged thumping of the desks by Assembly members. I was present and could see that the mood was electric; the speech would be remembered for a long time in Nepal. India–Nepal relations were at an all-time high. People joked that Modi would win any election hands down in Nepal.

Modi entranced the parliamentarians and common people alike, hundreds of whom had gathered by the roadside waiting for his motorcade to pass. He would make impromptu halts of the motorcade, get down from his bullet-proof BMW specially flown in from Delhi, stroll to the crowd and shake hands, do namaste and wave. There would be a sudden surge of the ordinary folk towards him, much to the dismay of his security entourage. Modi seemed to revel in this public approbation, a personality characteristic very different from his predecessor, who was more aloof and of an academic bent of mind. No Nepali leader had ever done this, let alone a foreign head of government. As the ambassador, I was worried about the PM's security and urged him to avoid these impromptu stops. He responded that there was no threat to his security since no one knew where he would stop the motorcade. He, however, agreed to discontinue this practice the next day. Come Monday, the auspicious first Shravan Somvar, on his visit to Pashupatinath, he again mingled with the roadside crowds by stopping en route. So much for my advice.

I remember the banquet hosted by Prime Minister Sushil Koirala at the Soaltee Hotel, the most prestigious hotel in Kathmandu, owned by Prabhakar Shumsher Rana in partnership with the ex-king. It was a grand occasion with several hundred guests. The ballroom was laid out with one long table and several smaller circular tables. And as most of those who have attended these events know, they have little interesting conversation. Our prime minister made a short but meaningful banquet speech. But Prime Minister Sushil Koirala, who was not in the best of health and coughing, read out a long speech covering all aspects of India-Nepal relations. It had already been a long and tiring day for the delegation, and the banquet seemed to go on forever, course by course. At one stage, I could see that Modi was finding it tiresome. I was sitting diagonally across from him; he gestured to me and when I went up to see him, said that I should expedite things if I could. I conveyed this to the Nepalese Chief Secretary, Leelamani Poudel, who was seated close to me, but I am not sure that things got expedited.

For some reason, the Nepalese serve western food at their banquets. Here was a delegation from India; we had similar culinary habits and tastes like the Nepalese; the Nepalese have fabulous cuisine, especially that of the Newar community. I once mentioned this to the Nepalese foreign secretary Shankar Bairagi, an outstanding diplomat, and he agreed with what I said. On several subsequent occasions, we were served Newar Thali meals at Hotel Dwarika, a unique hotel run by the elegant Ambica Shreshta and her daughter Sangita, with an internal façade covered with exquisite Newar woodwork. This was my favourite place to house our VIP guests. Unfortunately, the PM's security did not agree for him to stay there and insisted that he stay in one of the standard modern facilities.

The auguries for Modi's second visit to Nepal for the SAARC Summit from 25–27 November that year were not good. Debates in the Constituent Assembly were progressing with little contribution and participation from the Maoists and Madhesi alliance. The ruling NC-CPN (UML) coalition had presented a joint proposal on key elements of the Constitution on 7 November 2014, viz., Parliamentary system, seven-province model, etc. The most contentious issue related to the federal demarcation of the seven provinces with the Terai fragmented into five states. The joint proposal was rejected both by the Maoists and the Madhesis. As the one-year deadline to adopt the Constitution was approaching, there was a sense that the majoritarian alliance was moving rapidly towards finalizing a Constitution with or without the support of the agitating parties. It is in this context that the PM's second visit was being organized. We were also aware, after the first visit, that some sections of society, such as the Madhesis, had felt somewhat left out since the PM had made no mention of them in his famous speech to the Constituent Assembly.

For his second visit it was felt that Modi should see a little more of Nepal. During his earlier visit, he had expressed an interest in visiting Janakpur and Lumbini, the birthplace of the Buddha, as well as Muktinath. Muktinath, located in the high Himalayan district of Mustang, was ruled out because of the cold weather at that time of year. Eventually, Lumbini too was dropped due to paucity of time and logistical problems. Janakpur remained on the agenda. I had wanted the PM to see the sorry state of infrastructure on the Bihar–Nepal border in the hope that this would expedite road construction in border areas. In one of my meetings with the PM, I suggested that he travel by road to Janakpur. He readily agreed and told me that I should quietly make this intention public so that the roads would, hopefully, be improved in time for his visit. For a prime ministerial visit, even the lackadaisical PWD Department would pull up their socks and work with alacrity! Other elements of his visit to Janakpur would include the presentation of a token few bicycles to school-going girls before launching a larger programme. This scheme had been a big success in Bihar and had resulted in a huge reduction in the number of school dropouts among girls. Further, there would be a mass civic reception where he would address the people of the Terai. Due to the open border, we also expected a large number of people from the bordering districts of Bihar. I had even gone to Janakpur and visited the Bara Bigha Cricket Ground that was found to be suitable for the reception.

Within Nepal, even as people were squabbling about who should be on the dais, etc. the government started developing cold feet about the visit to the Terai. They were probably not sure what message Modi would give to the people of the Terai, who wanted equal participation and representation in Nepal. Also, they had reservations on the scheme for distribution of bicycles.

Indeed, the leadership may have been worried that due to Modi's popularity, his personal and Indian influence in the Terai would become even stronger. I was called by Foreign Minister Mahendra Bahadur Pandey, who was close to Oli, and informed that they would not be able to arrange for Modi's visit to Janakpur since the administration was overstretched due to the SAARC Summit and they could not make adequate arrangements for security. He added that they could not make special arrangements for one SAARC leader and had to treat all equally! I reported this to Delhi and Modi cancelled his Janakpur visit. The whole episode left a sour taste in our mouth.

When Modi did visit for the SAARC Summit, a visit that was now limited to Kathmandu, he also had several bilateral issues on the agenda. These included the handing over of the trauma centre, a military helicopter and inaugurating the first direct bus service between Kathmandu and Delhi, thereafter known as the Modi bus in local parlance. His primary public speaking engagement was at the handover ceremony of the trauma centre. In the presence of PM Sushil Koirala and the Speaker Subhas Nemwang, Modi made an impassioned speech[7] on the need for early adoption of a new Constitution on the basis of *sahmati* (unanimity) not brute majority, that voices of all sections of society, Madhesi, Pahadi and Maoists, should be heard. He said that it was for the people of Nepal to decide the type of constitution they wanted and India had no role in the matter. He also uttered a word of caution. If the Constitution was not adopted by *sahmati*, there could be problems later on. I could see that faces of the Nepalese leaders on the stage fell. They possibly interpreted Modi's stress on *sahmati* as a veiled warning to accommodate Madhesi aspirations.

The political mood in Nepal became increasingly vitiated as the deadline of 22 January to adopt the Constitution approached. Maoists and Madhesis, who had formed an alliance for a more progressive constitution, were worried that the NC and CPN (UML) were rushing ahead with the Constitution and that they would adopt it without their consent, given that they could easily rustle up a two-thirds majority. Opposition parties started agitating and also disrupting the proceedings of the house. This culminated in complete mayhem in the house on 20 January 2015. Microphones were thrown by Maoist and Madhesi members at their colleagues from the Congress and especially CPN (UML). K.P. Sharma Oli, leader of the parliamentary party of the CPN (UML), had taken a particularly strident position on several key issues, including federalism and inclusion that were dear to the Maoists and Madhesis. Oli told me later that he was planning to respond in kind but that it was Bidya Devi Bhandari, seated next to him, who restrained him from doing so. Oli felt that the whole incident had been planned in advance by the Maoists. In any event, the house could not adopt the Constitution on the due date.

While there was a broad consensus that Nepal should be a federal democratic republic, as agreed in the interim Constitution, there remained major differences on the issues of federal boundaries, inclusion and representation, on which the most contentious debates took place without a consensus emerging. As a result of the changed composition of the Constituent Assembly, with the NC–CPN (UML) combine in pole position, there was a rollback on commitments made following the end of the Maoist insurgency and the Madhesi uprisings that were enshrined in the interim Constitution. Political ground realities had changed.

The key demands of the Madhesis during their agitation, prior to and following the promulgation of the Constitution, related to the nature of federalism, political representation, inclusion in state structures and citizenship.

The demand for an autonomous Madhesh Pradesh was linked to the growth of identity politics encouraged by the Maoists during the insurgency and reflected a sense of exclusion felt by Madhesi and Janjati communities. However, despite a commitment to this effect enshrined in the interim Constitution, there was deep reluctance on the part of both the Nepali Congress and CPN (UML) to accommodate this demand. Nepalese leaders were accustomed only to a unitary state. If at all they were looking at federalism, it was merely in administrative terms, whereas the demand for federalism had its genesis in the exclusionist policies of the ruling hill elites vis-à-vis Madhesis and Janjatis. When linked to identity or regional aspirations, the Nepali Congress and CPN (UML) saw federalism as a step that would weaken national unity and cohesion. An autonomous Madhesh Pradesh stretching from the Mechi to the Mahakali rivers was anathema. It was viewed as laying the ground for fissiparous tendencies in the country, given their innate suspicions of the dual loyalties of the Madhesis and an existential fear of India. The annexation of Crimea by Russia in 2014 evoked great angst in Nepal. It revived memories of 1975. Nepal did not want to become Sikkimized. Indeed, the first draft of the Constitution had deferred federal delimitation altogether. It was only after the verdict of a single-judge Supreme Court bench headed by Justice Girish Chandra Lal in July 2015[8] that the draft was revised and delimitation of state boundaries, however imperfect, was included in the Constitution.

Instead of honouring the commitment of one (or two)[9] Terai province(s) covering the twenty Terai districts enshrined in the interim Constitution that Madhesi parties were willing to accept, the Terai was carved out into five units. They received only one truncated Madhesh Pradesh, province number 2 comprising eight Terai districts stretching from the Kosi to the Gandak rivers. The remaining twelve districts of the Terai were merged with hill provinces. Even the earlier NC-CPN (UML) joint proposal of two Madhesi states in the Terai, which had left out the three districts of the east and two of the far west, was jettisoned. The dispute over these five districts was the proximate cause for the Madhesi Andolan prior to promulgation of the Constitution that resulted in many deaths, mostly through police firing.[10]

The leaders of both the Nepali Congress and the CPN (UML) represented a conservative mindset and narrow political agendas. Unlike Girija Prasad Koirala, the tallest political leader of his time who had signed the famous Comprehensive Peace Agreement with the Maoists and the eight-point agreement with the Madhesis and who was personally committed to honouring these agreements, after his death, his successors were more timid in their approach. I had innumerable meetings with Nepal's leading politicians over several hours on the contentious issues of the Constitution. Sushil Koirala, the prime minister, was not in favour of many provinces. He felt that a small country like Nepal could not afford the cost of federal and provincial governments. He would say to me that the Government of Nepal had been unable to even construct a new Parliament building for themselves (the old Rana-period building in Singha Durbar was structurally unsuitable and, in any event, since the Singha Durbar was the seat of the government, it was not appropriate for it to house Parliament as well) and had to operate from rented premises of the Convention Centre built by the Chinese. Who would construct the Assembly buildings for provinces? Who would provide for the separate judiciaries and bureaucracies? He would say that at most, Nepal should have three provinces. From India too, there may have been some mixed messages. I was told by a Nepali interlocutor that one or two politicians from India too had expressed scepticism about the suitability of the federal model for Nepal. Nepal was also afloat with rumours that China was not in favour of federalism.

The most contentious issue related to the two far western districts of Kailali and Kanchanpur and the three far eastern districts of Sunsari, Morang and Jhapa, all of which fell in the Terai but where migrants from the hills had strong commercial and political interests. The far western Terai was an area with a significant Tharu population. Though they were not a majority, they constituted the single largest group in the area. Historically, the Tharus had been discriminated against; many had become serfs on their own land, community-owned but not recognized as such by the state. The Tharus had been major supporters of the Maoists and suffered the largest number of casualties during the insurgency; it was the Maoists who had planted the seeds of Tharuwan, or a state for the Tharu community.

The eastern Terai also had an interesting history. Historically, this was an area populated by the Santhals, Koche-Rajbanshis, Meche and other communities, some of whom lost their lands and migrated to India as labour in the tea plantations of North-east India. Jhapa district, for instance, was settled by migrants from the eastern hill districts such as Tehrathum, to which both K.P. Oli of the CPN (UML) and K.P. Sitaula of the NC originally belong. The demographic composition of this part of the Terai had been transformed over the decades with the Pahadis in a dominant position. Morang district, and specially its largest town Biratnagar, was the hometown of the Koiralas. Indeed, Biratnagar town had been developed by the Koirala patriarch, BPK's father Krishna Prasad Koirala. This was their fiefdom. Sunsari was divided between the Madhesis and Tharus in the Southern part of the district and Pahadis in the upper areas.

Generally, in the Terai districts, following the construction of the East–West Highway and the settlement of hill migrants in new towns along the highway such as Birtamod, Damak, Itahari, Lahan, Bardibas, Butwal, Kohalpur, etc. the demographic composition had changed. Madhesis, the original inhabitants of the Terai, were in areas close to the Indian border connected by the famous Hulaki or Postal Roads that linked the headquarters of districts in the Terai such as Bhadrapur, Inaruwa, Rajbiraj, Janakpur, Jaleshwar, Malangwa, Gaur, etc. To this day, whenever the government wishes to move some district administrative office from the district headquarters to one of the new towns along the highway, there are large protests in the Terai.

Given the strong interest of some of the key leaders in both the eastern and western Terai, these five districts became a major bone of contention. Sher Bahadur Deuba of the NC and Bhim Rawal of the CPN (UML) took a very strong stand that Kailali and Kanchanpur could under no circumstances be separated from the hill districts of the far west. Oli of the CPN (UML) and Sitaula of the NC argued that Sunsari, Morang and Jhapa could similarly not be separated from the hill districts in the east. In other words, even if the Madhesi parties were willing to agree to two provinces in the Terai, these five districts would have to be separated. In many meetings with Sushil Koirala, I would ask him to find an amicable compromise that would satisfy all stakeholders; the idea that these five districts could be governed directly by the Centre, somewhat akin to Union Territories of India, or that a final decision on their location could be kept in abeyance for the time being or sent to a Commission did not find favour. He used to throw up his hands and say, 'What can I do? Deuba does not agree'; or, 'Sitaula does not agree.' As president of the party and PM, Sushil Koirala could have taken a position but was reluctant to do so. Since positions were rigid on one side, it became easier for a similar unwillingness to compromise on the other side as well. In the event, the Terai was divided in five separate parts, with eight districts from Parsa to Sarlahi forming the truncated Madhesi Province Number 2 and the other twelve districts merged with the hill provinces. As a result, the demographics of the Terai were altered, with hill communities dominating in six of the seven provinces even though Madhesis represent one-third of the population.

Another key Madhesi demand was that representation in legislative bodies should be in proportion to their population. Hill Nepalese leaders, however, felt that due significance also needed to be given to geographical factors to ensure that every district of Nepal was adequately represented in both houses of Parliament. The Terai, while comprising 51 per cent of the population, represents only 17 per cent of the land mass of the country. The hills, on the other hand, comprise 49 per cent of the population with 83 per cent of the geographical area. Clearly, introduction of geography as a determinant of seats, particularly in the lower house, implied that the Terai would get less than 50 per cent of the seats. After the first amendment to the Constitution, which decided that representation would be on the basis of population and geography rather than geography and population (the order between the two was reversed), the Terai received seventy-eight seats of the 165 directly elected members of the lower house. It was also ironic that the unit for determining geographical representation was the district and not the federal province, although the role of the district would lose salience in the new constitution.

The membership of the upper house, too, was controversial. Every province was to be provided eight seats. In a fifty-nine-member upper house, fifty-six members would be elected by seven provinces and three nominated by the government. Given that six states had a Pahadi majority and only one with Madhesi majority, the composition of the upper house would always be one where Madhesis were in a small minority!

A related issue was the ratio between First Past the Post (FPTP) seats and Proportional Representation (PR) seats in the Pratinidhi Sabha or lower house. In the first CA, the ratio between PR candidates to FPTP candidates was 60:40. The proposal in the new constitution reversed this to 40:60, viz., in a 275-member lower house, 165 members would be elected on an FPTP basis and only 110 on a PR basis. In effect, the proportion had been altered in favour of FPTP candidates. It was felt that such an approach worked against a more equitable representation of disadvantaged groups.

Poor representation in state organs and security forces has been a long-standing grievance of the Madhesi and Janjati communities. There are few Madhesi-origin officials in senior positions either in the army and police or indeed, in civil administration. Janjatis are reasonably well represented at junior levels in the army and the police, but not in the higher echelons of the bureaucracy. Accordingly, these communities, and especially the Madhesis who were better organized, demanded proportionate inclusion in state administration and security services, a demand that had already been accepted in the interim Constitution. The term 'proportionate' was eventually added to 'inclusion' following the first Constitutional Amendment, even though some influential hill leaders were not in favour of any quota system for jobs.

In many conversations that the writer had with Oli, it was clear that despite being a communist, Oli was rather conservative in his thinking on issues of affirmative action for the disadvantaged communities. He once narrated a story from his childhood to me. Growing up in Athrai village of Tehrathum in a small, poor Brahmin household, he said that he went to the village school. He referred to two of his classmates, one a Dalit and the other the son of a rich trader. He said that because of the conducive atmosphere in his house, he studied hard and did well. The rich man's son was spoilt and not interested in studying and the Dalit neither studied nor had a suitable atmosphere at home. Basically, he was trying to convey that though he belonged to the upper-caste Brahmin community, he did well due to his merit and hard work, and conversely others did poorly because of the lack of it. On another occasion, he rhetorically asked me, 'Suppose you fall sick and need to visit a doctor, would you go to the best doctor or to one who has benefited from reservations and the quota system?' Unlike in India, where the founding fathers of our Republic decided early on that reservations were needed for the underprivileged communities not only as recompense for the centuries of discrimination but for them to realize their true potential and become equal productive citizens, in Nepal, some key political leaders did not see merit in reservation; they saw it as a zero-sum game. It is only the long and persistent struggles of the underprivileged communities that have secured this right for them, albeit in an abridged manner and not in the full measure that had once been promised. Even though there is 45 per cent quota in government jobs today, it covers several categories of people, including women, Dalits, Adivasi Janjatis, Madhesis, the differently abled and those from backward regions. In effect, the quota is so dispersed that its impact stands diluted.

The Nepali ruling elite has traditionally had a deep-seated fear that migration from Bihar and Uttar Pradesh was altering the demographic composition of the country. This fear of being swamped by outsiders (known colloquially as *Fijikaran* of Nepal) with presumed dual loyalties made the issue of citizenship extremely sensitive. Madhesis, on the other hand, have always complained of difficulties in obtaining Nepalese citizenship certificates, with some being denied citizenship over several generations. The new constitution brought in certain changes with regard to citizenship by marriage; for instance, citizenship by descent would be available to a person whose father or mother was a citizen of Nepal at the time of the commencement of the Constitution; this provision would, however, not be applicable to a female citizen married to a foreigner. The Constitution also abolished the category granting citizenship by birth. It only includes citizenship by descent and by naturalization. Further, restrictions were placed on naturalized citizens holding high positions in the federal government and provinces as well as security forces. The debates on this issue also reflected an existential fear of India and Nepalese leaders wanted to ensure that no sensitive position in Nepal would be held by a naturalized Nepali of Indian origin.

Though the debates on the draft Constitution progressed largely between the senior leaders of political parties, President Ram Baran Yadav, a Madhesi from Janakpur and an erstwhile leader of the Nepali Congress close to Sushil Koirala, played an important role behind the scenes. He tried hard to persuade SK to accommodate Madhesi demands. I had known him when I was JS in the Ministry when he had been injured during the crackdown following King Gyanendra's takeover in 2005. He always faced a huge dilemma in his mind. He was from the

Terai, but acceptable to the Pahadi leaders. Indeed, he had
been critical of the Madhesi agitations of 2007 and 2008. His
entry into politics was facilitated by the fact that he had been
B.P. Koirala's physician. Mahant Thakur's departure from the
NC to form the Terai Madhesh Loktantrik Parishad (TMLP)
had left the NC bereft of any senior Madhesi leader. This was
an anomalous situation given the fact that the NC had a huge
support base in the Terai; indeed, it was known as a party of
the Terai. During the Presidential elections, when the Maoists
fielded Ram Raja Prasad Singh, a famous revolutionary leader of
yore and a Madhesi, the NC fielded Ram Baran Yadav, who won
with the support of CPN (UML). Even though the Madhesi
parties were officially supporting the Maoist candidate, several
MPs from Madhesi parties violated the whip and indulged in
cross voting in favour of Ram Baran Yadav.

Ram Baran Yadav was educated at Jadavpur University and
PGI Chandigarh. He believed deeply that for Nepal to be stable
and prosperous, it needed to have close and cordial relations
with India. Indeed, he mentioned to every Indian visitor about
the great support and contributions of India in the political and
economic transformation of Nepal, from the Delhi Pact of 1950
to the twelve-point agreement of 2005. As President, he played
an important role in supporting a progressive constitution that
accommodated Madhesi aspirations.

I had established a close working relationship with the
President and was a frequent guest at his palace, Shital Niwas, a
large Rana structure with a red façade, not far from Lainchaur, the
seat of the Indian embassy. The palace was badly damaged during
the earthquake, making the top floor, used as the President's
living quarters, uninhabitable. In an earlier avatar, Shital Niwas
had been the Indian embassy and had hosted King Tribhuvan
for three weeks in 1950 when he fled from the clutches of the
Ranas. Sir C.P.N. Singh was then ambassador, and I was told
a fascinating tale, possibly apocryphal but interesting, by B.L.

Sharma, a sweets-maker and father-in-law of Binod Chowdhry, the founder of Wai Wai noodles, reputed to be the richest businessman in Nepal. Sharma told me that King Tribhuvan was in captivity at the Narayanhiti Palace. Since he was fond of sweets, Sharma would regularly deliver boxes of delicacies to the palace. The communication between the king and the ambassador was carried out through messages hidden in the boxes. That is how the plan was hatched to get King Tribhuvan to come to India House. On the appointed day, the king went on a picnic to the hills of Shivpuri. Shital Niwas stands on the wide road from Lainchaur to Budhanilkantha and Shivpuri. As the king's motorcade approached India House, his vehicle swerved into the open gates of Shital Niwas. Later, Shital Niwas became the office of the Foreign Ministry, and I had the pleasure of visiting it several times when Bhekh Bahadur Thapa was Foreign Minister. I had known him well from his time in Delhi as ambassador.

Ram Baran Yadav was quite disturbed at the manner in which the dominant parties, the CPN (UML) and the NC, were forging ahead with the Constitution, disregarding the demands of the Madhesis. He was also angered at the manner in which the protests in the Terai were being handled by the SK government. Several protesters had been killed by police bullets.[11] President Ram Baran Yadav also used to threaten political leaders that he would not accept any Constitution that was not acceptable to the entire population. At a late stage during the Constitution drafting process during the first fortnight of September 2015,[12] he had even sent a letter to the Constituent Assembly formally conveying his views, but the Chairman of the Constituent Assembly, Subhas Nemwang, refused to even share the message with members on the grounds that there was no provision in the interim Constitution for the President to send a message to the house. President Yadav was, therefore, in a deep dilemma when the Constitution was finally drafted. He decided that his duty and responsibility as head of state was to accept the document

produced by the CA irrespective of any reservations that he may
have. He was worried that had he not done so, he would have
gone down in posterity as someone who had betrayed his own
country.[13] I could understand this sentiment and the reasons
why he felt compelled to perform his constitutional duty, but I
thought his reverential gesture of holding the new Constitution
to his head, in a sign of great obeisance and respect before the
house, was odd.

President Ram Baran Yadav lived a very simple life. He
was a widower. I had the pleasure of dining with him on several
occasions over simple *dal, bhat, tarkari* and the ubiquitous
saag. Knowing my sweet tooth, he would have delicious *kheer*
prepared for me. Being a diabetic, he himself refrained from
such indulgence. Having been educated in Jadavpur, he was
fluent in Bengali and close to President Pranab Mukherjee. In
fact, he sent his constitutional adviser, Professor Surya Dhungel,
to New Delhi from time to time to brief our President. I also
took care to brief President Mukherjee on virtually every visit to
Delhi. During my courtesy call prior to leaving for Nepal, the
President had told me of his interest in Nepal and that he wanted
to be kept informed of developments there. Subsequently, at the
end of every meeting, and some of them went on for over an
hour, he would again ask to be briefed on my next trip. Initially,
the secretary to the President and the joint secretary would be
present in my meetings, but after a while, I used to meet him
alone. I was struck by the depth of his knowledge on the working
of the Indian Constituent Assembly and his memory for names
and composition of various committees, how each member was
selected, as well as the debates. Consequently, our President's
messages to his Nepali visitors, rooted in India's own experience
on the importance of accommodating diverse aspirations and
taking all sections of society along, were profound and visionary.

The great earthquake of 25 April 2015 was a game changer
with regard to the Constitution-drafting process. PM Koirala

had frequently been talking about fast-tracking the Constitution writing process that had already overshot the one-year deadline. With the massive earthquake, the uncertainties that it had created and the inadequacies of governance that it had revealed, for the leaders it became a now or never moment. The CPN (UML) and the NC were already in agreement. An effort was now made to reach out to the Maoists and Madhesis to forge a grand compromise. The Maoists decided to part company with the Madhesis and joined forces with the NC and the CPN (UML). From among the Madhesi parties, only the wily Bijay Kumar Gacchedar of the Madhesi Janadhikar Forum joined this compromise. He was a prominent Tharu leader from eastern Nepal and had good relations with political leaders across the board. He was also known to prioritize self-interest above everything else. Accordingly, he broke away from the other Madhesi parties and joined the sixteen-point 8 June agreement, which mentioned that eight provinces would be created but their boundaries would be determined later after the report of a federal commission set up for this purpose. The 8 June agreement also diluted a key Madhesi demand for proportionate inclusion in state structures.

This agreement, which was criticized by the Madhesi parties, was subsequently challenged in the Supreme Court that passed an interim order by a single-judge bench that the Constitution could not be promulgated without the demarcation of state boundaries. While the signatories to the agreement criticized the order, Madhesi parties welcomed it as being in conformity with the provisions of the interim Constitution of 2007. Ultimately, the four signatories abided by the court decision and demarcated state boundaries in the new Constitution.

Following the 16-point agreement, a draft Constitution was tabled in the Constituent Assembly on 30 June 2015. It had the support of the Nepali Congress, CPN (UML), the Maoists and Gacchedar's Madhesi Janadhikar Forum. Together, they had more than the required two-thirds majority to adopt the Constitution. Developments proceeded rapidly after the 8 June agreement. The number of states swung like a pendulum from the initial eight to six before settling down at seven. Boundary demarcation was determined by the political and economic interests of several influential politicians while ignoring the demands of the Tharus and Madhesis of the Terai and the Janjatis. Even Gacchedar's MJF Democratic withdrew from the four-party alliance following the announcement of the seven-state model.

As a result, protests began in different parts of the Terai, in Sarlahi, Rautahat, Siraha and Janakpur, the political heart of the Terai, in Birgunj, the business capital, and in the western districts of Dang and Bardiya. The Tharu-dominated region of Kailali in the far west saw huge protests and violence in Tikapur, where police personnel and civilians were killed. Thereafter, curfew was imposed in most of the Terai districts and the army called in, the first time since the Maoist insurgency. Even as the agitation continued in the Terai and the police used heavy-handed tactics, the ruling political leadership did little to assuage fears and try and forge a compromise with the agitating parties. Indeed, some leaders, such as K.P. Oli, further inflamed passions with provocative speeches. In one, he referred to a large human chain of protestors in the Terai against the draft Constitution as a *Makhe Sanglo* or a chain of flies.[14] After the death of a Madhesi protestor, Oli would insensitively say that a mango has fallen from the tree.[15] On another occasion he asked Terai leaders such as Rajendra Mahato, who was in the forefront of protests and also suffered serious head injury from a police baton, to claim territory in Bihar and UP instead of Nepal.[16] Instead of reaching out to protestors, hill politicians decided to speed up the adoption of the Constitution even in the face of the protests.

Of course, the Madhesis were divided into several political parties, each with its own niche constituency. Upendra Yadav's party represented the large Yadav community in the Terai, Mahant

Thakur's TMLP was considered to be a party of the Brahmins, since its top leaders, including Thakur, Hridayesh Tripathi and Sarvendra Nath Shukla, belonged to that community. Bijay Kumar Gacchedar's MJF (D) represented the Tharu community. Rajendra Mahato's Sadbhavna Party represented the other caste groups in the Terai. Despite the fact that they were divided along caste lines, they were united in resisting the discrimination against them by the hill communities. They came together to form a loose coalition, which coordinated the movement in the Terai against the Constitution.

The movement was the strongest in the Birganj Janakpur belt, the centre of Madhesi politics. It was not as successful in the far Eastern Jhapa and Morang region, the stronghold of Oli and the Koirala family, respectively. In the far west, the Tharus under the charismatic leadership of Resham Chowdhry had protested, but the protests had turned violent in which several persons were killed, including a police officer. In the heavy-handed crackdown that followed, members of the hill community went on a rampage and destroyed Tharu property with some leaders, including Resham Chowdhry, crossing over to the Indian side. On his return to Nepal, Chowdhry was arrested and imprisoned, but like George Fernandes in India, he won his parliamentary election sitting in jail!

One incident that caused considerable suspicion in Nepal was a document erroneously leaked to the media by our External Publicity Division. The embassy had been regularly briefing the Ministry of External Affairs on the developments with regard to the Constitution and feeding them with position papers and other documents. What had been a Madhesi position paper on their demands was projected by the *Indian Express* in a front-page headline story on 13 July 2015[17] as India's demands with regard to the Nepalese Constitution. This was completely untrue. The official spokesman issued a public denial, but the *Indian Express* stood by its story and no one in Nepal believed us. In a fraught atmosphere, it appeared to confirm the Nepali perception that the Indians were solidly backing the Madhesis and would do everything to ensure that their demands were met. This was very different from what we were doing in reality. India's approach during the Constitution-drafting process was motivated largely by a desire to see that interests and concerns of all sides were accommodated to the extent possible in order to ensure durable peace and stability in the country. At no point did we give any prescriptive demands to the Nepalese in terms of the specifics of their Constitution.

Given the historical background of agitations for greater political representation and inclusion, as well as the solemn commitments made by the Government of Nepal, following the Maoist insurgency and Madhesi Andolan and India's own role in facilitating these agreements, it was our assessment that failure to accommodate Madhesi and Janjati concerns could result in prolonged instability and turmoil in the country. Madhesi groups were split into three categories: there were the political parties that were working through the Constituent Assembly and whose protests were peaceful; there was another section that had taken up arms in the past. These had been armed vigilante groups such as those led by Jai Prakash Goit and Jwala Singh in the Terai that had split from the Maoists and had created terror in the region. We did not want a revival of such groups. Finally, there was the group led by C.K. Raut that advocated secession and was gathering support among the educated youth for the creation of an independent Madhesi state. We were also worried that this secessionist sentiment, currently at a nascent level, may gather strength if Madhesi demands were not accommodated. It is for these reasons that India emphasized at high political levels the need for the Constitution to be owned by all communities and all citizens.

On the contrary, and even in the face of the ongoing mass agitation in the Terai in which almost fifty people had lost their lives, largely in police firing, the Nepalese political leadership rushed through the Constitution. A specious rumour was spread that India did not want Nepal to adopt a constitution; that India wanted to keep Nepal in a state of 'controlled instability'; pages from a book written by one R.K. Yadav, a former Cabinet Secretariat official, suggesting that India had planned to Sikkimize Nepal were circulated among Nepal's parliamentarians. A rumour gained currency that India would prevent adoption of the Constitution; that the Constituent Assembly (II) would fail like the first Constituent Assembly. Maoist leaders such as Prachanda were worried that in such an eventuality the achievements of the Maoist insurgency, particularly a republican Nepal, would become nullified or even seen as a criminal enterprise, ergo any constitution was better than no constitution. Above all, there was pressure, particularly from the CPN (UML), for swift adoption of the Constitution since this would trigger implementation of a power-sharing deal between the Nepali Congress and the CPN (UML) that would enable the leader of the CPN (UML) K.P. Oli to become prime minister. The NC, too, was keen that the credit for the historical achievement of promulgating the Constitution should go to a government led by them.

In the event, more than 300 Articles of the Constitution were adopted within one week. Unlike in India, where the Constituent Assembly debates are essential reading to interpret our Constitution, crucial discussions on controversial issues in Nepal took place behind closed doors between key leaders of the parties of whom five were Brahmin (Sushil Koirala, K.P. Oli, Madhav Nepal, Prachanda and Baburam Bhattarai) and one Chhetri (Sher Bahadur Deuba). Three-line whips were issued to members of Parliament by their respective political parties to vote in favour of all articles. Amendments introduced by members were withdrawn at the behest of party bosses and the Constitution was adopted by an overwhelming (almost 90 per cent) majority. Madhesi members of the NC and CPN (UML) who had been urging accommodation of Madhesi concerns fell in line despite their reservations. It was also argued that the Constitution was a work in progress and that it could be amended in the future to accommodate the concerns of those who were unhappy. It is another matter that the procedure for amending provincial boundaries is extremely difficult. Following its promulgation on 20 September 2015, Diwali was celebrated in Kathmandu, whereas the Terai was plunged into a long dark night of despair and gloom. The ongoing agitation of the Madhesis was further exacerbated. Protestors began picketing the no man's land between India and Nepal that resulted in an interruption of supplies from India to Nepal, causing considerable hardship not only to the people of the hills but also the plains.

What was clear is that the Maoists, including both the top leaders Prachanda and Baburam Bhattarai, who had waged a ten-year insurgency in which 17,000 people had lost their lives, were willing to give up the progressive agenda of identity-based federalism and inclusion that they fought for. As a result, the new constitution turned out to be regressive on several issues of interest to the marginalized Madhesi and Janjati communities when compared to the interim Constitution.

As ambassador, I had been conveying to the Government of India that the Constitution was being rapidly fast-tracked by dispensing with a lot of procedures as well as time for debates on various clauses and articles. I had urged the government to send a suitable envoy to convey our assessment and concerns about the situation, and particularly the fact that the views of a significant section of society were being ignored; that the Constitution was being rushed through even in the face of protests in the Terai in which several people had been killed. Further, that it was important for India to issue a statement expressing our concern at the developments. I recall being called to Delhi a few days before the visit of Foreign Secretary S. Jaishankar during 18–19 September 2015. During my visit, EAM Sushma Swaraj agreed that India should try and make a final attempt to see whether a negotiated compromise could be found to take the agitating forces on board. The time between approval of the Constitution by the Constituent Assembly and its promulgation provided one last opportunity. In the Indian case, even as the Constitution was adopted by the Constituent Assembly on 26 November 1949, it was promulgated only two months later, on 26 January 1950. The logic was that even at this late stage, if a settlement with the Madhesis could be arrived at, it could be accommodated in the Constitution. If not, the Constituent Assembly had already endorsed the Constitution and it would be promulgated. There was some discussion on whether to send a political envoy or a bureaucrat. Sushma Swaraj felt that since a clear message needed to be conveyed, it would be better to send a bureaucrat rather than a politician who may tilt with the wind. Given the importance of the mission, it was decided to send the foreign secretary as the PM's special envoy. Unfortunately, and I say this in retrospect, the Nepalese political leaders were unwilling to listen. Instead, they decided to kill the messenger by leaking reports to the media about his supposedly arrogant behaviour. Some of these reports found their way to India and were also mentioned in a speech in the Rajya Sabha by Mani Shankar Aiyar on 7 December 2015.

Much has been written about the foreign secretary's visit to Kathmandu after the Constitution was adopted by the Nepalese Constituent Assembly. Nepalese sources have argued that our foreign secretary projected an arrogant body language and behaved badly with Nepalese leaders.[18] I participated in all his meetings with senior Nepalese politicians, including Deuba, Oli and Prachanda, and saw no evidence of this whatsoever. In all his meetings, the FS conveyed one simple message: it was still not too late to try and bring the agitating parties on board. He also pointed out how deeply India had been committed to supporting Nepal from the time of the peace process that began with the agreement in Delhi in November 2005 between political parties and the Maoists, failing which the Maoists would still be fighting a guerrilla war; he also conveyed that it was important for Nepal that the new Constitution had the fullest international support and endorsement. Even if the rest of the world supported it, without India's support, there would remain a major void. All interlocutors conveyed that the visit was too late in the day and at this stage not much could be done; that if the visit had taken place earlier perhaps there may have been time to further negotiate with the Madhesi groups, but now that the Constitution had been adopted by the Constituent Assembly and the date for proclamation by the President had been announced, nothing more could be done.

The Constitution was promulgated on 20 September 2015. There was a state function in the Parliament and the diplomatic corps was invited. I was in a dilemma and unsure about what to do. The constitution had deeply divided various communities in Nepal. India was unhappy with the manner in which the Constitution was rushed through without making the necessary effort to take everyone on board. On the other hand, I was the accredited representative of the President of India and had been invited to a formal state occasion in the Nepalese Parliament. The media was covering the occasion and had already been speculating on whether the Indian ambassador would attend or not. I finally decided to attend and was one of the last ambassadors to arrive at the New Conference Centre. I was received by the chief of protocol and ushered to the gallery upstairs where the corps was seated. The chief also requested me to attend the brief reception with the President and senior leaders of Nepal after the formal ceremony. During the course of the ceremony, he came to me at least three times to remind me to attend the reception, but I had already made up my mind. Without letting him know, I quietly slipped out of Parliament as soon as the formal ceremony was over and headed home. I did not want to put myself in the awkward position of having to congratulate the leaders of Nepal when we had major reservations on the nature of the process adopted and when the people of Nepal were so deeply polarized. The Government of India merely 'noted' and did not 'welcome' the adoption of the Constitution.

4

The Post-Constitution Fallout

Following the promulgation of the Constitution in September 2015, the Madhesis stepped up their protests in the Terai, particularly in the no man's land between Nepal and India. They started picketing border checkposts that were critical supply routes into Nepal for oil and gas and other commodities. Over a few days, shortages became visible in Kathmandu, with long lines at petrol stations and cooking gas depots. Influential voices in Nepal began pointing fingers at India, suggesting the latter was behind the Madhesi protests and particularly the border disruptions. Even as there was a growing perception in Nepal that India was extending considerable support to the Madhesis and colluding with them in blocking the border, and anger that India only 'noted' and did not welcome the Constitution, a leftist–royalist coalition government, headed by the CPN (UML) under the leadership of PM K.P. Oli, had taken over from the Nepali Congress-led coalition in October 2015.

The coalition included the Maoists, Kamal Thapa's royalist Rashtriya Prajatantra Party (RPP) and Bijay Gacchedar's Madhesi Janadhikar Forum (MJF [D]). There is an interesting backdrop to the formation of this coalition. India had become increasingly disenchanted with the utterances of Oli, who was dismissive about Madhesi demands for a more inclusive constitution. Known for his sarcastic speech, *Ukhan Tukka* in Nepali, he would taunt the Madhesis; on federalism, he said that they should make a demand for territory in UP and Bihar, implying thereby that that is where they have come from.[1] Though several senior leaders from both the NC and CPN (UML), including Sushil Koirala, Sher Bahadur Deuba and Krishna Prasad Sitaula, were not in favour, it was Oli who became the public face of the opposition to Madhesi demands. He became a deeply polarizing figure, despised in the Terai.

Under the agreement with the CPN (UML) after the CA II elections, Sushil Koirala was expected to hand over the prime ministership to Oli following the adoption of the Constitution. However, the situation both before and after the adoption of the Constitution was fraught, with the agitation picking up momentum in the Terai and the blocking of major trade and transit points between India and Nepal. In such a situation, the installation of a divisive leader like Oli would in all likelihood add fuel to the fire, further deteriorating the situation in the country. This was the thinking in Delhi at the time and we were hoping that a Congress-led coalition would continue.

Within the Congress party, too, there were different opinions. Sushil Koirala was in two minds on whether to hand over power to Oli as committed earlier or to renege, given the ground situation in the country. In the latter instance, the Congress–CPN (UML) coalition would collapse, and a new alignment would be required since one of the two parties would now sit in the opposition. Koirala was in a dilemma and kept postponing a decision, giving time to the Oli camp to consolidate and expand its support within the other parties that could have gone either way.

In the event, Sushil Koirala announced his candidature on the day of the election for the PM, but it was too late by then. Prachanda, considered to be progressive on constitutional issues, blithely announced that he would support Oli, who was vehemently opposed to the agenda of inclusion; Kamal Thapa, a conservative royalist and leader of the RPP, went incommunicado and refused to meet with SK's emissaries. He told me later that he may not have been averse to supporting a Congress-led coalition had it been headed by Deuba, with whom he had worked well in the past. Gacchedar, a wily Tharu politician heading the MJF (D), sensing the direction in which the wind was blowing, decided to throw in his lot with Oli.

Oli was elected PM with 338 votes to Sushil Koirala's 249. Only the Madhesis, excluding the MJF (D), supported the Nepali Congress. This was taken to be a tacit acceptance by the Madhesis of the new Constitution since they had participated in the election. Oli was sworn in on 12 October 2015. His coalition was to last for ten months till July 2016 when a new coalition of Maoists and NC was formed with Prachanda as prime minister.

Oli's ten months in office were marked by major developments in Nepal. The first point on the agenda of the new coalition was to address the supply shortages that had now started to bite, especially in the Kathmandu valley. Kamal Thapa, who was appointed deputy prime minister and foreign minister, was sent to India to see whether there was some way in which the supply situation could be improved. Though cordial, the visit did not result in any major breakthrough. India conveyed that the problem of supplies was created by the Madhesi protesters and that a political solution needed to be found to ease the situation. There were long lines of trucks and tankers at some of the important border crossings, especially Raxaul–Birganj, which were blocked from entering Nepal by protesters sitting in the no man's land. Meanwhile, we conveyed that we would do what we could to re-route supplies from other checkposts that were still open or partially open; medicines and Aviation Turbine Fuel (ATF) would be airlifted if required. Kamal Thapa, on his return, must have conveyed to Oli that it was essential to find a political solution to the problems.

A few weeks after his visit to India, I was called by Thapa to his office and we discussed a handwritten four-point paper that went some way in meeting Madhesi demands on proportionate inclusion and constituency delimitation, giving primacy to population and to geography as a secondary basis. He then asked for the document to be typed and handed me a copy, which I promptly forwarded to Delhi. Overall, our reaction was positive. Thapa soon thereafter visited India in a personal capacity; he had gone to the ashram of Sri Sri Ravi Shankar in Bengaluru and was stopping by in Delhi en route to Kathmandu. In his meeting with EAM Sushma Swaraj, we conveyed our support to the proposal as a step forward. The EAM inquired whether this had the endorsement of PM Oli. Thapa replied in the affirmative, but in order to be fully sure, he arranged upon Swaraj's request, a phone call between her and Oli. The latter confirmed what Thapa had told us. This paper became the basis for the first amendment to the Constitution, which was adopted in January 2016.

Meanwhile, there was some domestic criticism that India was enforcing an unannounced blockade that was causing untold misery and suffering to the Nepali population; UNICEF came out with a report that three million children would be at risk; there were dire reports of shortages of medicines.[2] There was also speculation that India would not end the 'blockade' until the elections to the provincial assembly in Bihar were over since some twenty-one seats in the Bihar provincial legislature belonged to districts of north Bihar along the India–Nepal border, which have a *roti-beti-rishta* with the Nepalese Terai. Several Indian members of Parliament wanted a discussion on the situation in Nepal in the house. Indeed, a discussion was arranged in the Rajya Sabha in the first week of December, with the EAM making a comprehensive opening statement laying out our overall policy. I was also in Delhi at the time and had asked her whether it would be useful for me to meet some of the opposition leaders prior to the debate. She encouraged me to do so. I briefed Dr Karan Singh of the Congress (I used to meet him regularly on my visits to Delhi, given his interest in Nepal since, as he was fond of telling his Nepali interlocutors, he was a *jamai* or son-in-law of Nepal), Sitaram Yechury of the CPI (M) and D.P. Tripathi of NC (Pawar). The debate was largely balanced, with the exception of a very critical analysis presented by Mani Shankar Aiyar, where he was dismissive of Madhesi claims and Madhesi leaders, who coincidentally were visiting Delhi at the time. Though both belonged to the Congress party, the statements of Aiyar and Dr Karan Singh were diametrically opposed to each other. Most members expressed concern at the situation in Nepal and urged the government to do everything possible to see that things improved. The debate took place just after Kamal Thapa's private visit to India where some headway had been made in terms of the constitutional amendment and hence the situation appeared to be moving towards a resolution.

Even as Oli tried to mend fences with India and sent Thapa on two visits in quick succession to Delhi, the left parties continued to whip up anti-India sentiment, including virulent attacks on social media; anti-India demonstrations and burning of effigies of Indian political leaders were organized by leftist student organizations.[3] Oli was projected as the tallest nationalist leader of Nepal who could stand up to India's 'bullying' tactics.

Oli also made a huge outreach effort to China. Following a well-publicized visit in March 2016, wherein several agreements, including one on transit of goods through China, were signed, the Nepalese government and Kathmandu-based media created a perception that Nepal had a serious alternative to India, that if things became difficult on the India–Nepal border, Nepal could turn to China for alternative supply routes, including for fuel. In fact, during the period that supplies to Nepal were disrupted from India, China made well-publicized deliveries of petroleum products and supplies by road and rail from the Kerung–Rasuwagadhi checkpost. These were symbolic deliveries but received huge media attention in Nepal, with leaders welcoming Chinese trucks with garlands of marigold. Such events also generated considerable criticism in India, with some commentators suggesting that India had 'lost' Nepal to China. In addition to the new Transit Treaty with China, agreements included the opening of several checkpoints on the Nepal–China border, construction of roads leading from Tibet to Nepal, as well as railway linkages between Kerung, Kathmandu and Lumbini, and between Kathmandu and Pokhara. The grounds for an upgradation of Nepal–China military ties were laid. Subsequently, the Chinese defence minister visited Nepal and for the first time a joint military exercise on counter-terrorism and disaster management between the PLA and the Nepali Army was held in 2017.

Historically, it is the monarchists and the leftists that have played the 'China card'. This was evident during the 1960s, following Mahendra's takeover, and more recently in 2015–16, when the government was headed by the CPN (UML). Given Nepal's geographical location and overwhelming dependence on India in terms of trade, transit, investment and employment opportunities, there is clearly little possibility of China replacing India or becoming a viable alternative to India for Nepal in the foreseeable future. However, China's role and activity have increased significantly, not merely in terms of financial assistance and projects but also in the support extended to political parties. While in the past, China's advice to visiting Nepali leaders was to maintain harmonious relations with India, today China does not appear to be averse to taking advantage of frictions in the India–Nepal relationship and interfere overtly and covertly in domestic political issues.

During my stay in Kathmandu, I got to know Oli well, both when he was in power and in the opposition. He is a remarkable, wily leader. He has not allowed his illnesses, two kidney transplants, complications thereafter, trips in and out of hospital, and frequent intake of fistfuls of medicines, steroids and immuno-suppressants, to cramp his no-holds-barred style: acerbic, crisp and cutting. His nephew through the wife's side, Rajesh Bajracharya, is the keeper of Oli's health and much else besides. Oli is garrulous and every meeting lasts for a long time. Consequently, his atrocious time-management leaves his personal staff in a quandary, constantly apologizing to visitors. On occasion, I have had to wait for a long time for him to complete some other meeting! But sometimes this had a plus side. Once, Pradeep Gyawali, then a close aide of Oli and till recently the foreign minister, had to fill in till Oli arrived and I learnt a lot on the origins and history of the CPN (UML) from him.

Oli is a shrewd politician, possibly the shrewdest in Nepal. Since he spent fourteen years in the king's jails following his role in the Jhapa uprising of the early 1970s, similar to the Naxal movement in Siliguri of 1972, Oli is largely self-educated. Though he is fluent in English, conversations were in Hindi, which was his preferred language of communication with me. Unlike some of the other leaders, Oli speaks his mind on issues and there is no double talk. You know where he stands. Though he is a communist, he is conservative in his outlook and against affirmative action and inclusion. He was contemptuous of Madhesi leaders and could not understand why India was supporting them. He said that they could not do anything for India, only he could. Oli disliked his projection in Indian media as a China camp follower and said that he could never go against India; that everything—culture, civilization, language and climate—binds Nepal with India; Chinese culture is alien. Since he was not personally involved in the peace process—it was Madhav Nepal, general secretary of the CPN (UML) at the time—Oli appears less committed to it. He was scornful of some of his colleagues, both within his party as well as the Maoists.

At one time, Oli was India's great friend. It was during his time as home minister in the early 1990s that close cooperation between our respective intelligence and police services was established. He played an important role in the approval of the

Mahakali Treaty of 1996 in the Nepalese Parliament, even at the cost of a split in his party, when the Bam Dev Gautam faction separated.

Oli is a close personal friend of President Bidya Devi Bhandari, widow of the charismatic Madan Bhandari, general secretary of the CPN (UML) who died in a car accident in May 1993. She has a deep influence on him and is perhaps the one politician that he trusts implicitly. Oli also loves to entertain. I have enjoyed his hospitality on several occasions, including at his home, with his wife Radhika Shakya playing the gracious host. He had once invited me to a lunch together with Bidya Bhandari at a Nepalese restaurant at Baber Mahal Revisited, a more charming version of our own Santushti Complex in what were the stables of General Babar S.J.B. Rana's palace and an oasis in the dust and din of Kathmandu; he was fretting and fuming that Bidya Bhandari was late, but was quiet as a mouse and full of charm as soon as she arrived; not a word of censure escaped his lips. When I told him that I was vegetarian, he shook his head in mock horror and said that he was a carnivore. He could not do without his daily quota of meat!

Even at the height of our disagreements, we always kept our channels of communication open. Since he would not want to be seen receiving me at his residence and he would not come to India House, we would meet at the house of a businessman in Kathmandu! He had to live up to his nationalist credentials as the only political leader in Nepal who could stand up to India. In the past, when he was a rising star, all his medical treatments, including the kidney transplant, were arranged in India. After he developed this image of being a great nationalist, he never visited India for treatment; he would go to Bangkok and Singapore. And the second kidney transplant he arranged for in Nepal, at a time when most politicians went abroad. This won him great accolades from the public.

Our relations with Oli during his ten-month rule were marked by considerable distrust. Though he had accommodated

Madhesi demands to an extent and paid an official visit to India in February 2016 after the Madhesi 'blockade' had ended— India pulled out all stops to welcome him; he was housed in Rashtrapati Bhavan, arrived to a spectacular reception in Bhuj, where he went to see the earthquake reconstruction activities, and thereafter visited the Tehri Dam; we provided new trade and transit points, including the port of Visakhapatnam—no joint communique was issued due to differences on a reference to the new Constitution. India was keen that a commitment of Nepal to address remaining issues in a time-bound manner be included; the Nepalese merely wanted India to welcome the Constitution. Further, Oli's strategy to play the anti-India nationalism card and his overtures to China did not sit well with India. Thereafter, in May 2016 he abruptly cancelled the state visit of the President of Nepal to India. I had dined with the President and her charming daughters just two days before the visit was cancelled. Separately, there were insinuations that the Nepalese ambassador in India, Deep Kumar Upadhyaya, was conspiring against the Oli government with the Indian ambassador in Kathmandu and they were both meeting secretly somewhere in western Nepal[4]—we had planned to go there to promote tourism opportunities in what was a relatively less developed region. Indeed, the Oli government decided to recall Upadhyaya. During the same month some Indian TV channels ran a story that Prime Minister Oli was considering expelling the Indian ambassador by declaring him persona non grata. I was completely oblivious of this till Foreign Secretary Jaishankar called me to ask whether there was any truth to it; he also told me that I had the solid backing of the Government of India and that I should convey to the Nepalese side that taking any such step would have consequences. I immediately spoke to Foreign Minister Kamal Thapa on the phone, and he expressed complete ignorance about any such proposal; he promptly issued a tweet denying that the Government of Nepal was contemplating any such step. I found out later through journalist friends in Delhi that the story had originated from a highly placed source in Kathmandu. Clearly, since the foreign minister was not aware of it and Oli's press officer had been a *Kantipur* correspondent in New Delhi with good contacts in Delhi media circles, the needle of suspicion pointed to the Prime Minister's Office.

Meanwhile, Prachanda was increasingly disenchanted by Oli's autocratic style of functioning and his refusal to honour the gentleman's agreement to hand over power after a year. Prachanda was also fearful that Oli was making overtures to Sher Bahadur Deuba of the Nepali Congress for an NC–CPN (UML) coalition as was the case during the time of drafting of the Constitution. It is in these circumstances that Prachanda eventually broke away from Oli, pre-empted him and formed a government under his own leadership with NC support. The understanding was that Sher Bahadur Deuba would take over after a year. Sushil Koirala had earlier passed away on 9 February 2016. Prachanda became prime minister in August 2016 and handed over the reins to Sher Bahadur Deuba in May 2017.

Pushpa Kamal Dahal, who likes to be known by his nom de guerre, Prachanda, the fierce one, is an engaging personality in Nepalese politics. It is difficult to comprehend that he led a movement that was responsible for the death of 17,000 Nepalis. Within the CPN Maoists, he and Baburam Bhattarai were like yin and yang. Baburam was cerebral, highly educated, a national topper in school, an architect from Chandigarh and a PhD from JNU. He was the intellectual, the ideologue, the brains behind the movement. Prachanda was the charismatic leader, a superb orator who could arouse public emotions at will, a tactician who would sup with the devil to advance his own cause. At a function commemorating the birthday of Mahatma Gandhi organized by the Mahendra Narayan Nidhi Foundation in Kathmandu, when asked how he felt while bowing before the apostle of non-violence, he said without guile that he was like Emperor Asoka who transformed his life philosophy after seeing the death and despair on the battlefield of Kalinga and pursued the path of the Buddha. He was fond of referring to the '*Yudh to Budh*' and '*Shastra to Shashtra*' remarks of PM Modi during his address to the Constituent Assembly in 2014!

Prachanda is warm and friendly, says what you want to hear, makes you feel happy and then goes and does what he wants. Dependability is not his strongest point. For several months he had been telling me that he was a progressive leader and that his alliance would be with the democratic forces, namely, the Congress and the Madhesis, and then he decided to link up with the CPN (UML), led by Oli, a diehard conservative!

He has a relatively simple lifestyle: wakes up very early in the morning, plays a good game of table tennis with his security personnel and is ready for meetings by 7 a.m. In my early days as ambassador, he would invite me to meet him at unearthly morning hours till I conveyed to him through a mutual friend that the earliest that was convenient for me was 8 a.m. He always kept this in mind for the rest of my tenure. On most occasions, I would meet him in his residential office near Lainchaur, but there were some occasions when I dined with him in his family quarters. When the weather was good, especially in winter, we would meet on his terrace and bask in the sun.

I recall a meeting between Sushma Swaraj and Prachanda, probably at his Parliament office, during one of her visits to Kathmandu. She said to him in Hindi, '*Aap to hamare Kamal Pushpa hain*', playing on his name Lotus Flower, which was the symbol of her party, the BJP, in India. Prachanda was delighted, grinning from ear to ear.

Prachanda has not allowed the personal tragedies in his life to affect his political role. He lost a daughter to cancer; his son, Prakash, also his personal secretary, died tragically at a young age. Prachanda's wife Sita Dahal has been ailing from a neurological disease that apparently has no cure.

For a man who led such a violent insurgent movement, Prachanda, shockingly for me, displayed a sense of insecurity in some of our conversations. Once, over the course of several weeks, I noticed that Prachanda was tense and worried in my meetings. When pressed, he eventually said that the Indian intelligence agencies were gunning for him. When I told him this was laughable and asked for proof, he gave me a piece of paper purportedly written on our agency letterhead that appeared to corroborate his fears. I had the matter examined and demonstrated to Prachanda that the paper was a forgery with a false watermark. It is possible that someone who wanted to create a misunderstanding between Prachanda and the Indian establishment was playing mischief. Eventually, Prachanda accepted this.

There has been considerable speculation both in Nepal and in India that one of the reasons why India was unhappy with Nepal was that the new Constitution did not declare Nepal to be a Hindu state. This is a complex issue. It is true that India had a BJP government with a strong belief in Hindutva, but there was a subtle distinction between the BJP party, the Sangh Parivar and the government. I recall that early on in her tenure in July 2014, EAM Sushma Swaraj had paid a bilateral visit to Nepal prior to Prime Minister Modi's visit. She participated in a programme organized by the Hindu Swayamsevak Sangh of Nepal that she had accepted on her own; this was not a programme proposed by the embassy. At the programme, some speakers started waxing eloquent on Nepal as a Hindu Rashtra; also that now that the BJP was in power in Delhi, India too would become a Hindu Rashtra. Sushma Swaraj was very angry at this event and publicly stated at the forum that she had sworn an oath to the Constitution of India and could not associate herself with the remarks of some of the speakers and walked out in a huff. Later that year in September, Home Minister Rajnath Singh was in Kathmandu for a SAARC Home Ministers' meeting. At a press interaction he was reminded that as BJP president he had been a strong advocate of Nepal being a Hindu Rashtra and whether he thought that the new Constitution should declare this. I was worried about how he would react to this question, but his response was perfect. He said that as the representative of the Government of India, he did not have any view on the matter, and it was for the leaders and people of Nepal to decide whether Nepal should or should not be a Hindu state. Of course, there were organizations and individuals in India that would like to see Nepal as a Hindu state, but as far as the Government of India was concerned, we did not have any view on the matter. I used this formulation for my entire tenure in Nepal.

I should also state that this issue was never discussed in any of our formal bilateral meetings with Nepal. Nor, as ambassador, was I ever requested by anyone in the Government of India to work for Nepal as a Hindu state. I am told by some friends from Nepal that the matter did come up in one-on-one meetings of Nepalese leaders with some of our leaders; also that the RSS affiliates in Nepal as well as gurus like Sri Sri Ravi Shankar were advocating the concept of Hindu Rashtra.[5] The only time that a related issue came up was in a briefing in Delhi where I had mentioned that Nepal was going to be a secular country and there was some discussion on whether secularism would be defined as *Sarva Dharma Sambhava* or *Sarva Pantha Sambhava*, but nothing more.

That this was a sensitive issue in Nepal was clear. The communists did not want a Hindu state. In Nepal, this had connotations connecting it to the monarchy. Indeed, it was only in 1962 that King Mahendra declared Nepal to be a Hindu Rashtra and claimed that since he was an avatar of Vishnu, he had a divine right to rule. As a dear friend, the renowned journalist Vijay Pandey, once told me, in Nepal the last bogey of the Hindu Rashtra train carries the king; the monarchy was inseparable from the concept of Hindu Rashtra and it was not possible to have one without the other. When this was explained to Sri Sri Ravi Shankar, he started campaigning for a Hindu republic.[6]

Even though the public discussion on the first draft of the Constitution had shown that an overwhelming majority of Nepalese, especially from the Terai, were keen to retain Hinduism as the state religion in Nepal, this was strongly opposed by the Janjati communities. I recall a huge procession by the Janjatis in Kathmandu in 2015 during the drafting of the Constitution, demanding that Nepal be a secular state. International NGOs, not only from some Western countries, but also South Korea, and evangelical organizations were active in undertaking proselytization activities and large groups, mainly of Janjatis such as Tamangs, had converted to Christianity. I have seen for myself how churches have mushroomed in Kathmandu in ordinary houses in several neighbourhoods. The idea of secularism was also supported by Western countries, especially the US. I recall meetings at UN House of the diplomatic corps, and one of the main issues that the US ambassador would raise was freedom of religion and secularism.

Eventually, Nepal went with secularism, but they adopted an interesting definition, a sort of halfway house: Article 4 of the Constitution provides for 'religious and cultural freedom, along with the protection of religion and customs practised from ancient times'. This is a reference to '*sanatana dharma*'. The Constitution also imposed penalties for proselytization activities and declared the cow as the national animal.

I left Nepal on 1 March 2017 upon retirement from the Indian Foreign Service. The period thereafter saw a further evolution in our policy. First, we suggested to the Madhesis that they should participate in local elections even in the absence of any forward movement on their demands for a constitutional amendment. In effect, we gave up our support for a more inclusive Constitution, implying thereby that the Madhesis should accept it as it is. This was partly due to the fact that the first amendment to the Constitution had partially met some Madhesi demands and partly due to our perception that we had alienated the ruling elite, which had as a consequence made strong overtures to China.

Over a period of time, the Maoist–Nepali Congress–Madhesi coalition that had replaced the CPN (UML) coalition under Oli began showing cracks. Though Prachanda had once told me that he got along well with Deuba, that they were family friends and would meet socially from time to time, Deuba started putting pressure on Prachanda to resign as the date for the general elections was approaching. General elections were to be conducted in November 2017. It was also decided that provincial elections would be held coterminous with the federal elections. The longer Prachanda continued in power, the shorter would be the tenure of Deuba as PM. Eventually, under considerable pressure from Deuba, Prachanda resigned and paved the way for the latter to take over as PM in May 2017. Thereafter, differences started emerging between the Nepali Congress and the Maoists on the one hand, and the Nepali Congress and the Madhesis on the other. Since the ruling coalition comprised the Nepali Congress, the Maoists and the Madhesis, it was expected that this coalition would jointly fight the elections on the basis of some seat-adjustment formula. However, this was not to be. The Maoists decided to part ways with the Nepali Congress and agreed to a seat adjustment with the CPN (UML); the Madhesis decided to fight separately in the Terai since no seat-sharing agreement could be finalized with the Nepali Congress. Though it is true that a seat-sharing agreement between the Maoists and the Nepali Congress was more problematic since they were deadly enemies during the insurgency and it was difficult for grassroots-level cadres of the two parties to work together, poor coalition management by the NC is also responsible for pushing the Maoists towards the CPN (UML). Similarly, though both the NC and Madhesis were competitors in the Terai, with some effort a seat-sharing formula could have been worked out, but for the short-sightedness of the Nepali Congress. There was thus a two-way contest in the hills between the NC and the CPN (UML)–Maoist combine. The plains witnessed a three-way contest between the Nepali Congress, the

Maoist–CPN (UML) combine and the Madhesis. The election results decimated the Nepali Congress, which was reduced to sixty-three seats in the Pratinidhi Sabha, the lower house. It did not win a single province. The Maoist and CPN (UML) secured 174 seats in the 275-member house, just short of a two-thirds majority, and won in six of the seven provincial assemblies. The Madhesis did much better than before, winning thirty-three seats in Parliament, and formed a government in Province No. 2 in the Terai.

The results set off a chain of events that included the formation of a coalition government of the CPN (UML) and the Maoists, eventually leading to a merger of the two parties. It is believed that China played an important role in this process.

India had to accept this new reality. Oli, a larger-than-life leader who had played the anti-India nationalist card successfully, was now expected to lead a stable government. India sent EAM Sushma Swaraj to Kathmandu in early February 2018 to make amends with Oli and the communists, even before Oli was elected leader of the parliamentary party, let alone prime minister. The visit was seen as a huge political gesture to Oli that bygones were bygones and that India would make a fresh start with the Oli government. Since the Nepali Congress was decimated and even Madhesi parties were extending outside support to the communist government, we had no option but to extend support to the Oli government, which we did in full measure. Our expectation was that with the re-establishment of cordial relations, Oli would go slow on his outreach to China. Instead, as we shall see later in the book, the role and influence of China increased steadily, to the extent that today, China is an important player in the domestic politics of Nepal.

There has been some domestic criticism of India's policy vis-à-vis the Constitution-drafting process. It has been stated that India went out on a limb to support the Madhesi cause; this pitted it against the dominant hill elite which in turn made a strategic move to embrace China. Had India not become too deeply involved in the Constitution-drafting process and, in particular, assisted in swiftly ending the Madhesi blockade, the situation would not have come to such a pass.

This argument ignores the fact that India, historically, has been deeply involved in supporting the aspirations of the Nepalese people for progressive change. India facilitated the democratic mainstreaming of the Maoists in 2005 and the resolution of the Madhesi agitations of 2007 and 2008. In effect, India stood as a neutral referee to some of these agreements. Had these agreements not been reached, the killings and turmoil would have continued. Time and again during the period of Constitution drafting, the Madhesi leaders argued that India had a moral responsibility to ensure that these agreements were implemented and incorporated into the Constitution.

Further, in Nepal, the population is evenly divided between the hill Bahun Chhetris, Janjatis and Madhesis. In fact, the Janjatis and Madhesis comprise two-thirds of the population. They are not an insignificant minority group that can be ignored. If their concerns and aspirations are not met, it will be difficult to achieve durable long-term stability in Nepal. And instability in Nepal, especially in the Terai plains, will make it vulnerable to growing external presence that could be inimical to India's interests and security. We are familiar with the role of the ISI and Pakistan-sponsored terrorist activities[7] from Nepalese soil; the Terai has been particularly vulnerable. The number of mosques and madrasas along the border areas have also increased. In more recent times, there is a growing presence of Western NGOs involved in proselytization, especially in the hill districts but also in the Terai.

Unfortunately for us, we have multiple strategic objectives in Nepal that sometimes lead to mutually conflicting policy approaches. We would like to see durable stability, democracy and constitutional governance in Nepal; at the same time, we are wary of Nepal drawing closer to China. Long-term stability in Nepal, which is also in India's strategic interest, requires a more inclusive state. However, the ruling elite sees this as a threat to their position; they renege on solemn agreements committing Nepal to a policy of inclusion and equity that were facilitated by India. They then turn to China and encourage a growing Chinese presence in Nepal in order to balance what they see as India's intrusive policy. We see this as a threat to our interests, and then move away from our approach to support a more inclusive, democratic Nepal. In other words, we embrace the Oli government and jettison the Madhesi cause in the hope and expectation that Nepal will step back from its embrace of China. In reality, this has not happened. Not only has the Chinese role increased in Nepal, we have alienated elements within political groups such as the Nepali Congress and some Madhesi leaders that have traditionally been close to India in the past. We now see that even the Nepali Congress is not averse to copying the strategy of the Oli-led communists to play the anti-India nationalism card. In fact, as we shall see in the next chapter, it was the Deuba-led Nepali Congress that agitated for redrawing the map of Nepal to include large chunks of Indian territory in Uttarakhand.[8]

Despite the massive electoral victory scored by the Oli-led coalition in 2017 and the subsequent merger of the two communist parties, political stability remained elusive in Nepal. Even as Nepal was reeling from the COVID-19 pandemic and its economic fallout, the Nepal Communist Party was plagued by inner-party rivalries and differences. Oli was criticized by Prachanda and former prime ministers Madhav Kumar Nepal and Jhalanath Khanal for centralizing considerable authority within his own office, including power to appoint individuals to constitutional bodies such as the powerful anti-corruption Commission to Investigate the Abuse of Authority. His autocratic behaviour and unwillingness to honour his commitment to share power with Prachanda or even to consult with other senior leaders on matters of policy and appointments created a chasm of distrust between the two factions. Oli was seen as being increasingly isolated within the NCP as a group of former CPN (UML) colleagues, led by Madhav Nepal, teamed up with Prachanda against Oli. Reduced to a minority in several bodies of his party, Oli dissolved the lower house of Parliament on 20 December 2020 and announced fresh elections. This dissolution was ruled as unconstitutional by the Constitutional Bench of the Supreme Court, which restored the house in February 2021.[9] The move was a huge setback to PM Oli but a separate judgment of the Supreme Court effectively annulling the creation of the ruling party, the NCP, and restoring the status quo ante pre-merger, i.e., re-establishing the erstwhile CPN (UML) and NCP (Maoist Centre), created a new political dynamic that significantly strengthened Oli's position.[10] As a result of this judgment, Oli became the leader of the largest party in Parliament with 121 MPs. The Nepali Congress, with sixty-three MPs, and the NCP (Maoist Centre), with fifty-three, were a distant second and third parties. The Janata Samajwadi Party, largely from the Terai Madhesh but also including Janjatis, was the fourth largest party.

Following the restoration of the house, Oli sought and lost a vote of confidence and resigned. The NC, the Prachanda-led NCP (Maoist Centre) and the Upendra Yadav faction of the Janata Samajwadi Party voted against him, and a section of the CPN (UML), led by Madhav Kumar Nepal, and a faction of the JSP led by Mahanta Thakur and Rajendra Mahato absented themselves/abstained. Despite Oli's defeat, the opposition parties were unable to muster a majority, largely because the JSP was divided with one faction supporting Deuba and Prachanda, and another in favour of Oli. In accordance with Article 76 (3)[11] of the Constitution, the President again invited Oli, as the leader of the single largest party, to form a government and gave him thirty days to prove his majority. Oli was sworn in as PM again, even though he had lost the support of the house just a few days before.

Instead of seeking the vote of confidence, Oli recommended to the President that Article 76 (5) of the Constitution be invoked, namely to identify a member of the house who could gain majority support and form a government. He did so without resigning his post as PM. In other words, even without a legal vacancy in the position, a fresh search for a PM was instituted. Even though the President only allowed for less than one day for formation of a new government, Deuba was able to muster the support of 149 MPs belonging to the NC, NCP (Maoist Centre), the Madhav Nepal faction of the CPN (UML) and the Upendra Yadav faction of the JSP. Accompanied by a large number of MPs, including former prime ministers Madhav Kumar Nepal, Jhalanath Khanal and Baburam Bhattarai as well as Upendra Yadav, a former deputy PM, Deuba presented the signatures of 149 members of Parliament supporting his candidature to the President. Though at a press conference the same day, Oli had publicly stated that he did not have the requisite support, in his submission to the President he claimed support (without individual signatures of MPs; Oli merely submitted letters signed by himself as Chairperson of the CPN [UML] and of Mahant Thakur as co-chairman of the JSP) of 153 MPs, 121 belonging to his own party, including those belonging to the Madhav Nepal faction and thirty-two belonging to the JSP, including those from the Upendra Yadav faction that was supporting Deuba. The President rejected both candidatures on the grounds of overlapping names, thereby enabling Oli to continue as PM. Later that night, on the recommendation of the cabinet, the house was dissolved for a second time in May 2021 and elections announced for November. Effectively, the country was back to the situation in December 2020, when Oli had dissolved the house for the first time. A large number of writ petitions were filed in the Supreme Court, challenging the actions of the prime minister and the President.

What is deeply intriguing is that the JSP, a party dominated by Madhesis, remained divided in its response to the political developments, with leaders such as Mahant Thakur and Rajendra Mahato, who were in the forefront of the Madhesi agitations of 2015–16, eager to team up with Oli should some of their demands be met. This would have been unthinkable some years ago, when Oli was seen as the leader most adamantly opposed to Madhesi demands. But politics can make for strange bedfellows. The President swore in a Council of Ministers, with three deputy prime ministers, including Rajendra Mahato from the JSP, with a total of eleven members from the JSP on 4 June 2021. Another cabinet expansion took place on 24 June 2021. The ostensible reason provided by the JSP in defence of their decision to support Oli was that he had moved forward with some of their demands for withdrawal of cases against Madhesi workers as well as on the citizenship issue. On the latter, however, the ordinance brought in by the Oli government remains suspended following a decision of the Supreme Court.[12] Meanwhile, the Supreme Court, in another decision on 22 June 2021, has nullified the two cabinet expansions undertaken by PM Oli following the dissolution of the house, thereby removing twenty ministers, including two of the three DPMs from their posts.[13] Madhesi leaders have not progressed on their demands on the citizenship issue and now have even lost their cabinet positions.

In a landmark unanimous decision on 12 July 2021, in response to petitions filed challenging the dissolution of the lower house by the President in May 2021, a constitutional bench of the Supreme Court again ruled that the dissolution was unconstitutional. What is more, the court appointed Sher Bahadur Deuba, leader of the Nepali Congress, as the prime minister. Deuba was sworn in as prime minister for the fifth time on 13 July 2021.

The decision of the Supreme Court has far-reaching political repercussions. First, it is a sharp indictment of the actions of both Prime Minister Oli and President Bidya Devi Bhandari that have been judged to be in contravention of the Constitution. The President's actions have been brought under judicial scrutiny and the court has reserved the right to 'correct' presidential decisions if they are not in conformity with the Constitution. Second, it is for the first time that the Supreme Court has directly appointed the prime minister. Third, the court has adjudged that under Article 76 (5) of the Constitution, party whips do not apply and individual members are free to decide whom they wish to support as prime minister.

Deuba secured a comfortable majority of 165 votes in Parliament (he needed 136 for a majority), with the Maoists, both factions of the JSP and some members of the CPN (UML), including Madhav Kumar Nepal, supporting his government. His government is now likely to continue for the full term of Parliament, with elections likely in early 2023 (the term of the lower house expires in March 2023). The government is expected to be stable since under Article 100 of the Constitution, a no-confidence motion can only be introduced after a period of one year. This provision was brought in by the framers of the Constitution to prevent political instability and frequent change of governments in the past. If, however, the coalition falters due to political differences between partners or poor coalition management, elections could conceivably be held earlier than scheduled.

India's relationship with the Oli government during the time of the COVID-19 pandemic has swung like a pendulum. Even as Oli became isolated within his own party, the erstwhile NCP, he played the nationalism card by engaging in cartographic aggression and issuing a new map of Nepal that included the territories of Limpiyadhura, Lipulekh and Kalapani in Uttarakhand state; the new map was provided parliamentary cover through a constitutional amendment. Separately, Oli publicly stated that India was trying to unseat him, implying that opponents within his party, namely, Prachanda and Madhav Kumar Nepal, were working at the behest of India. Oli made fun of the Indian national emblem and motto, averred that the Indian virus was deadlier than the Chinese one and ludicrously stated that Lord Ram was born in Nepal[14] (and more recently, on the International Day of Yoga on 21 June 2021, that yoga originated in Nepal). Bilateral relations plummeted to a new low and political level engagement between the two countries came to a standstill. Over the course of several months, both countries realized that the long hiatus in dialogue was not a sustainable one, given the nature of the bilateral relationship. India realized that this vacuum was facilitating a greater role for and the influence of other countries, such as China. India was also worried about the adverse impact of the no-dialogue situation on our extensive development partnership programme in Nepal. Oli too was keen to resume a dialogue with India, particularly on the boundary issue. Beginning September 2020, a series of high-level visits, including that of the head of India's external intelligence, the army chief and the foreign secretary to Nepal, and of the Nepalese foreign minister to India for the Joint Commission have taken place. The head of the Foreign Affairs Cell of the BJP also visited Nepal at the invitation of Oli. Since then, with the annulling of the merger of the CPN (UML) and the NCP (Maoist Centre) by the Supreme Court, the communist force has been weakened and Chinese efforts for a strong united communist party have suffered a setback, at least for the present.

As a result of the resumption of high-level engagement and the fact that some key Madhesi leaders close to India have teamed up with Oli, there is a perception in Nepal that India was solidly backing the Oli government, even though it had thrown constitutional propriety to the wind and undermined democratic norms; that India's primary goal was to weaken the communist dominance in Nepal and China's influence. Kathmandu was abuzz with conspiracy theories that India would like Nepal to become a Hindu state and may even have sympathy for the monarchy in some form,[15] and that somehow Oli may have promised forward movement on these matters. That Oli, a diehard communist, perhaps for the first time ever paid obeisance at Pashupatinath temple in January 2021 and his close associate Mahesh Basnet recently proposed at a central committee meeting of the CPN (UML) that both secularism and federalism, key features of the Constitution, should be reviewed, appear to suggest that these issues may become political planks in elections in the future.[16] Five former Nepali prime ministers issued a statement on 12 June 2021, warning against foreign influence in internal matters of Nepal. The statement said that 'Nepal and Nepalese should decide on internal matters. We urge everyone to remain alert against direct or indirect foreign influence or interference in the country's politics and internal affairs'.[17] This was an unusual statement, interpreted by observers as aimed at India.

Though there may not be any substance to these conspiracy theories, it would be wise for India to recall its own historical experience in Nepal. In the past, the monarchy was singularly responsible for the development of anti-India nationalism and playing the China card; furthermore, the fact that Nepal was a Hindu Rashtra may have struck a chord with certain sections of society in India, but it did not contribute to an improvement in state-to-state relations. India's long-term interest is for Nepal to be a strong and vibrant democratic state that accommodates the interests and aspirations of its diverse communities. This will strengthen national harmony and cohesion, and bring long-term stability, which is also in India's interests. Historically, India has always supported movements for progressive change, inclusive democracy and rule of law. A tactical approach by India may yield short-term gains but complicate the longer-term engagement with Nepal and weaken democratic governance. While we must work with the government of the day, it is important that we continue to engage intensively with all political forces in Nepal and not be seen to be partisan.

5

Disputed Boundary: Kalapani, Lipulekh and Limpiyadhura

On 20 May 2020, Nepal published a map showing a new external boundary with India.

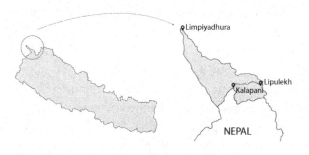

Outline of new map of Nepal

This map is only for explanatory purposes and does not in any way imply acceptance or endorsement of the boundaries depicted. It is based on a map originally published in Scroll.in ('Territoriality Amidst Covid-19', 19 May 2020, https://scroll.in/article/962226/territoriality-amidst-covid-19-a-primer-to-the-lipu-lek-conflict-between-india-and-nepal).

About 335 sq. km of Indian territory,[1] including Kalapani, the Lipulekh Pass and Limpiyadhura was added to Nepal through a cartographical amendment, shown in the map above, viz., the beak jutting out in the extreme north-west of Nepal. With one stroke of the pen, Nepal had created a major territorial row with India in a sensitive Himalayan frontier area bordering Tibet. Not only did Nepal shift its boundary with India several kilometres westwards, it also altered its already settled boundary with China. This cartographical aggression was provided legislative cover when a constitutional amendment to the coat of arms of Nepal, which includes the map of Nepal, was adopted by overwhelming majorities in both houses of Parliament and received Presidential assent on 18 June 2020. There was considerable dismay, even anger, in India, with the official spokesperson of the Ministry of External Affairs stating that 'artificial enlargement of territorial claims will not be accepted by India.'[2]

Why has Nepal suddenly claimed a large chunk of Indian territory? How did things come to such a pass between Nepal and India? What is the impact on the inhabitants of the region and the broader people-to-people relationship? How can this emotionally sensitive issue be resolved at a time of heightened nationalism in both countries?

Nepal has argued that it was the publication of a new map of India in November 2019, following the reorganization of the state of Jammu and Kashmir into two union territories, which showed Kalapani as an Indian territory, that prompted Nepal to protest.[3] Interestingly, the press statement issued by the Ministry of Foreign Affairs of Nepal on 4 November 2019 only talks about the 'Kalapani area' and does not refer to Lipulekh and Limpiyadhura. The Nepalese also claimed that they did not receive any response to their proposal to send Madhav Kumar Nepal, a senior leader of the former NCP, to India for discussions on the boundary matter; nor did their request for formal talks elicit a response. Thereafter in May 2020, Defence Minister Rajnath Singh inaugurated a segment of the Dharchula Lipulekh Road, to which the Nepalese again protested and summoned the Indian ambassador, claiming that a part of this road runs through Nepalese territory. When India did issue a response to the official note from Nepal,[4] they saw it as a dilatory tactic since it stated that the matter would be discussed after the COVID-19 pandemic was over. Later that month at a virtual seminar at the MP-IDSA, Army Chief M.M. Naravane, in response to a question, said that Nepal may have raised the boundary issue at the instance of a third country, implicitly referring to China.[5] Though the Nepalese Army did not respond to this statement, the Nepalese defence minister Ishwar Pokhrel said that General Naravane's comment was a 'political stunt'.[6] Meanwhile, Chief Minister of Uttar Pradesh Yogi Adityanath further inflamed passions by suggesting that Nepal should think of the long-term consequences of its actions and also remember what happened to Tibet.[7] All of these developments, according to Nepal, precipitated matters and expedited their decision to first issue a new map by an executive decision and subsequently provide legislative cover through a constitutional amendment in June 2020.

Nepal's new map is based on a unilateral assertion that the source of the Kali River is at Limpiyadhura and not Kalapani, as asserted by India; that the Kuti Yangti River, the western headwaters of the Kali with its source at Limpiyadhura, is actually the Kali since it is the biggest stream in hydrological terms, i.e., in terms of the distance, water carrying capacity and river basin area compared to several other streams in the east that descend into the Kali. Limpiyadhura is several kilometres north-west of Kalapani. Accordingly, all territory east of the river beginning from Limpiyadhura belongs to Nepal. The area that Nepal is now claiming lies in the Byans Patti close to the borders with Tibet and Nepal.

There is a two-hundred-year-old history to the India–Nepal boundary as it exists today. The 1816 treaty signed in Sugauli between the British East India Company and Nepal and the 1860 treaty signed in Kathmandu between British India and Nepal had fixed the external boundaries of Nepal with India.

The Sugauli Treaty, signed after the Anglo–Nepal Wars of 1814 and 1815 in Article 5 declared that: 'The Rajah of Nipal renounces for himself, his heirs, and successors, all claim to or connextion with the countries lying to the west of the River Kali and engages never to have any concern with those countries or the inhabitants thereof.'[8]

Accordingly, all of Kumaon, Garhwal and territory up to the Sutlej Rivers that had earlier been captured by the Gorkhas were ceded to the East India Company government.

In other words, Nepalese territory lay to the east of the Kali River and Indian territory to the west, in effect making the Kali the boundary river dividing the two countries in the far west of Nepal. However, the treaty did not refer to the source of the Kali River nor was any map attached to the treaty.[9] This is the source of the considerable problems and tensions between Nepal and India today.

Anyone who has trekked through this part of Kumaon, Uttarakhand en route to Kailash and Manasarovar is struck by the beauty of the landscape. Relatively untouched by modernity, these valleys nestled in the high Himalayas are full of verdant pastures, rivers and streams. The Kali River, known by that name because of its dark waters, emerges here from the sacred springs at Kalapani and begins snaking down to the plains, where it transforms into the Sharda and eventually joins the mother river Ganga, as do all other rivers of Nepal that flow from the north to the south. Not far from Kalapani, one gets a spectacular view of Om Parvat, where the snowfall takes the form of the Hindu holy symbol.

According to Indian mythology, aeons ago, the great Maharishi Veda Vyasa had also walked this area en route the sacred pilgrimage to Kailash Parvat after the end of the Mahabharata war between the Pandavas and Kauravas. He was so charmed by the Rung/Bhotia people of this region that he wanted to spend the remaining years of his life in the valley that takes his name, but was taken back to Hastinapur by Bhim since Yudhistir wanted

to conduct the Rajasuya Yagya. The Manas Khand of the Skanda
Purana has several references to this area as well as to the Lipi
Parvat and Shyama (Kali) River.[10] In the minds of the people of
the region, Kalapani has always been the sacred source of the Kali
River.[11] Charles A. Sherring, in his *Western Tibet and the British
Borderland: The Sacred Country of Hindus and Buddhists, with an
Account of the Government, Religion, and Customs of Its Peoples*,
published in 1906, states that 'then passing through the country of
the Bhotias, viz. Chaudans and Byans, he is to worship at Kalapani,
the springs, which the devout Hindu considers the sources of the
River Kali, and most sacred to the Goddess of that name'.[12]

The nine villages of the Byans Patti—including five villages of
the Kuti Valley, namely, Kuti, Nabi, Napalchyo, Rongkong and
Gunji, two villages of the Kali valley, Budi and Garbyang, and
two of the Tinkar valley, Chhangru and Tinkar—are united by
ethnicity, religion, economic engagement and relations of kinship
and marriage. It was common for the people of one village to graze
their animals in pastures in areas belonging to another. It was also
not uncommon for the people living on one side of the Kali to
own land on the other side. Thus, villagers from Garbyang owned
land in Tinkar. Similarly, villagers from Gunji and Budi also
owned land on the other side of the river. During winter months,
some schools on the Indian side would shut and education was
carried on in schools on the Nepalese side, where the villagers
migrated. Villagers paid taxes on both sides of the border, to the
Indian authorities for their homes on this side and to the Nepalese
for the property they possessed on the other side or for grazing
rights. Even after the Treaty of Sugauli was signed between the
British East India Company and the Nepalese in 1816 and the
river became an international border between the two countries,
the pattern of interchange that existed earlier continued. The river
did not divide the people, rather it united them.

The Rung/Bhotia people of Byans were also involved in border
trade with Tibet. Lipulekh was the primary pass used for trade and

pilgrimage. Till the 1962 India–China War, the inhabitants of the valley were engaged between June and November in trade of food grains (gur, barley, wheat, rice, etc.), salt and wool, borax, carpets, sheep, ponies and mules, silver items, musk, Tibetan tea and thankas with Tibetan traders at the big mandi in Taklakot, Purang and other market towns in Tibet. Ancient pilgrims and travellers have documented the flora and fauna and the lives of the local community of this frontier land. Swami Pranavananda speaks of the ethereal beauty of this region and has documented the great pilgrimage that he had undertaken scores of times.[13] He has described the mandi and also states that Mahatma Gandhi was revered by some monks as an avatar of Guru Padmasambhava and that there was vigorous trade of a coarse white cloth known as Gandhi *khaddar*.

I recall my own pilgrimage to Kailash and Manasarovar three decades ago. In those days, one had to walk up all the way from Tawaghat in Pithoragarh district of Kumaon. After a gruelling trek over several days, one reached the beautiful village of Gunji that the Nepalese are now claiming. It must have been quite prosperous in the old days when border trade with Tibet was thriving. Many houses had beautifully carved wooden doors and windows. Most inhabitants of this small village would move down to Dharchula in the winters when the climate became too cold and inhospitable. Though the Byans valley was a remote frontier area, literacy was high and the seven villages on the Indian side, including Gunji, have provided several civil servants to the IAS, IPS and other services. Gunjiyals, Garbyals, Napalchyals, Budiyals and Kutiyals are surnames that would be familiar to some of us, though we would probably not be aware of their origins.

This area was captured by the advancing Gorkha Army in 1790. Following the defeat of the Gorkha Army in the Anglo–Nepal wars of 1814 and 1815 and under the terms of the Treaty of Sugauli of 1816, it reverted to India (British East India Company). The treaty was signed in the small town of Sugauli in

East Champaran along the Nepalese border near Birganj in Parsa district. The town, known to the British as Sewgolee, is also the setting for Rudyard Kipling's story of the mongoose Rikki-Tikki-Tavi.

Part II of the *Himalayan Gazetteer*, recorded by Edwin Felix Thomas Atkinson and published in 1884 at Allahabad, has a detailed account of the Anglo–Nepalese wars as well as the discussions between the British East India Company and the governor of Doti, Bam Shah, who was a representative of the Raja of Nepal, on several issues, including an interpretation of the Sugauli Treaty, and documents the exchange of letters between the two sides.

To quote Atkinson, 'By treaty the Kali was made the boundary on the east, and this arrangement divided into two parts parganah Byans, which had hitherto been considered as an integral portion of Kumaon as distinguished from Doti and Jumla. In 1817, the Nepal Darbar in accordance with the terms of the letter of the treaty, claimed the villages of Tinkar and Changru lying to the east of the Kali in parganah Byans, and after enquiry had shown that the demand was covered by the terms of the treaty possession was given to Bam Sah, who was then Governor of Doti.'

In the initial period after the signing of the treaty, the British had kept all of Byans Patti as part of Kumaon and handed over the two villages only later, after entreaties by the Nepalese. This was done on a legal basis in accordance with the terms of the Sugauli Treaty, with little regard to the situation on the ground. Indeed, the officials dealing with the matter had perhaps no knowledge of the historical and geographical context of the area they were dealing with. The transfer of Chhangru and Tinkar actually created significant problems for these two villages since access to and from this area was largely through the Indian side. For travelling to Tibet, these villagers used the Lipulekh Pass[14] and to access other areas in the South, Dharchula on the Indian side was the convenient route. Even today, there is no road access to these villages from the Nepalese side and the Nepalese are dependent on helicopter services. Of course, due to the open border between India and Nepal, the Nepalese villagers can and do use India to access their own country. Furthermore, once the Darchula (Nepal) Tinkar road is ready, the Nepalese would no longer need to enter Indian territory to access either Tibet or the southern parts of their own country.

Not satisfied with receiving only Chhangru and Tinkar villages, the Nepalese subsequently claimed two more villages, Kuti and Nabi, in 1817 on the grounds that the Kuti Yangti was the Kali River and these villages lay to the east of the river. This claim was rejected by the British.

The *Himalayan Gazetteer* states:

> But not satisfied with this advantage, the Nepalese claimed the villages of Kunti and Nabhi as also lying to the east of the Kali, averring that the Kunti Yankti or western branch of the head waters should be considered the main stream as carrying the larger volume of water. Captain Webb and others showed that the lesser stream flowing from the sacred fountain of Kalapani had always been recognised as the main branch of the Kali and had in fact given its name to the river during its course through the hills. The government therefore decided to retain both Nabhi and Kunti, which have ever since remained attached to British Byans.

The Gazetteer also footnotes the correspondence between the British and Nepalese officials. The letters are from 4 February, 5 March, 11 August, 20 August, 5 September,[15] 20 September and 10 October of the year 1817. There is no evidence to suggest that Nepal did not accept this decision of the British. The matter was not raised again during the remainder of the period of British rule in India nor was it raised with the government of independent India for five decades!

Then again, Volume III of Part II of the Gazetteer states the following about the River Kali:

> Kali, the largest river of Kumaon . . . has two headwaters; the Kalapani to the east, which takes its rise in the southern slopes of the ridge crossed by the Lipulekh pass into Hundes; and the western branch, which has the longest course and the largest volume, is known as the Kuthi-Yankti. The latter has its rise in the glaciers lying along the upper portions of the patti of Byans from the foot of the passes of Mankshang or Mangsha and Lunpiya leading into Hundes. From a little below Kalapani encamping ground southwards the Kali forms the boundary with Nepal.

The next significant alteration in the India–Nepal boundary happened in 1860. In view of the significant assistance provided by Jung Bahadur Kunwar and the Nepalese Gorkhas to the British to suppress India's First War of Independence in 1857, and following entreaties from the Nepalese, the British returned the territories of the so-called Naya Mulk, the present-day districts of Kailali, Kanchanpur, Banke and Bardiya, the lowland area between the Kali and the Rapti rivers, to Nepal in 1860. The preamble of the 1860 treaty begins with the following words:

> During the disturbances which followed the mutiny of the Native army of Bengal in 1857, the Maharaja of Nipal . . . freely placed troops at the disposal of the British authorities . . . and subsequently sent a force to cooperate with the British Army in the re-capture of Lucknow and the final defeat of the rebels. On the conclusion of these operations, the Viceroy and Governor-General . . . rendered to restore the Maharaja the whole of the lowlands lying between the River Kali and the District of Goruckpoer, which belonged to the State of Nipal in 1815 . . .[16]

Article 2 of the treaty states that:

> The British govt hereby bestows on the Maharaja of Nipal in full sovereignty, the whole of the lowlands between the Rivers Kali and Raptee, and the whole of the lowlands lying between the River Raptee and the District of Goruckpore, which were in the possession of the Nipal State in the year 1815, and were ceded to the British government by Article III of the Treaty concluded at Segowlee on the 2nd of December in that year.

While the Nepalese sought a return of the lowland territories between the Kali and the Rapti rivers and between Rapti and Gorakhpur after 1857, there is nothing to suggest that the Nepalese raised their claim on any of the villages of the Byans Patti in the Kumaon highlands or asserted that the Kuti Yangti was actually the Kali River and that the areas east of the Kuti Yangti belong to Nepal. In any event, if there was any such claim, it was clearly rejected by the British since it would otherwise have been reflected in the treaty of 1860. The fact that it is not mentioned suggests that it was not raised, in which case the matter is presumed to have been settled in the year 1817 itself, when it was first raised. In either case, the boundaries were deemed to have been finally established between Nepal and British India in 1860 and there has never been any major territorial dispute since.

Even in the face of this incontrovertible proof, the Nepalese have now renewed this claim on the same grounds, rejected some 203 years ago by the British, and have published a new map showing Limpiyadhura (the source of the Kuti Yangti River) as the source of the Kali River. They have included not only the villages of Kuti and Nabhi but Gunji and Lipulekh Pass as well in addition to Kalapani in their new map. India has rejected these claims and has termed them as an untenable cartographical assertion by Nepal.

A Nepal–India Border Joint Technical Committee was constituted in 1981 to finalize demarcation of the India–Nepal boundary. Over the course of its work for more than two decades, the committee completed the demarcation of 98 per cent of the boundary and finalized 182 strip maps; it however, identified two areas, Kalapani and Susta[17] on which no consensus could be forged. The matter of Kalapani was raised at the level of the prime minister during I.K. Gujral's visit to Nepal in June 1997 and found mention in a press statement. Thereafter, it was included in a formal joint statement issued by the two governments for the first time after the visit of Prime Minister Sher Bahadur Deuba to India in March 2002.[18] At that time, no reference was made to the villages of Kuti, Nabhi or Gunji or Lipulekh Pass. Since the technical group could not resolve the remaining issues, it was decided in 2014 that this would be done at the level of foreign secretaries of the two countries. Not much progress has been made.

Prior to 2020, Nepalese maps had generally shown the Kali River as a stream flowing from Lipulekh Pass. If this lesser stream, the Lipu Gad/Kalapani River, was taken to be the Kali River, the Kalapani area, comprising some 35 square kilometres of land[19] would fall on the east bank and hence under the Treaty of Sugauli would become Nepalese. India's understanding of the Nepalese claim at the time was thus restricted to 35 square kilometres of territory. This position was clearly stated by Prime Minister Girija Prasad Koirala in the Nepalese Parliament in the Nepali month of Asoj 2055 (Vikram Samvat), corresponding to 1999. This would bring the trijunction between India, Nepal and China (Tibet) close to the Lipulekh Pass. This position was in conformity with the 1850 map issued by the East India Company but was not in conformity with the map issued by British India in 1879.

India had not accepted the Nepalese position. The considered Indian view remained that the source of the Kali River was the Kalapani Springs itself; that Lipu Gad/Kalapani River became the Kali River only after it was joined by various streams, including Lilingti Gad and another stream Pankha Gad a little below

Kalapani; that it is the ridge line from a point below Kalapani going north-east towards Tinkar Pass that is the boundary between the two countries. In other words, the India–Nepal border lies east of the Lipulekh Pass in the vicinity of the Tinkar Pass as contained in the Survey of (British) India Map of 1879 and all subsequent maps. Accordingly, the Lipulekh Pass as well as the Kalapani area fall fully within Indian territory.

Sam Cowan refers to the shift in the boundary eastwards between 1850 and 1879 in his November 2020 article.[20] Referring to the Anglo–Nepal Wars of 1814–15 he argues that, 'Far from Lipulekh being an afterthought, it was a key driver for the whole war plan' given its importance for the trade with Tibet. Indeed, he cites 'Papers Respecting the Nepal War from the General List of Papers Regarding the Administration of Hastings', including a letter from John Adam, Secretary to the government to Edward Gardner, Commissioner of Kumaon, dated 3 May 1815, and quotes the following passage:

> As soon as the Goorka troops shall have withdrawn from Kamaon and the passage of the Sarda be secured, your attention will be directed to the introduction and establishment of the authority of the government throughout the province. On this subject, no instructions are deemed to be necessary, beyond which you have already been furnished; except in as much as refers to the boundary which should be assigned to the province. All the Maps in possession of this government are so incorrect, that no satisfactory judgement can be framed from them with regard to what the interests of the Company may require in that respect. To the eastward, the Sarda appears to present a natural limit. Still the important object of securing the trade with Tartary through the Himmaleh mountains against the interference of the Goorkhas might not be attained by fixing that river as the boundary; you are therefore requested to satisfy yourself on this point: and should it appear that a frontier beyond the Sarda, in

the part where it approaches the mountains, will be required for
the purpose above-mentioned, the extent of it must be defined,
so as that the cession of that tract must be made a stipulation in
any negotiation with the Goorkha government.[21]

Though no records have been found explaining the shift in the
boundary between 1850 and 1879, it is possible that the Crown,
which had taken over the administration of India from the East
India Company after the First War of Indian Independence in
1857, wanted to ensure tighter control of and unhindered access
to the Himalayan trading routes. As a token of their gratitude
for Nepalese help in 1857, the British returned the Naya Mulk
territories of the Awadh plains to Nepal. However, the British
expanded territory in the Himalayan region further east of the
Lipulekh Pass, a principal trading route. Another relevant factor
is that it is only in the 1870s that the Great Trigonometric Survey
was completed, and India was mapped for the first time on a
scientific basis.

It is highly unlikely that the Nepalese were unaware of this
shift in the British position reflected in the 1879 map. Indeed, on
the basis of the first regular survey of Nepal undertaken during
1924–27 by the Survey of India on the request of and under the
authority of the Rana prime minister of Nepal and under the
supervision of Nepalese officers Lieutenant Colonel Ganesh
Bahadur Chhetri and Captain Ganga Bahadur Karki,[22] a map
was published in 1927, the so called 'Skeleton Map of Nepal'[23]
that clearly excludes Kalapani,[24] i.e., it is in conformity with the
1879 Indian map. The Nepalese therefore could not have been
unaware of the 1879 position. There are no records to show that
the Nepalese protested against this development at the time. It is
only after a hundred years that Nepal has raised the issue bilaterally
with India.

Meanwhile, the issue has become far more complicated
since Nepal has now increased its claim from about 35 square

kilometres to 335 square kilometres.[25] In effect, Nepal has reverted to its maximalist claim of 1817, which was specifically rejected by the governor general at the time,[26] without regard to all the developments that have taken place since. They are now claiming territory in the Kumaon that was briefly under their possession for 25 years between 1790 and 1815 and which they had ceded to the British following the Anglo–Nepalese wars of 1814 and 1815. Since then, these territories were always administered by the East India Company, British India and following independence, the Government of India.

No official documentary evidence has been presented by the Government of Nepal to substantiate their claim; it has simply been asserted with the publication of a new map, though certain knowledgeable individuals, retired surveyors, journalists and former politicians have variously averred that Nepal has sufficient evidence to justify its claims. If that were the case, there would have been no need for the Government of Nepal to establish a team of experts to gather evidence in support of their claim. Ironically, this was done after the publication of the new map became a fait accompli.

Nepal's claim, as evidenced from the public domain, comprises maps produced between 1817 and 1860, some inferential evidence on the basis of military checkposts set up by India in the early 1950s on the Nepal–Tibet border, recollections of high-ranking politicians of the early 1960s as well as tax receipts of Byansi villagers and evidence that they participated in Nepalese elections. Nepalese experts and journalists have further argued that India has dug an artificial pond at Kalapani, constructed a temple and has created the myth that this is the source of the Kali River. The Nepali magazine *Mulyankan* published a detailed report by journalist Sudheer Sharma on the Kalapani issue.[27]

Former Surveyor General Budhi Narayan Shreshta of Nepal has asserted that there are several maps that depict the Kuti Yangti as the Kali River.

It is true, in the past, in the absence of maps based on proper surveys, some British East India Company maps that were issued till 1860 depict the Kuti Yangti as the Kali River, even though this had been categorically rejected in 1817 by Captain Webb. Thus, for instance, a map produced by hydrographer James Horst Surgh in 1827 shows the Kuti Yangti as the Kali on grounds that it is this stream that is the largest. Similarly, a map of 1829 also depicts the Kuti Yangti as the Kali. Neither of these maps identify the Lipulekh Pass. It was in 1846 that the Lipulekh Pass and the Kali River were shown as marking the boundaries of Kumaon with Tibet and Nepal, respectively. Even when the Kuti Yangti was shown as the Kali River, it was always depicted as an internal river, never as a boundary between India and Nepal. There is no published map, Nepali or Indian, that shows the Kuti Yangti as the boundary between India and Nepal other than the new map that Nepal has published in 2020.

It is only in 1879, however, that the first proper map, based on a scientific survey, was prepared and published. It depicts the Lipulekh Pass in India and marks the source of the Kali River at Kalapani and the Kuti Yangti as one of the Himalayan headwaters flowing into the Kali River a short distance before Gunji. Headwaters of the Kali River were not taken into consideration in determining the source. The map depicts the boundary of Nepal beginning from the south of Kalapani running north-east along the watershed somewhat west of the Tinkar Pass. Subsequent maps reflect the position of the 1879 map and support the Indian position today.

Budhi Narayan Shreshta, in his book *Border Management of Nepal*, 2003, has also stated that India had set up 18 military checkposts[28] on the Nepal–Tibet border areas very early in the 1950s. This was around the time that there was considerable disquiet in both India and Nepal following the communist victory in 1949 in China and their manoeuvres in Tibet. It is striking that the list of the checkposts mentioned by Shreshta does not include

Kalapani or Lipulekh, from times immemorial the passage to Tibet for pilgrimage and trade. If these belonged to Nepal, clearly, these would have been important places for establishing a military checkpost.

Another Nepalese narrative relates to the presence of the ITBP checkpost at Kalapani. It is argued that India forcibly occupied the Kalapani territory and established an armed presence there. In his article Sam Cowan[29] refutes Budhi Narayan Shreshta's contention that the checkpost was established by retreating Indian forces after the Sino–Indian conflict of 1962. According to Cowan there was not much fighting in the middle or central sector of the India–China boundary. The fighting was confined to Ladakh and the eastern sector. Other Nepali writers have argued that the post existed as early as 1959, and some have mentioned 1961–early 1962. Some have argued that after the government of Kirti Nidhi Bista had sought the withdrawal of the Indian checkposts in 1969, the post at Tinkar Pass was removed and established once again at Kalapani.

To the question as to why Nepal did not protest when India occupied Kalapani, if indeed Nepal claimed Kalapani as its own, there are various speculative responses. In his *Mulyankan*[30] article, Sudheer Sharma states that when Rishikesh Saha was Finance Minister he had raised the matter with the king; Mahendra simply responded by saying that India was upset with him (after the coup of 1960) and he did not want to do anything that would irritate India further. This did not prevent Mahendra from making overtures to China with the agreement on the Kathmandu–Kodari Road. Nor did it prevent Nepal from asking India to withdraw all border checkposts in 1969.

In reality, the presence of an Indian checkpost was a fact, at least as early as 1956, when the UP Special Police Force set up camp along the border areas.[31] This post was transformed into an ITBP checkpost later in 1979. Shyam Saran, in an article in the *Indian Express*, recalls that when he was ambassador in Nepal, Kirti

Nidhi Bista told him that one of the proudest moments of his life was when he 'stood down' Indira Gandhi and compelled her to *withdraw each and every military post* from Nepal's territory. This was reiterated in his statement to the Panchayat where the names of the posts were spelled out.[32] It is only later in 2017, before he died, that he said that the Indian post at Kalapani continued to be on Nepalese territory.

That Nepal's latest claim to Lipulekh Pass is an afterthought is also evident from the fact that Nepal did not protest the signing of the famous Panchsheel Agreement between India and China in 1954, which contains several references to this pass that has traditionally been used for the Kailash Manasarovar pilgrimage as well as trade between India and Tibet. Thereafter, the pass is referred to in several agreements between India and China signed over the decades. It is only in 2015 that Nepal protested following the India–China joint statement issued after PM Modi's visit to China in May that year since it contained a reference to Lipulekh Pass.

Even the Mahakali Treaty of 1996 relating to the integrated development of the Mahakali River marked a deviation from the Sugauli Treaty of 1816 when it said in the preambular part that the two governments recognize 'that the Mahakali River is a boundary river *on major stretches* between the two countries' (italics mine). The fact that the treaty did not refer to the source of the river became an issue of major domestic political upheaval in Nepal and the then CPN (UML) split with a faction led by Bam Dev Gautam forming the CPN (ML). At the time, Oli was a major supporter of the treaty and he ensured that the Deuba government received adequate votes for the treaty to be adopted by the Parliament. As prime minister, Oli did a volte-face.

Nepal has also claimed that it has tax records and evidence that people from Byans Patti participated in Nepalese elections in the past. Indeed it is quite possible that Indian villagers participated in local polls on the Nepalese side on the basis of tax receipts relating to properties that they owned on the other side of the Kali River. As stated earlier, all of Byans Patti was a cohesive, unified unit with considerable engagement and the demarcation of the Kali River as the boundary did not alter this system, which continued unhindered even after the signing of the Sugauli Treaty. I was told by Nrip Singh Napalchyal, a former Chief Secretary of Uttarakhand who belongs to Byans Patti, that it is only in the mid-1980s that Byansi villagers with land and properties in Nepal (Dhuligarha, Deothala and Barbakhiya) were told that they would have to decide about their citizenship. They left Nepal and settled down in Khotila and Phoolbasti near Dharchula on the Indian side. The Byansis have voted in every Indian election since 1952. They obtained Scheduled Tribe status in 1967 and this is likely to have played a role in their decision to stay in India as Indian citizens.[33]

India also has adequate revenue records to prove that the seven villages of Byans Patti paid taxes to the British. Part II of the Revision of Settlement in Kumaon District prepared by J. O'B Beckett for the period 1863–1873, published in 1874 at Allahabad, clearly prescribes the Jumma of the last year of the expired settlements from the seven villages of Byans Patti, namely Goonji, Gurbyang, Kootee, Nabee, Napalchyoon, Roonkang and Waree Boodee as Rs 24, Rs 68, Rs 45, Rs 41, Rs 20, Rs 34 and Rs 61 respectively. It then goes on to prescribe the rates under the next settlement.

Another clinching argument from India's perspective is provided by the China-Nepal Boundary Agreement of 5 October 1961.[34] Article 1 of the Agreement states that:

The Chinese-Nepalese boundary line *starts* from the point where the watershed between the Kali River and the Tinkar River meets the watershed between the tributaries of the Mapchu (Karnali) River on the one hand and the Tinkar River on the other hand, thence it runs south eastward along the watershed between the tributaries of the Mapchu (Karnali) River on the one hand and the Tinkar River and the Seti River on the other hand . . . (emphasis added).

Clearly, the Nepal–China boundary *starts* from a point to the East of Lipulekh Pass according to this agreement. Accordingly, Boundary Pillar No. 1 demarcating the Nepal–China boundary has been placed near Tinkar Pass. This is well east of Lipulekh Pass.

In the absence of a watertight case, why has Nepal unilaterally chosen to publish a new map, knowing full well that it would create major problems in its relationship with India? The answer lies in the internal politics of Nepal. In November 2019, it was the Nepalese Congress that had first started protesting India's new map on the grounds that Kalapani was shown as Indian territory. For them it was a political ploy to embarrass the Oli government and the Nepalese Communist Party, which had successfully used anti-India nationalism to bolster its own popularity. The Nepali Congress perhaps felt that using similar tactics may boost its own sagging fortunes and chose to take a leaf out of Oli's copybook. Thereafter the matter was raised in the State Affairs Committee of the Nepalese Parliament and directions given to the government to issue a new map. Oli had initially been going slow and merely protesting to the Indian government. His government claims that the lack of a positive response on the part of India to the official notes sent by Nepal seeking foreign secretary-level talks to resolve the boundary issue precipitated matters and, given internal pressures, he had no option but to go ahead and publish the new map. Nepal felt that India was not interested in discussing the matter and was using the COVID-19 pandemic as an excuse to delay talks, particularly since Indian leaders were regularly engaged in conversations with world leaders through videoconferencing.

Though there may be some truth that India may have initially downplayed the importance and urgency of the matter, the fact is that Oli was under considerable pressure from within his party. The long litany of complaints against Oli included his poor handling of the COVID-19 pandemic and its economic consequences, his autocratic style of running the party and government without consulting other leaders, which was in violation of several agreements and understandings that he had with the co-chair Prachanda, and his unsuccessful attempt to bring in a bill making it easier for political parties to be split.

In May 2020 itself, senior leaders of the NCP, namely, Prachanda, Madhav Kumar Nepal, Jhalanath Khanal and Bam Dev Gautam, had got together against Oli. Within the standing committee, the highest decision-making body of the NCP as well as in the Central Committee, Oli was reduced to a minority. At that stage, with the active mediation of the Chinese, including a phone call between Presidents Bidya Bhandari and Xi Jinping, shuttle diplomacy of the Chinese Ambassador who met the President, Oli, Madhav Nepal and Prachanda on the same day to patch things up, the Oli government survived. However, this was short-lived, and the problems resurfaced in July 2020 when Prachanda requested Oli to give up both his positions as PM and party president, which Oli refused to do. Once again, the Chinese Ambassador was active and urged Communist leaders to refrain from doing anything that may split the party.

In the midst of these internal tussles, the boundary issue became a lifeline, a God-sent opportunity for Oli. He used it to refurbish his nationalist credentials and rouse national public opinion in his own favour as the only leader who could stand up to India, the only leader who could get the territory back from the Indians, etc.

In various webinars, senior officials of Nepal who have since retired from government service have argued that the boundary issue is an emotive one in Nepal; that like India, Nepal considers its country to be the motherland. Territory, therefore, arouses deep inchoate emotions among the people. If that were the case, surely the Government of Nepal would have repeatedly raised the issue in all high-level bilateral engagements with India. The truth is that even when Oli, who has taken anti-India nationalism to new levels in Nepal, visited India in 2018, he did not raise the boundary issue.

From the author's perspective, the reality in Nepal is that the far west of the country is a remote area that was directly linked to Kathmandu only after the construction of several river bridges by India in 1999. Prior to that period, access to the Kathmandu valley from far western Nepal was through the Indian territory. The Byans valley is an even more remote and distant part of far western Nepal. Even to this day, it does not have direct road access from within Nepal. Not many political leaders from Nepal would have visited this area. It is only now that the army has been instructed to construct a road from Darchula to Tinkar Pass that would give the Nepalese access to both Tibet and other parts of Nepal, without going through the Indian territory. The strategic implications of such a road in the context of the present deterioration in India-China relations would have to be kept in mind by India.

Overall, we are confident that territories now claimed by Nepal have always belonged to India and there is enough evidence available to prove this. Our broad sense is that Oli has raised this issue to divert attention from his own domestic political problems. This perception is further buttressed by the fact that the Oli government rebuffed Indian offers to begin talks, informally conveyed prior to the unilateral publication of the new map. What is particularly distressing for India is that Oli has raked up the matter at a time of crisis between India and China, particularly in Ladakh. This has given rise to the suspicion that Nepal is acting at the behest of China. Even if this is not the case, public perception in India, also created by the media, has turned against Nepal. For the first time in living memory, the Indian sentiment has turned negative vis-à-vis Nepal.

By pushing through a constitutional amendment, Oli has tied the hands of his successor governments. With what confidence can India negotiate with Nepal if there is no guarantee that the Nepal government will be in a position to obtain parliamentary endorsement by two-thirds majority for any future boundary settlement? This would be particularly difficult if it involves loss of territory for Nepal. It is relatively easy to forge consensus when you gain territory; loss of territory will inevitably imply that the opposition will cry foul, domestic public opinion would be negative and prospects for obtaining a two-thirds majority almost impossible. Before entering into negotiations, India would need a commitment from leaders of political parties in Parliament that they would accept the outcome of any future India–Nepal boundary talks.

6

Historical Treaties: Is It Time for Revision?

This chapter discusses two issues that have become or have the potential to become irritants in the relationship. They have been raised over the years from time to time. The selected issues are the 1950 Treaty of Peace and Friendship and the question of Gorkha recruitment into the Indian Army.

The 1950 Treaty of Peace and Friendship[1]

The 1950 treaty is a long-standing irritant in the relations between India and Nepal. Nepal argues that the treaty was signed at a time when the geopolitical circumstances in our region were very different, and it needs to be altered to reflect the current realities. There is nothing unusual about this argument. India too has argued in the United Nations, for instance, that the structures of the UN, particularly the Security Council, needs reform and should reflect current global realities. Prime Minister Modi, during his visit to Nepal in August 2014, had categorically stated, publicly, that India was prepared to go along with whatever Nepal desired, to abrogate the treaty if they did not find it useful, or to review it and, if necessary, amend it through negotiations. India is prepared for both the options.

The treaty was negotiated by the autocratic Rana regime at a time when the communists had taken control of China and Chinese activities in Tibet were causing concern in the Himalayan states on the southern flanks. The Nepalese rulers were worried about the departure of the British from India, with whom they had established a cosy relationship. On the other hand, several Nepalese political leaders, including B.P. Koirala, had participated in the Indian freedom struggle and were keen to introduce democratic political freedoms in Nepal. The Rana regime wanted to ensure its own survival in the changed political situation in the neighbourhood. From the north, they saw an existential threat; from the south they were worried that the winds of political change would engulf them. This was the context in which the 1950 treaty was signed. Indeed, political developments occurred at a rapid pace and the Rana regime did not survive in its earlier form; the dramatic escape of King Tribhuvan to India and his triumphant return to Nepal following the Delhi Pact that led to a power-sharing arrangement between the Ranas and the political parties happened soon after the treaty was signed.

Over the years, Nepal came to see the treaty as derogating from its full sovereignty. Though in public leaders have argued that the treaty is unequal since on the one hand it was signed by the prime minister of Nepal and on the other by the Indian Ambassador, their main reservations relate to Articles 2 and 5.

Article 2 states that, 'The two governments hereby undertake to inform each other of any serious friction or misunderstanding with any neighbouring State likely to cause any breach in the friendly relations subsisting between the two governments.'

From the Indian perspective, since Nepal only has two neighbours, Article 2 was a clear reference to China. India, of course, has several neighbours including Pakistan and China and, as we shall see later, it has been argued in Nepal in the past that since India did not inform Nepal about its wars with China and

Pakistan in 1962 and 1965, respectively, the treaty has been in breach.

Article 5 states that, 'The Government of Nepal shall be free to import, from or through the territory of India, arms, ammunition or warlike material and equipment necessary for the security of Nepal. The procedure for giving effect to this arrangement shall be worked out by the two governments acting in consultation.'

Basically, the treaty was a compact that recognized Nepalese independence and sovereignty and provided national treatment to citizens but brought Nepal under the Indian security umbrella through the security clauses requiring mutual consultation as well as those relating to arms purchases. This is even clearer from the secret side letters exchanged at the time of signature of the treaty that were made public by Pandit Nehru in 1959.[2] Our stance had already been made clear by Pandit Nehru's statement that India saw its frontier as the Himalayas.[3] Sardar Patel's letter of 1950[4] had also made this explicit; further, the stationing of Indian personnel at the Nepal–Tibet border checkposts was with the concurrence of the Nepalese authorities.

Since then, however, the situation has dramatically changed. The security clauses of the treaty have become more or less redundant. Kirti Nidhi Bista in the 1960s had said that Nepal was never consulted by India in the context of the wars with China and later Pakistan[5]. The treaty did not prevent Nepal from developing cordial relations with China even in the wake of tensions in the India–China relationship. The Nepal–China boundary was agreed upon in 1961 following the agreement for the construction of the road between the Tibet border and Kathmandu, the famous Arniko Highway linking Khasa (Zhangmu) in Tibet with Kodari in Nepal and on to Kathmandu. And this, at a time when the relationship between China and India had plummeted to a new low from the Hindi–Chini Bhai–Bhai days of 1954.

Nepal's desire for full sovereignty and freedom in the exercise of its foreign policy is understandable. This has also been the quest of the Bhutanese. However, while the Bhutanese have succeeded in amending the 1949 treaty with India relatively smoothly without negatively impacting on bilateral ties, Nepal has been unsuccessful so far. This in a sense reflects the different foreign policy trajectories followed by the two countries. Bhutan is deeply committed to its friendship with India and has not established diplomatic relations with China. Nepal, on the other hand, has not been mindful of India's concerns. Indeed, at times it has worked to deliberately undermine our interests. The high decibel criticism of the merger of Sikkim with India and their proposal for equidistance between India and China, reflected in the Nepal as a Zone of Peace Proposal, were not well received in India. Nepal has also used the 1950 treaty to whip up anti-India sentiment. It is perhaps useful to have some permanent irritants in the relationship to use when politically expedient.

Nepal does not wish to abrogate the treaty, which it easily can in accordance with the procedure laid down in the treaty. Rather it wishes to cherry-pick elements of the treaty; retain those that are in its favour and delete those that it does not like. An unbalanced treaty may not be in our interest. The situation today in de facto terms conforms to what Nepal wants. The security clauses are more or less inoperative whereas the national treatment clauses, theoretically reciprocal, are operative and have brought immense benefit to the people of Nepal.

An Eminent Persons Group, headed by Bhagat Singh Koshiyari, a senior BJP leader and now governor of Maharashtra, and Bhekh Bahadur Thapa, former Foreign Minister of Nepal, has prepared a report that is thought to contain recommendations on the way forward on the treaty. The fact that the report has not been accepted by India, even two years after it was finalized, suggests that we are unhappy with the contents. For Nepal, the key issue in the report, the contents of which have not been disclosed in the public domain, is a review of the 1950 treaty. Perhaps, the time has now come for a serious discussion at the foreign secretary level between the two countries to work out a new compact that accommodates the concerns of Nepal while recognizing India's security interests. That this is doable is clear from our experience with the treaty with Bhutan. That could be a template for the revision of the India–Nepal Treaty.

The Tripartite Treaty; The Gorkha Connection

If you travel to Pokhara, a twenty-minute flight slightly north-west from Kathmandu, you are transported to a different world. This is a lovely lake town known for its views of Macchapuchare, the fish tail mountain, and also the point from where the famous Annapurna trekking circuit begins. This region is home to sturdy mountain people, the Gurungs and the Magars who, together with the Kirati Rais and Limbus from eastern Nepal, have formed the backbone of the Gorkha Regiments of the Indian Army. The valley is dotted with pretty houses belonging to ex-servicemen of the British and Indian armies who live on the generous pensions that they receive for their service. Pokhara town itself is littered with billboards advertising training services for those interested in joining the two armies.

A few miles from Pokhara, paragliding enthusiasts heading to Sarangkot will, in all likelihood, meet young men huffing and puffing up the hill carrying heavy *pitthus* or backloads, preparing for the recruitment tests for the Indian and British armies. This is one of the most popular career options for a young man (and now women as well) and possibly the easiest way to break out of a life of poverty. The pay and perks of service offered by the two armies are better than anything that can be achieved for equivalent service within Nepal.

There is a 200-year-old history to this association of the Gorkhas with the Indian Army. In the early decades of the founding of the state of Nepal by the Shah dynasty, the Shah kings launched several expeditions to expand their territory.

Having captured Kumaon first and then Garhwal in the west, they were eventually stopped by Maharaja Ranjit Singh's army in Kangra (now in Himachal Pradesh) in 1809. Some of the defeated Nepalese soldiers found employment in the Sikh army. To this day in vernacular, Nepali soldiers who join the Indian Army are referred to as *lahure*, after Lahore, Maharaja Ranjit Singh's capital.

Subsequently, the Nepalese battled the British East India Company in 1814 and 1815 and were defeated. They sued for peace and signed the Sugauli Treaty in 1816. Even though the Nepalese had lost, the British were deeply impressed by the military prowess, courage and valour of the Nepalese forces. It is said that a junior British officer, Lieutenant Frederick Young, impressed with the bravery of the Gorkhas, had requested General Ochterlony to be allowed to seek recruits from the Gorkha war prisoners.[6] Under an agreement entered into between Kajee Ummer Sing Thappa and Major General David Ochterlony on 15 May 1815,[7] it was agreed that, 'All the troops in the service of Nepaul, with the exception of those granted to the personal honour of the Kajees, Ummer Sing and Runjore Sing, will be at liberty to enter into the service of the British government, if it is agreeable to themselves and the British government choose to accept their services . . .' Thus began the first Gorkha Regiment of the Indian Army, known as the 'Nasiri' regiment.

Even prior to Independence, the question of continuing the recruitment of Gorkha soldiers into the Indian Army was under active consideration. On 1 May 1947, the prime minister of Nepal, Maharaja Padma Shumsher Jang Bahadur Rana, had conveyed that he would 'welcome the proposals to maintain the Gurkha connection with the armies of the United Kingdom and India'. He went on to say that 'If the terms and conditions at the final stage do not prove detrimental to the interest or dignity of the Nepalese government, my government will be happy to maintain connections with both armies, provided men of the Gurkha regiments are willing so to serve (if they will not be looked upon as distinctly mercenary).'

Thereafter the terms and conditions were worked out, accepted by the prime minister of Nepal and attached to the Memorandum of Agreement among the Government of the United Kingdom, the Government of the Dominion of India and the Government of Nepal, the so-called Tripartite Agreement[8] under which recruitments by the Indian and British Armies continue to this day.

Since then, the Gorkha regiments have distinguished themselves in the service to the nation. The Gorkha Rifles have won three Param Vir Chakras (PVC), the highest award for bravery during combat, and numerous other battle honours and awards. They have produced three Army Chiefs, General, later Field Marshal S.H.F.J. Manekshaw, General Dalbir Singh Suhag and General, later Chief of Defence Staff Bipin Rawat.

In an article in the *Sunday Guardian* of 6 June 2020, Major General (retd) Ian Cardozo describes the Gorkhas in the following words: 'They are cheerful in disposition and nothing disturbs their equanimity. They are loyal to the core and fearless in battle. They are cheerful in adversity and however bad the situation they never complain. All this makes them among the best soldiers in the world and they are much sought after. Soldiering for them is a natural profession and Gorkha regiments have men from the same family who have served with the regiments for five generations and more.'

He then refers to an incident during the India–Pakistan war of 1971: 'My battalion, the 4th Battalion the 5th Gorkha Rifles (FF) was tasked to capture a Pakistani post which was protected by marshes, minefields and barbed wire. The battalion decided to assault the enemy position through the marshes which had three to four feet of water. The commanding officer, Lieutenant Colonel Arun Harolikar, led the battalion in what has come to be known as the last *khukri* attack in modern military history. The enemy came to know of our presence only when the Gorkhas were upon them. *Khukris* flashed that night and Pakistani heads rolled to the dexterous use of this Gorkha weapon. The enemy was decimated. Those who managed to escape passed the word around: 'Don't mess with the Gorkhas. If you do, you may lose your head!'

There are numerous similar stories of the valour and courage of Gorkha battalions in the 1962 conflict with China as well as wars with Pakistan and as part of the Indian Peace Keeping Force (IPKF) in Sri Lanka.

It is not for nothing that the regimental motto of most of the Gorkha Rifles (GR) regiments is *Kayar Hunu Banda Marna Ramro* (It Is Better to Die in War than Live like a Coward).

In recent years, particularly after the restoration of multi-party democracy in Nepal, the Tripartite Agreement has become the subject of some controversy. Some communist leaders have argued that it does not behove a self-respecting sovereign nation to allow its people to join foreign armies and fight in foreign wars. Some of these conflicts could be against countries that are friendly to Nepal. The Maoists included in their famous forty-point demand of 1996, the closure of Gorkha recruiting centres in Nepal. Subsequently, pursuant to a recommendation from the Nepalese Parliament, a Maoist-led government tried to stop the recruitment of Gorkhas in 2012 but was unsuccessful. The previous communist government under Prime Minister Oli has again raised this issue. Foreign Minister Pradeep Gyawali, in a webinar on 31 July 2020, stated that the Tripartite agreement was 'redundant'. It was a legacy of the past. Nepal would like to have two separate agreements with the UK, and India. In 2019, it was reported in the media that PM Oli, during his visit to the UK, had raised the issue with his British counterpart, Theresa May, but this did not find mention in the joint statement issued after the visit. Oli subsequently told the media that the UK did not agree to a revision of the Tripartite pact.[9] In February 2020, the Nepalese government has again sent a formal letter on the subject to the

UK. It is not clear whether the Nepalese have similarly raised this matter with the Government of India.

Discrimination against British Gurkhas[10] in terms of pension and leave concessions as well as the right to remain and live in Britain is an issue that has received considerable media attention in the UK. Joanna Lumley, the British actress, has been at the forefront advocating the cause of the Gurkhas (her father belonged to the Gurkha regiment). Some progress has been made in improving the terms and conditions of service, but all grievances have not been settled. It is likely that this is the proximate cause for the Nepalese to seek separate agreements with the UK and India.

As far as India is concerned, there is equal treatment of Gorkhas with other soldiers of the Indian Army in terms of pay and allowances, pensions and medical benefits. Revisions of pay following Pay Commissions as well as One Rank One Pay are applicable to Nepalese Gorkhas as well, as is the Ex-Servicemen Health Scheme (ECHS) for medical care. Accordingly, there are no complaints of any discrimination by India.

Overall, the Indian Army employs about 30,000 Gorkha troops from Nepal. Some 1,25,000 retirees from the Indian Army and related forces receive their pensions in Nepal. Every year Rs 4200 crore is provided to serving and retired Gorkhas in pay and pensions. This represents about 2 per cent of Nepal's annual GDP.

The pensions are provided both through the banking system as well as in cash by holding a series of Pension Camps in far-flung areas of Nepal. I had the opportunity to visit one of the Pension Camps. It had a festive atmosphere akin to a *mela*. Temporary stalls selling all kinds of products were set up by local villagers. For the pensioners it was an opportunity to interact with the Gorkha Officers of the embassy and with each other and relive past memories. I recall an audit team once recommending that these pension camps should be discontinued, and payments should be sent electronically to the bank accounts of the pensioners. This was recommended on grounds of both efficiency and security. I had argued against such a clinical approach on the grounds that the camps were one way of being in regular touch with the retirees. Increasingly, as we move to a more virtual world with declining human contact and interaction, particularly in COVID-19 times, I fear that we will lose this personal connect with an important constituency for India in Nepal.

If one visits the area near our Pension Paying Office in Pokhara, a whole town has arisen in its neighbourhood with a large number of shops catering to the needs of the pensioners. The gold and jewellery shops are particularly prominent in advertising their wares.

After spending the prime of their working lives with the Indian Army, most Nepalese Gorkhas return home to their villages and towns. They represent a disciplined, trained manpower that should be put to use. In their mid-40s, these men can make significant productive contributions to their motherland. Several retirees have started their businesses in the tourism and travel trade. Some organize homestays, others have established small hotels for trekkers and backpackers.

One enterprising retiree from the Indian Army is Honorary Captain Dam Bahadur Pun. He is one of the pioneers of the Poon Hill trek, popular with tourists who visit Pokhara. It is a short three-day trek and the ascent to Poon Hill provides the most spectacular views of the sunrise against the Himalayan range. Ghorepani is the base camp for the trek up to Poon Hill. This is a small village of a few dozen households. Most villagers provide accommodation for trekkers. Captain Pun has built a small hotel of a couple of rooms with en suite facilities. During a trek, the writer stayed in these basic but comfortable lodgings. Captain Pun is a highly respected member of his community. The same story is repeated in many villages where the pension received by retirees enables them to live a comfortable existence and, generally, they are better off than their local counterparts.

As far as the Government of Nepal is concerned, there is a certain distance that is maintained from the Indian Army retirees. I recall a conversation with former Chairman of the Interim Council of Ministers Khil Raj Regmi when I suggested to him that instead of recruiting untrained hands for security-related work during elections, the government could consider using the Indian Army retirees who are well trained and disciplined. Though he did not say anything, my suggestion did not find favour. My feeling is that the Nepalese establishment suspects these citizens of holding dual loyalties.

We have tried to involve the ex-soldiers, for instance, in monitoring some of the Small Development Projects undertaken by India in various parts of Nepal. They are also active in community forestry projects. Some such as Colonel D.B. Thapa have tried to enter politics but have been unable to make much headway. Nevertheless, there are several senior Nepali leaders, including Ram Bahadur Thapa 'Badal', the former home minister, who have close relation(s) who have worked in the Indian Army.

I recall an interesting incident about a Gorkha soldier from my tenure in Nepal. While serving in Kathmandu, I used to occasionally call on Tulsi Giri, a former prime minister of Nepal. He was a bit of a maverick, brilliant mind but he had crossed sides in both his political and personal beliefs several times. He started off as a member of the RSS, became a private secretary to the leader of the Nepali Congress B.P. Koirala, dumped multiparty democracy and joined forces with King Mahendra and became PM following the royal coup of 1960. Hailing from a high caste Hindu family, in later life he married Sara Yonjan, a Christian, and converted to Christianity. He had the distinction of serving two monarchs, Mahendra and his son Gyanendra. The latter also appointed him vice chairman of the Council of Ministers following the second royal coup of February 2005.

Tulsi Giri's father-in-law was more than a hundred years old when I met him on one of my visits to Giri's residence. He had been told that the Indian Ambassador was visiting and was decked out in a formal suit and tie. Yonjan told me that he used to receive a military pension from the office in Darjeeling, where he had lived in the past, but ever since he had moved with his daughter to Kathmandu, he had stopped receiving his dues. He showed me his identity card. It was from the late 1930s or early 1940s and stated that Yonjan was deployed in the Signals unit of the Azad Hind Fauj (Indian National Army). The ID was signed by Subhash Chandra Bose.

On returning to my office, I asked Defence Attache Colonel M.R.S. Mann (there was a framed certificate in his house from one of his military courses referring to him as Major MRS Mann) to personally ensure that Yonjan's pension was restored and given to him. This happened a few months later, alas some days after Yonjan passed away.

As far as India is concerned, we are proud of the Gorkha connection with the Indian Army and would want this tradition to continue unhindered. But only time and the thinking of political leaders in Nepal will determine the future.

7

The Economic Partnership: We Can Grow Together

Trade and Investment, Cooperation in Water Resources,
Development Partnership

The year was 2005. It was the month of June. I had taken a couple
of days off from work and decided to do the most famous trek in
Nepal, the Annapurna Circuit. It was known colloquially as the
Apple Pie Trail since it was popular with western backpackers and
was lined with tea houses en route that served excellent pizza and
apple pie! It was a difficult trek since you climbed to an altitude
of 5,400 metres, to the Thorung La (Pass) between Manang and
Mustang, two districts of Nepal that lie in the trans-Himalayan
zone with Mustang touching the Tibetan plateau. My companions
on this trek were the deputy chief in our Mission in Kathmandu,
V.P. Haran, and his daughter Anupama. We only did a truncated
seven-day version rather than the long three-week trek, beginning
our walk from Humde, which in those days was connected to
Kathmandu by air, rather than lower down in Besisahar. Apart
from the great natural beauty of the area and the magic of Manang

and Muktinath, one abiding memory that has stayed with me is of a young adult, nineteen or twenty at most, carrying a backpack that must have weighed not less than 20 kilogrammes held by a strap attached to his forehead, wearing shorts and the rubber *hawai chappals* popular all over South Asia. He belonged to western Nepal and was lugging his load over high mountain terrain; looking at his attire, he must have been from an impoverished family. Of course, the situation has improved since then but even today, Nepal remains one of the poorest countries in the world, including in South Asia.

Almost a third of Nepal's population works abroad. Four to six million Nepalese are believed to live and work in India, to which they have easy access, given open borders since times immemorial and national treatment under the 1950 Treaty of Peace and Friendship; another four million are employed in the Gulf and Malaysia. It is estimated that two Nepalese workers die abroad every day; some are working in temperatures of 55 degree Celsius in places such as Qatar that is preparing for the World Cup in football. A former Nepali ambassador to Qatar, Maya Kumari Sharma, told me in Chitwan where she lived, that the Nepalese worked in pathetic conditions for a pittance. She had publicly commented that they were working in an open jail! The Qataris were upset and asked for her recall. Nepal obliged.[1] She believed that it was important for South Asian countries that send workers to Gulf countries to join forces to ensure proper terms and conditions for expatriate labour.

Increasingly, the widespread poverty in Nepal forces its young adults to leave home for work. Women too are going abroad for work, some as domestic help. Why are the Nepalese voting with their feet? Of course, to some extent, it is difficult to find work in the mountain areas and down migration to the plains is inevitable. We see that in the population of Uttarakhand that depends significantly on remittances. As PM Modi said in his famous speech to the Nepalese Constituent Assembly in 2014, '*Paani aur jawani to pahad pe rukti nahin* (water and youth do not remain in the hills).' In the case of Nepal, the Maoist insurgency between 1996 and 2006 also took its toll. But today it is not only the people of the hills who are leaving; the highest out migration is now from some of the districts of the Terai plains! Why are there no jobs in Nepal? Why is Nepal the poorest country in South Asia, an LDC (least developed country)? Even Bangladesh, which was considered to be a basket case in 1975— remember the Concert for Bangladesh—with famine stalking the land, is today a rapidly growing developing country. And Bhutan, which is comparable in terms of its location, habitat and resources, though not in size, has a GDP per capita that is three times that in Nepal! Why has the much talked about peace dividend remained elusive in Nepal?

Several reasons are cited for the relative lack of prosperity in Nepal. Political instability involving over two dozen governments in as many years, the Maoist insurgency and the transition from a unitary to a federal state has implied that the economic project did not get the attention that it deserved, barring the initial euphoric years after the end of the Panchayat system and the advent of multiparty democracy. Devendra Raj Pandey, formerly Finance Minister and a respected figure in Nepal, has argued that the state's policies of exclusion are fundamentally responsible for the lack of development.[2] Added to this are the usual problems of corruption, lack of good governance and inadequate economic reform programmes, particularly with regard to land, that most developing societies face. An important reason has also been Nepal's inability to fully benefit from the dynamism and the buoyancy of the Indian economy, largely because of the mistrust and historical baggage that exists in the political relationship.

Nepal has established a clear economic vision of graduating from the LDC category by 2022 (it already meets the Human Assets and Economic Vulnerability criteria and needs to achieve the threshold GDP per capita of US$1230), becoming a developing country by 2030 and a developed country with a per capita income of US$12,000 by 2043. Of course, the ravages caused by the COVID-19 pandemic will push these dates further into the future. To achieve this goal of a *Samriddha Nepal Sukhi Nepali* (Prosperous Nepal, Happy Nepali), it would require a sharp increase in the rate of economic growth to double digit figures and a corresponding increase in investment. Significant assistance in the form of grants and loans as well as FDI would be needed to push up the investment rate. Fifty-eight per cent of GDP is derived from the services sector, with industry contributing 15 per cent and agriculture 27 per cent. Remittances from abroad represent one-third of total GDP. In most economies, as they grow, the share of agriculture in GDP declines relative to that of services and manufacturing. Nepal too is aiming to achieve this with a focus on key growth-driving sectors—hydropower; infrastructure; manufacturing; agriculture, by moving from subsistence to commercial farming and high-value produce; and skill development and services sector, particularly tourism. With a young, hardworking population—40 per cent Nepalese are in the 16–40 age group—there is a huge demographic potential that Nepal can exploit, provided the right policies are set in train.

Given Nepal's geographical location, resource basket and landlocked status, it is critical for the country to develop an India-specific strategy as part of its overall strategy for economic growth. How can Nepal leverage India's economic dynamism for its own benefit? In the past, it has tended to follow a policy of benefiting from arbitrage, differentials in customs duty rates between the two countries that have not generated economic development but have only enriched a few traders and politicians. Nepal also needs to focus more on the economic opportunities in its dealings with India rather than an overweening focus on the political aspects of the relationship where it tends to see India as a threat. It should draw up specific policies for its economic engagement and try, to the extent possible, to keep the political sphere distinct from the economic relationship. Of course, this is easier said than done in a highly charged environment where political fortunes may depend on playing the anti-India nationalism card.

India, too, needs a clear vision for its cooperation with Nepal and other neighbours. The neighbourhood first policy visualizes the BBIN (Bangladesh, Bhutan, India and Nepal) sub-region as an integrated economic space where the economic comparative advantage of each country can be exploited. Development of the connectivity infrastructure, roads, railways, integrated checkposts (ICPs), transmission lines, oil and gas pipelines and seamless digital interface, will create the enabling environment required to achieve this vision. It will reduce logistic costs, facilitate trade and enhance market access. Considerable headway is being made.

Most Indian connectivity projects are financed by grants or concessional lines of credit at terms that are very favourable, even when compared to Chinese loans. But project delivery is less than satisfactory. And this is a common complaint that one hears in Kathmandu. There are a series of problems in the implementation of these projects, some of which are on a G2G basis. The tendency is for India to implement projects in neighbouring countries in the same manner and using the same procedures that are employed for infrastructure development in India. There is a preference for public sector consultants and contractors; the policy is to allot the project to the L1 bidder, even though it may not have international experience; antiquated methods are used for making payments to contractors leading to major cash flow difficulties. Though some of the issues have to be resolved at our end, and the creation of the Development Partnership Division in the MEA is a step towards streamlining project delivery abroad, there are also serious problems that arise in the recipient country. The lack of adequate land reforms in the host country makes land acquisition an uphill task.[3] Nepal's experience of spending budgeted amounts is pathetic as is its pattern of aid absorption. In order to resolve these and related problems, a new bilateral mechanism for project monitoring was established during my tenure at the level of the ambassador in Kathmandu and the Nepalese foreign secretary. The meeting involves all stakeholders on the two sides and the problems are thrashed out at the meeting that is held at regular intervals. This is a pragmatic way of resolving issues at an early stage before they assume larger proportions and find their way into the media and lead to allegations and counter-allegations and public mudslinging between the two sides.

Nepal is blessed with two hundred major rivers and three major river systems, Kosi, Gandak and Karnali, that flow from the mighty Himalayas to the plains of India. It is estimated that 50 per cent of the water flows at Farakka Barrage, after which the Ganga enters into Bangladesh, come from the rivers of Nepal. Nepal's key driver or comparative advantage for sustainable development is exploiting this white oil. Of the estimated 80,000 MW of hydropower potential in Nepal, about 45,000 MW is commercially exploitable. Current installed hydroelectric capacity in Nepal is less than 1500 MW! Ironically, Nepal is a net importer of electricity from India. Almost a third of Nepal's total electricity consumption comes from India. Water becomes a valuable resource only if it can be stored and regulated. For millennia it has simply flowed away into the Bay of Bengal. Why has this potential not been exploited? This is a saga of missed opportunities. Not only are the people of the two countries deprived of power and irrigation benefits, the annual flooding in Bihar, UP and the Nepalese Terai causes untold human suffering through loss of life and property.

Cooperation in the water resources sector represents a win-win situation for both countries. Power, irrigation and flood control benefits of such projects and the fact that this is clean green energy, fully compatible with other renewable energy sources such as solar, make these projects attractive. Of course, the environmental and seismological factors would need to be fully considered before going ahead. The experience of the Tehri Project in India, which ran into a lot of opposition in the past but is today a symbol of success, sets a good precedent for similar projects in Nepal.

Exploiting the water resources potential depends in large part on intensive engagement with India, since it is potentially the largest market for Nepalese energy. This requires mutual trust and confidence. Nepal should have the confidence that it will derive the maximum gain possible from such projects. Unfortunately, the widespread anti-India sentiment in Nepal has made it very difficult for any government in Nepal to do a deal with India. Indeed, before any bilateral visit to India, various political parties exhort the prime minister not to sign any agreement with India that is against Nepal's interests. The Mahakali Treaty was termed a sell-out by Nepal and even led to a split in the CPN (UML). Even the Project Development Agreements for the Upper Karnali and Arun III projects faced huge political opposition from within the CPN (UML), though both projects were won against global tenders and offered extremely favourable terms to Nepal. It is this negative domestic environment that makes for uneasy India-Nepal cooperation in the hydropower sector, which is critical for Nepal's development.

Even when agreements are entered into by brave PMs, such as the Bilateral Investment Promotion and Protection Agreement (BIPPA) by Baburam Bhattarai in October 2011, there is strong domestic criticism in Nepal. The Fast Track Road project won by an Indian company in March 2016 on the basis of a competitive bid was cancelled due to opposition from the left parties.

Further, this lack of trust at the political level also seeps lower down into the bureaucracy, which is therefore worried about taking any initiatives vis-à-vis India. They are reluctant to wade into turbulent waters for fear of all kinds of allegations being raised against them. Even after an Indian company wins a project, the bureaucracy has a tendency to create hurdles or at the very least is not proactive in solving the problems faced by promoters. With the establishment of the Nepal Investment Board, there is some handholding, but not enough. No wonder many foreign companies find Nepal to be a difficult environment to work in, especially when compared to the red carpet rolled out for foreign investors in other countries.

Post-Independence, our focus was on large projects such as the Kosi High Dam that never took off.[4] If the waters of the Kosi could be regulated by the construction of a high dam, there would be huge benefits in terms of flood control and management in the Nepalese Terai and in Bihar, areas that witness a colossal loss of lives and property year after year due to the Kosi floods, irrigation and power generation. A barrage was constructed on the Kosi (and the Gandak) but resulted in some misunderstanding between the two countries, with allegations from Nepal that they had been short-changed by India. Steps to rectify the situation were taken in later years but the damage was done. To this day, the embassy in Kathmandu receives claims for compensation from farmers in Nepal for their land that they assert was never paid!

The Kosi High Dam project was revived with the establishment of the Joint Project Office (JPO) in 2004. Following the embankment breach on the east afflux bund in 2008, there was renewed focus on the project though there has been less than fulsome cooperation from the Nepalese authorities. The feeling in Nepal has been that it will bear an overwhelming proportion of the costs, since the entire submergence would be in Nepal, whereas the benefits in terms of irrigation and flood control would largely flow to India. The Sun Kosi Storage cum Diversion project was included as an integral part of the Kosi High Dam project, keeping in mind Nepal's interests. Further, an equitable framework for sharing of costs and benefits would need to be worked out to bring Nepal fully on board. But the JPO set up in 2004 for survey work and the preparation of a detailed project report (DPR) has been unable to complete even the preliminary survey work sixteen years later. There has been resistance from some of the local inhabitants, who would not even allow drilling work; indeed, in one incident, survey machinery and equipment was damaged by the locals.[5] At one stage there was even talk about closing the joint project office. Such a move would be unfortunate. We need to have a serious engagement at high levels to provide fresh impetus to the project. Another option that India should seriously consider is to associate Bangladesh, a lower riparian to the Ganga, with the project. Politically, a trilateral project involving India, Nepal and Bangladesh would be easier to implement from Nepal's perspective. If implemented, the project would also make the Kosi River partly navigable and allow for the possibility of Nepalese trade through inland waterways along the Ganga.

The present policy of embankment construction on various trans-boundary rivers between India and Nepal only provides a temporary solution to the flood problem. Since many of these rivers carry a lot of silt, as they debouch into the plains and slow down, the silt gets deposited, leading to a rise in the river bed. Indeed, the Kosi is now flowing above the surrounding land in some areas, thereby creating fresh dangers of possible breach of embankments. So far, there has been no case of the river overtopping the embankment since the east and west embankments are 10–16 kilometres apart. But the Kosi is known to be a river that has oscillated over 100 kilometres over the last two hundred years; straitjacketing it into an area of a few kilometres could create its own problems as witnessed in the breach of the left afflux bund when the river swung eastwards in 2008. Some experts have argued that due to heavy flows of silt and the fact that the location for the dam is in a seismic zone, the proposal for a high dam is not practical, but technological solutions would have to be found for these problems. Otherwise, the people of the Nepalese Terai and Bihar will have to live with the River of Sorrow as they have for the last many decades. India also needs to work with the Nepalese government on issues of soil erosion in the Himalayas and support the Rashtrapati Chure Conservation Project.

The Pancheshwar project on the Mahakali/Sharda River on the Nepal–Uttarakhand border was agreed upon with much fanfare in 1996—it resulted in a split in the CPN (UML)—

but even after it was revived during PM Modi's visit to Nepal in 2014, it has again got stuck and the joint DPR has still not been completed. The key points of contention are whether the waters of the Lower Sharda Barrage in India should be included as India's existing consumptive use and the sharing of irrigation benefits. India cites historical factors for its extant water usage, but Nepal refuses to accept this argument on the grounds that it is not mentioned in the Mahakali Treaty.[6] Though the electricity generation is shared equally between the two countries, in terms of irrigation India receives a disproportionate benefit since the irrigable land on the Indian side is much larger than in Nepal. Nepal wishes to also receive a share from this benefit. It is now six years since the project was revived. These contentious issues need to be resolved early, at the political level, failing which costs for the project will escalate further. Last time around, the estimated cost for the project increased from Rs 12,000 crores to Rs 34,000 crores at 2015 prices. If we account for inflation and the fact that the project will take about ten years for completion from the time of construction, we are looking at it coming on stream in 2031 if it starts in 2021. Even as costs have escalated, the overall capacity of the project has been reduced from 6750 MW to 5040 MW largely due to hydrological factors, namely, a reduced flow in the Mahakali River. The Nepalese wrongly feel that India is no longer interested in this project, partly because the submergence on the Indian side is much larger than in Nepal. These apprehensions must be addressed. The Pancheshwar High Dam is not only about electricity generation. It has the potential of transforming the economies of the region, both the underdeveloped far west of Nepal and the area of Kumaon in Uttarakhand. We should look at it as a strategic project that will further strengthen the economic interdependence between the two countries. An interesting model that should be studied is the Nam Theun 2 Project in Laos that has been commissioned for export of electricity to neighbouring Thailand. The World Bank and the Asian Development Bank played an important role in the financial structuring of the project.

Given the slow, lumbering pace of progress on the large dam projects, the two countries have moved towards run of the river projects that involve a much reduced submergence and hence displacement of populations. In addition to G2G projects, the sector is now open to companies, both state-owned and private. The Upper Karnali and Arun III projects are examples. Both projects estimated at 900 MW each were won by Indian companies, the former by private sector GMR and the latter by the public sector company Satluj Jal Vikas Nigam, through international competitive bidding. The finalization of the Project Development Agreements for the two projects was an uphill task. Even though the projects were secured on highly beneficial terms for Nepal, (GMR is providing 27 per cent free equity and 12 per cent free power for the Upper Karnali Project; SJVN is providing 21.9 per cent free electricity in the Arun III project) there was considerable resistance and opposition from within the CPN (UML). The then Chair of the party, K.P. Oli, played an important role in resolving the difficulties.

Unfortunately, the Upper Karnali project has got bogged down. Initially, there were some difficulties with the local community as well as threats by an extreme left group led by Netra Bikram Chand 'Biplav', but these have been largely overcome. Thereafter GMR faced some financial difficulties and has been looking for a strategic partner from abroad; the private sector arm of the ADB that had agreed to pick up a stake has backed out. A license for a separate 600 MW project that they had bid for and won on the Marsyangdi River was sold by them to another promoter. But a key difficulty for the company related to the guidelines for power trade issued by the Indian Ministry of Power that initially did not allow direct sale of power to Bangladesh. GMR was keen to finalize a Power Purchase Agreement with Bangladesh, which was offering a better price than India and in dollars, whereas Indian guidelines required the power to be first sold to an Indian buyer in rupees and thereafter India would sell the power to Bangladesh. This was a short-sighted approach that made it difficult for GMR to achieve financial closure. They were finding it difficult to finalize a PPA with an Indian off taker and hence were unable to arrange for the finances. Luckily, the Indian rules for cross-border power trade have since been amended. In this latter scenario, GMR would be able to sell electricity generated in Nepal directly to Bangladesh through the transmission line network in India. India would receive wheeling charges.

On the other hand, the SJVNL Arun III project is progressing reasonably well largely since it is fully funded by the GOI and does not need a PPA immediately. Despite initial security-related problems caused by the group led by Netra Bikram Chand 'Biplav', and some delays due to the COVID 19 crisis, it remains largely on track. The company has recently been awarded the 679 MW Lower Arun Hydropower project as well.

There are other possibilities in the hydropower sector as well. While there are several projects being implemented by Indian and Chinese companies, there are some other large and hyper large projects that remain dormant. A subsidiary of the Three Gorges Corporation had received the contract for the 750 MW West Seti hydropower project. The project is expected to evacuate power through a long transmission line up to the Indian border. Representatives of the Chinese company had met me in Kathmandu. They were keen to cooperate with an Indian company to construct the project, but no headway was made. I understand that the license for the project has since been cancelled.

Another massive project is the Karnali–Chisapani project that is expected to generate up to 10,000 MW of power. Though the Nepalese were keen on this project, partly since the Karnali region, which is now part of Province No. 6, is one of the poorest and most underdeveloped part of Nepal, currently, the Karnali project is in abeyance. The matter was raised by former DPM Bam Dev Gautam, who is from the region, in an informal meeting with me.

He was keen that it should be a collaborative venture between India, China and Nepal.

While such a proposal, given the current state of India–China relations, is only a distant theoretical possibility, given the fact that hydro-power projects require inordinately large sums of money, India should be open to collaborating with third countries and international funding agencies so that the hydro potential of Nepal can be exploited more rapidly. This will tie in the economies of the two countries even more, and indeed the sub-region of Bhutan, Bangladesh, India and Nepal eventually in a sub-regional electricity grid and provide a stronger foundation for regional cooperation. If third countries can help us in achieving this goal, we should welcome such cooperation.

Time is running out on some of these big-ticket projects given the changing electricity scenario in India. India is currently power surplus. In addition, there is a renewed focus on new and alternative sources of energy, such as solar, which is becoming increasingly economically viable as per unit electricity prices have plummeted, and nuclear power. Further the price at which electricity is sold shows a trend decline; large hydroelectric projects would become viable only when the unit cost of electricity sold is less than Rs 5 per unit, according to current estimates. The financial structuring of large projects such as Pancheshwar would need to take these factors into account.

In the past, our overall approach to development cooperation in Nepal was project based. It aimed to provide the basic infrastructure for Nepal coming out of a period of inadequate development and self-imposed isolation during the Rana rule. India assisted in developing roads—Tribhuvan Rajpath, Siddharth Rajmarg and the bulk of the east–west highway, airports in most of the towns of the Terai, hospitals, including Bir Hospital, National Trauma Centre, BPKIHS Dharan, laying of optical fibres and a large number of other projects. Today with a vision of an integrated and interconnected South Asia, particularly the BBIN region, our focus is on connectivity projects, including important link roads, railways, land ports or ICPs and inland waterways, oil and gas pipelines and electricity transmission lines. Our approach should be to facilitate rather than hamper economic cooperation and trade between countries such as Nepal and Bhutan with Bangladesh that are linked through land and riverine borders with India. We should develop regional supply chains for key products based on respective comparative advantages. This will promote intra-regional trade that stands today at a paltry 7 per cent, promote regional exports and tie in the entire region together, thereby contributing to a more meaningful and substantive relationship.

A new scheme that has been exceptionally successful is the Small Development Projects scheme; projects undertaken are of short duration, quick impact at the grassroots level with a maximum budget of Nepali Rs 5 crore. More than 500 such projects have been implemented in virtually every district of Nepal since the scheme was conceived in the early 2000s. Under the scheme, requests are received from different sources, governmental and non-governmental, from political and civil society organizations, and others for construction of schools, health facilities, rural roads, solar electrification, drinking water facilities, cold storages, etc. Under a tripartite umbrella MoU between the district official, normally the Local Development Officer who is in charge of project implementation, or a department of the planning ministry, the Embassy of India and the Ministry of Finance, projects are approved by the embassy and then implemented by the local district authorities. Indeed, if you travel through rural Nepal, you will see a large number of such projects. If you chance upon a modern building in a rural area, the probability is that it would have been constructed under this scheme. The scheme also provided India with an opportunity to interact at the grassroots level and is very important in strengthening goodwill for India among the Nepalese people. Unfortunately, despite the fact that we have undertaken several projects for most major political leaders of all parties, a sentiment was allowed to be built up in Nepal against the scheme; it was argued that this is not within the overall aid policy framework of the Nepalese government, that it is the government and not the embassy that should select projects; under the new Constitution the district level administrative framework has been transformed and hence the scheme cannot operate in its current avatar, etc. For three years, the continuation of the scheme was held up and it is only in 2020 that a new version has been approved.

Year after year, the Government of Nepal raises the issue of the burgeoning trade deficit with India. Two thirds of Nepal's total trade of US$11 billion in 2017–18 is with India. The India–Nepal trade is highly skewed in India's favour; exports to Nepal account for US$6.38 billion whereas imports from Nepal are a mere US$437 million. Nepal's trade deficit with India is a whopping US$5.9 billion.[7] The fundamental problem is that there is not much that Nepal can export to India. Indeed, even if all of Nepal's annual exports of about a billion US dollars are sold to India, there will still be a mammoth trade deficit. This is most visibly demonstrated if you travel to the Inland Container Depot at Birganj, which is run by the Indian company Container Corporation of India. Most of the containers that arrive at Birganj with imports for Nepal return empty since there is nothing to fill them up with. As a result, the logistics costs for Nepalese trade increase significantly, since the importer has to pay for the empty container to return to its destination.

It is also important to examine the composition of Nepal's trade basket. Roughly one third of Nepal's imports relate to POL products, most of which are also imported by India. Another significant amount comprises intermediate goods that are essential for Nepal's industry and agriculture. These two categories therefore represent essential imports for sustaining the economy. The balance remaining represents imports of consumer products. Similarly, if one looks at Nepal's exports to India, they largely comprise agricultural products, textiles, filaments and fibres and some iron and steel. The only way for Nepal to have more balanced trade is to either increase exports—India already provides duty and quota free access to Nepal for most products—or reduce import of consumer products. Indeed, the only realistic long-term solution is for Nepal to develop its hydroelectric potential, export electricity to India and hence improve its balance of payments situation.

Nepal also argues that a lot of its exports of perishable commodities get held up due to non-tariff barriers, some from the Central government in terms of public health regulations and testing requirements and others by the state governments. The lack of adequate testing laboratories close to the border complicates matters, with product samples having to be sent to faraway Kolkata or Lucknow for testing. Trucks carrying perishable agricultural produce have been known to be stuck at border customs for a week while awaiting test results. Similarly, Nepal complains from time to time of various levies imposed by state governments of UP or Bihar on products such as ginger, etc.

These are small problems but get magnified in the context of India–Nepal relations and can be easily solved. It should not be difficult for India to establish some testing facilities in Nepal. Insofar as issues relating to state governments are concerned, we need to devise a more effective and quicker problem resolution mechanism. Under the current framework, there is not much contact between the embassy in Kathmandu and the state administrations. Issues raised by Nepal, even if they pertain to the state governments, are sent by the embassy to the commerce and external affairs ministries in Delhi. They then further liaise with the state governments. This complicated channel of communication is time consuming. There needs to be direct engagement between the state governments and countries such as Nepal and Bhutan, with which we share open land borders. Indeed, for Nepal, many critical issues relate not to the Government of India but to the UP or Bihar authorities. We should facilitate a system for direct interaction between our states and the Nepalese government with the embassy as an intermediary. The embassy can keep the Central government informed. Indeed, following the adoption of the federal system in Nepal, we could even think of direct cooperation between the border provinces of Nepal with our state governments. Such regular and frequent interaction at both political and bureaucratic levels would go a long way in resolving problems that tend to become irritants in India–Nepal relations.

While we have a vast network of G2G mechanisms in diverse areas, these are still very formal. Meetings take place on an annual basis. In the period between meetings, in some cases there are sub-groups that meet. While this system is necessary, there is need for more informal and direct channels of communication between the concerned ministries in Nepal and their Indian counterparts, while keeping MEA in the loop. There is little email communication at the ministry-to-ministry level and almost all communication is routed through the foreign ministries in both countries. While this worked well in the past, when our ties were not as multifaceted as they are today, we need to move on to more contemporary systems of communication that are now available with modern technology.

Then again, there is inadequate coordination in India between our ministry of external affairs and other ministries, such as health or commerce, that legislate on issues that have a major impact on neighbouring countries, such as Nepal and Bhutan, with whom we have open borders and duty free movement of trade. The specific circumstances of these two countries are not taken into consideration in policy formulation. For instance, under our public health legislation, certain conditions were imposed on imports of agricultural and animal products. These also applied to Nepal and Bhutan without exception, leading to a sharp negative impact on traditional border trade that has being going on from times immemorial. Stronger coordination is needed between the MEA and concerned line ministries and within MEA between the territorial and functional economic divisions.

A key strategy for Nepal is to attract foreign investment in the manufacturing sector. Given the potential for electricity generation, Nepal could also consider investing in energy-intensive industries, such as cement, aluminium, iron and steel, where costs of production may be cheaper when compared to India. Many large Indian companies have been operating in Nepal since the early 1990s after the economic reforms programme undertaken following the advent of multiparty democracy. These include Hindustan Lever, Surya Tobacco, Asian Paints and Dabur, among others. Unfortunately, the pace of fresh FDI has slowed. In recent years, there have been few big-ticket investments from the Indian private sector outside the hydro-power sector.

The lack of interest by Indian investors in Nepal should be a matter of concern to both governments. Even though India represents the largest share of total FDI stock in Nepal, in terms of fresh investment into Nepal, China is the biggest contributor. And this is despite the fact that the extant Indian companies in Nepal have done well and have remitted significant dividend and royalty payments to their owners. Of course, not all companies have been successful; the Indian joint venture UTL in the telecom sector turned out to be a failure. At a time when Indian companies have invested abroad in a big way, in terms of acquisitions as well as greenfield and brownfield investments, why is there a reluctance to invest in neighbouring Nepal, a country that is next door, is culturally very similar and has a duty-free regime with India? Why can the Dabur success story of production in Nepal by an Indian company for the Indian market not be replicated? Is it due to a lack of opportunities, or a difficult working environment? If Indian companies are not investing in Nepal, will companies from other countries invest? As a former vice chair of the Nepal Planning Commission Govind Pokharel told me, when they were on a visit to Malaysia, the first question that industrialists there had asked was about Indian investment in Nepal. In other words, countries want to know whether or not Indian companies are investing in Nepal; if not, then the reasons thereof. Indian FDI would therefore have a multiplier effect for other FDI.

Nepal has established a Nepal Investment Board to consider foreign investments of more than US$100 million in the country. It is a single-window mechanism for foreign companies. But it needs to do much more on the question of advocacy and promoting Nepal as an investment destination. During high level visits of Nepalese leaders, there is usually a proforma meeting organized by the three Indian Chambers of Commerce, FICCI, CII and ASSOCHAM, where speeches full of generalities are made but with little follow up. A more focused approach that involves the preparation of a basket of bankable projects in different sectors followed by a targeted approach towards the relevant companies would be more effective. Nepal should consider holding road shows in different Indian cities to attract Indian FDI.

Common complaints from Indian companies that belong to the India Business Forum in Kathmandu, which interacts with the embassy on a regular basis, relate to inadequate IPR protection, antiquated labour laws and restrictions on remittance of profit and dividend. On IPR in particular, even though Nepal is party to the relevant international covenants, there is little protection of patents and trademarks. Thus, you have a Medanta Hospital, a hole in the wall operation in Kupondole, Kathmandu; you have billboards advertising Podrej steel furniture; a famous case on the use of the trademark Kansai of Kansai Nerolac Paints by a Nepalese went in favour of the Nepalese party. Theft of IPR makes it difficult for companies to operate or indeed launch new products in the Nepalese market, since many a time the copyright has already been registered by someone in Nepal. These problems need to be seriously addressed.

The services sector too offers huge opportunities for India–Nepal partnership. An added advantage is that this is a labour-intensive sector and hence would open up prospects for Nepal's youth. Tourism is already a major contributor to Nepalese GDP and the largest number of tourists that visit Nepal are Indians. Of a total visitor count of 1.1 million, some 2,00,000 tourists visit from India. These figures are understated since they only include arrivals at the Tribhuvan International Airport in Kathmandu. But even if we include the visitors across land borders, the number is insignificant compared to the size of our population. Clearly there is a huge potential waiting to be tapped. In 2018, 1.85 billion domestic tourist visits were made across India.[8] Given visa-free travel with Nepal, and the fact that all destinations are within three hours flying time from India, there is no reason why this huge market cannot be tapped. Plans to develop various religious circuits, Buddhist and Hindu, given the location of important pilgrimage sites such as Lumbini and Pashupatinath, Janakpur and Muktinath in Nepal received a boost with PM Modi's visit to some of these sites in 2018, but cross-border arrangements need to be speeded up vigorously. Including Nepal in the Leave Travel Concession Scheme for Central government civil servants would also encourage Indian tourists to visit Nepal. A rebranding of Nepal as a high value and high-quality tourist destination like Bhutan, rather than a backpacker's paradise, would bring high spending visitors.

Blessed with a salubrious climate, Nepal is also an ideal location for high-quality educational and medical institutions as well as sports facilities. Some Indian investors, such as the Manipal Group, have ventured into Nepal, though they have faced considerable problems in the smooth running of their teaching hospital in Pokhara.[9] Establishment of good international schools in Nepal could potentially attract rich NRI and NRN clientele. Similarly, development of international class sports stadia, for example, for cricket, could attract the money-spinning IPL to Nepal.

If you travel to the beautiful Himalayan resort town of Dhulikhel, an hour and a half's drive north-east from Kathmandu, a few kilometres before reaching Dhulikhel, you will come to the nondescript municipality of Banepa. It is an old trading village located on one of the traditional routes to Tibet. Today, Banepa is known for a state-of-the-art nursery and greenhouse belonging to the Indian company Dabur. The nursery produces saplings of several medicinal plants, such as ashwagandha and shatavari. These are then distributed to farmers who cultivate them on their land parcels and sell the produce back to Dabur, for use in their Ayurvedic products.

Nepal is well known for its biodiversity and an abundance of medicinal plants and herbs. As the demand for natural and herbal products increases worldwide, there is a great opportunity for Nepal to cultivate these on a commercial scale. Instead of traditional low value food crops, a switch by farmers to some of these high value plants will not only create new employment opportunities but improve rural incomes. To some extent, this is already happening in parts of Nepal. Companies like Patanjali are sourcing herbs from Nepal. But more needs to be done in a public-private partnership mode.

Similarly, Nepal has considerable potential in the field of high value agriculture, including items such as mushrooms, asparagus, etc. The same is true of floriculture as well as dairy products. Nepal produces world class Ilam tea and coffee. Nepal could become a niche producer of such products that can easily be sold in India. I recall meeting a young Frenchman, Francois Driard, whose stepfather had been an ambassador to Nepal. He settled down in Nepal and established a company selling Himalayan French Cheese. He had a regular stall at the weekly Saturday market at Le Sherpa, a beautiful restaurant, not far from the Indian embassy in Kathmandu. The market was frequented largely by expats in Kathmandu, though it was not uncommon to come across Radhika Shakya, spouse of Prime Minister K.P. Oli, who would arrive inconspicuously to shop for organic food products. Francois has set up a small enterprise, which is benefitting Nepalese farmers. He told me that he wanted to scale up his venture and export his products to India as well, but our health and quarantine regulations made it extremely difficult. Indeed, if we could establish adequate testing facilities and develop cold chains it should become feasible to export such products to India. Nepal could also follow the example of Sikkim and work towards becoming an 'organic' farming country over time.

Traditionally, the Nepalese rupee has been pegged to the Indian rupee in the ratio of 1.6:1. Further, the Indian rupee is freely usable in small denomination notes in Nepal. Bilateral trade is also conducted in rupees. Some Indian Army pensioners living in far West Nepal receive their payment in Indian rupees. The Indian currency is a safe haven for use during times of medical emergencies, for education, etc. The announcement of demonetization of Indian currency in November 2016 had a negative impact on Nepal. The demonetized Indian currency still in the custody of Nepal has to date not been exchanged by us. This is another in the long litany of complaints against India.

If Nepal is serious about using its demographic dividend, clear focus is required for the development and upgrading of labour skills both for domestic employment in priority sectors such as hydropower, tourism, commercial agriculture, etc. as well as for employment abroad. Skilled manpower will attract better salary terms for Nepal's expatriate work force. For instance, there is a major need for caregivers in countries such as Israel or construction workers in the Gulf countries. Appropriate nursing skills, or those required in the field of construction would move Nepali labour up in the value chain. There is a crying need for the establishment of training institutions in areas such as tourism, nursing, construction activities, etc., in Nepal. India has already set up a Vocational Training Institute in Morang district named after former prime minister Man Mohan Adhikari and is in the process of setting up another in Hetauda. To be truly successful, these institutions should be developed on a public-private partnership basis so that they can match the skills required with the available jobs, both in existing sectors as well as emerging ones.

On occasion, Nepalese friends have wistfully said to me that they wish their neighbouring states had been Maharashtra or one of the southern states. As if the growth impulses from these states would magically create prosperity in neighbouring Nepal. They somehow blame their location next to the 'Bimaru' states of Bihar and UP for some of their problems. I am afraid that the only road to economic prosperity is to adopt appropriate economic policies and create a favourable environment in which both domestic and foreign investors see opportunities for mutual benefit.

8

Humanitarian Assistance and Disaster Relief

The Great Earthquake of 25 April 2015

It was a Saturday morning, almost noon, in April. I had got ready to take my eighty-something mother for an espresso to the Hyatt Hotel. She was on a wheelchair and suffering from ISLD, an interstitial lung disease that had significantly reduced her lung capacity and left her dependent on supplementary oxygen 24/7. She looked forward to her Saturday outings with me. Just as we were about to leave India House, a sprawling ninety-year-old mansion in the heart of Kathmandu, the earth shook, and a low rumbling sound emerged from its bowels. I sensed immediately that it was an earthquake and ran to my mother's room. We were both on the first floor. She was sitting on her bed and I hugged her. She didn't immediately comprehend what was happening. Only when she saw the chandelier swinging from side to side did she realize that we were in danger. But there was nothing we could do; only wait for the tremors to subside. Even as the earthquake was underway, my security complement, including Personal Security Officer Sameer Singh and two constables from the CISF, without regard to their own safety, ran up two flights of stairs to our rooms to assist. Once the tremors stopped, they carried my mother to the ground floor and thence to the gardens where she would spend the next few hours.

This was the longest and scariest fifty-six seconds of my life. We found out later that it was a magnitude 7.8 temblor on the Richter scale with its epicentre at Barpak in Gorkha district about 150 kilometres north-west of Kathmandu. My driver Raju Lama who was outside later told me that he saw India House swaying from side to side and he expected it to collapse on its inhabitants. Luckily, we all escaped unhurt, but shaken. The house, unlike other Rana-era palaces of similar vintage that fell, suffered major cracks but remained standing.

After settling my mother in the gardens, I walked down to the Chancery and housing complex for an inspection. Unfortunately for us, we lost the daughter of an employee on our muster roll. As she was fleeing from her house, an old boundary wall fell upon her, killing her instantly and injuring her mother. Other than that, all our other employees and their families were safe, though badly shaken. And everyone had come out of their apartments to the safety of open ground where some would remain for a few days, as several hundred aftershocks continued to occur.

At that point in time, none of us knew the damage that the earthquake had caused but estimates of lives lost were in the tens of thousands. As it turned out, about 8,800 people lost their lives and 18,000 persons suffered injuries. Almost 5,00,000 houses were destroyed and 2,50,000 were damaged in the fourteen most heavily impacted districts. Most of the UNESCO World Heritage Sites in the Kathmandu Valley, including the iconic Kashtamandap from which the city takes its name, several palaces in the Hanuman Dhoka area, temples in the beautiful Durbar Square of Bhaktapur, the Dharahara tower, parts of the Buddhist stupa complexes at Swayambhu and Baudha and of the ancient temple of Changu Narayan fell to rubble.

Even before we could communicate with Delhi—electricity had failed and telecom connectivity had degraded sharply—I received a call from Foreign Secretary Jaishankar conveying that the GOI was ready to assist Nepal. Indeed, within six hours, our planes loaded with men, material and supplies arrived at Tribhuvan International Airport in Kathmandu, once approval of the Nepalese government was received. Later, I came to learn that our systems for disaster relief and management were activated almost immediately after the earthquake. Prime Minister Modi, who was driving in his motorcade, felt the tremor and immediately assessed from his own experience of the Bhuj earthquake of January 2000 that this was a major shock. Upon discovering that the epicentre was in Nepal, he convened an emergency Cabinet meeting to authorize the full support of GOI; he was the first to break the news to the Nepalese prime minister, Sushil Koirala, who was on a flight to Bangkok en route Kathmandu.

Over the course of the next few weeks, the Central government, the state governments, NGOs, the private sector and the people of India would provide several hundred crores of rupees worth of assistance. Our aircraft, helicopters, military doctors and engineers, NDRF (National Disaster Response Force) personnel and several teams of telecom providers, ham radio operators, electricity experts, teams from the Indian Oil Corporation and others provided relief and succour to those in need. A team headed by an Additional Secretary in the home ministry was deputed to assist the mission in Kathmandu. It was a mammoth logistical exercise and India assisted Nepal just as it would have if the earthquake had struck any part of India.

In all, Indian Air Force transport planes made thirty-one sorties to Kathmandu, carrying sixteen NDRF teams, three teams of army engineers, several medical teams and two army hospitals; 570 tonnes of relief material, medical supplies, oxygen concentrators, tents, tarpaulins, water and food items were airlifted. Eight MI-17 and five ALH helicopters were stationed in Nepal for several weeks for search, relief and rescue operations. Helicopters made 1800 sorties, evacuated 3000 stranded and 900 injured persons; these included 1500 Indian and 100 foreign nationals from countries such as Israel, the USA, France and China; injured persons and bodies of those that had died were also airlifted to India. Helicopters dropped 600 tons of relief material in remote, mountainous areas. Some 2000 trucks carrying 14,000 tons of relief materials from the Government of India, several state governments and others crossed into Nepal from the Indian border. About 1200 tons of relief supplies were sent by train. Several thousand Indians were evacuated in buses through the land borders. Our dynamic Consul General Anju Ranjan, based in Birganj, the main entry point on the India–Nepal land border, played a critical role in ensuring smooth clearance of our vehicles carrying relief material.

A high-level delegation comprising NSA Ajit Doval, additional principal secretary to the PM, P.K. Misra, and Foreign Secretary S. Jaishankar arrived six days after the earthquake to express solidarity with Nepal and renew India's commitment to do whatever was necessary to help Nepal in its moment of distress. This was followed by delegations from the National Disaster Management Authority (NDMA). A team of Indian experts led by V. Thirupugazh from the NDMA was sent to assist the Planning Commission of Nepal to prepare the Post Disaster Needs Assessment, which was pegged at US$6695 million. This became the basis for the pledging conference of donors convened in Kathmandu in June 2015. EAM Sushma Swaraj made a pledge of US$1 billion, the largest by any country, to help with the reconstruction efforts. Of this, US$250 million was a grant and the remaining US$750 million a concessional loan.

This was the largest ever Humanitarian Assistance and Disaster Relief (HADR) intervention abroad by India. Though our role in the 2004 tsunami has been written about, there is need for a greater awareness of India's role as the first HADR responder in Nepal. This chapter is an attempt to fill the gap. Not only was

India the first and fastest responder, our assistance was not limited only to rendering assistance to the Nepalese authorities. We helped foreign governments in the extraction of their nationals; our helicopters transported Nepali troops as well as relief and rescue teams from many countries, including the US and China, to their designated districts. We evacuated thousands of Indian nationals and several foreign nationals to India. Special facilities for visa on arrival were arranged at the Nepal-India land border for foreign nationals.[1]

The initial hours following the earthquake were very disorienting and difficult. Our first task was to get the Mission up and running. We also knew that on this occasion, our priorities would not only be the safety and security of the Indian community but assistance to the Nepalese government and people. The Nepalese authorities too were unprepared to deal with the enormity of the tasks. Prime Minister Koirala was away and it fell upon DPM and Home Minister Bam Dev Gautam to coordinate the rescue and relief effort. I knew him well and it was easy to work with him. But we had not bargained for the obstacles put in place by some in the bureaucracy. In the immediate aftermath of the earthquake, we had little difficulty in getting flight clearances for our military transport aircraft that were the first to land in Kathmandu within a few hours of the earthquake. But after some time, defence adviser, Colonel Mann, informed me that clearances were being delayed. Though it is true that the Kathmandu Airport has limited parking bays for aircraft and there was traffic congestion, knowing the thinking in the Kathmandu bureaucracy, we had a nagging suspicion that the Nepalese wanted to balance clearances to Indian aircraft with clearances to aircraft from other countries. Over some time, however, the situation improved, especially when the management of the airport was entrusted to the Nepalese Army. The age-old cordial ties between the Indian and Nepalese Armies stood us in good stead. And the Nepal Army was headed by General Gaurav S.J.B.

Rana, a no-nonsense professional soldier whose only priority was to get the work done.

We spent the next few weeks running the embassy from the small garden in front of the Chancery. Our coordination meetings, meetings with visitors and all media interactions took place in the open air. My deputy Piyush Srivastava played a critical role in ensuring coordination both within the Mission and with local authorities. Most embassies are required to develop a contingency plan in the event of a natural or man-made disaster or a conflict. The collegial preparation of this document and the brainstorming that is part of the process is as important as the final product. Every official must know in advance his or her role in the event of a contingency. Luckily for us in Nepal, we had completed preparing such a plan and thus were well equipped to handle the situation. At the very least, our officers were aware of their responsibilities and what was required of them. Coordination meetings twice daily made every official au fait with developments, essential to avoid duplication and confusion and ensure success.

The Nepalese government was woefully unprepared for the disaster. In the initial days, I recall urging both the prime minister (who had since returned to Kathmandu) and deputy prime minister that it was important for the government to be visible; that they should publicly offer reassurance and succour to the people. A senior official told me that the government did not have the capacity required to provide assistance to such a large number of people in far-flung areas; that if they went to the public, they would only face brickbats. It is only after some persuasion that he agreed to visit one of the NDRF locations with me to witness the stupendous efforts of Indian teams to extract bodies from the rubble. It is only after the Nepalese Army was entrusted with managing the bulk of the relief operations that some semblance of a systematic effort became visible.

In addition to the large number of rescue and relief teams from India and other countries, droves of media personnel, especially from India, descended on Kathmandu in the days following the earthquake. Some of the audio-visual media accompanied our helicopter teams on rescue and relief missions in far-flung mountainous areas of Nepal. As Indian television channels started beaming reports of the efforts of Indian teams, a perceptible sense of resentment developed in Nepal. Indian channels were quite popular and news reports appeared to suggest that the bulk of the relief efforts were being carried out by India, implying thereby that the Nepalese authorities were ineffective. The Government of Nepal had already suffered some embarrassment when it became publicly known that it was the Indian prime minister who had been the first to inform his Nepalese counterpart about the earthquake.

To be fair to the Nepalese, there were also some genuine reasons for their anger. A young Indian reporter with little knowledge of human let alone Nepalese sensitivities and the complex nature of the India–Nepal relationship, was found asking, for example, a grieving mother how she felt after she had lost her child.

As a consequence, a series of reports started appearing in the Nepalese print and audio-visual media critical of India. Television anchors and radio stations proclaimed that the Indian Army was only rescuing Indians; Indian helicopters were flying sub-optimal loads; Indians had taken over Tribhuvan International Airport; Indian supplies were rotten and unfit for human consumption and so on.

Meanwhile, the large Indian community in Kathmandu started clamouring for evacuation by air. The embassy had started evacuation of the sick and wounded as well as the bodies of those that had perished on returning Air Force planes. There was little capacity to carry the hundreds of Indians *gheraoing* the airport. Indeed, though they were shocked and possibly traumatized after the quake, as most of us were, they had by and large escaped relatively unscathed. Nevertheless, a huge crowd gathered outside the airport as Indian Air Force planes started arriving. The presence of these people created a law-and-order situation for the Nepalese security authorities as well as for the embassy. A further complication for us was catering to many requests from Delhi for evacuation of VIPs and relatives and friends of VIPs. Getting the specially privileged persons to the airport tarmac area quietly, without drawing attention, was a difficult task amid protesting crowds.

The attention of the Indian media was now diverted to the Indians at the airport as if this was the main story. The distress of the Nepalese was forgotten. This again irked the Nepalese as perceptions developed that India was in Nepal only to help their own and not the Nepalese.

My colleagues and I were getting increasingly worried and upset at some of the negative publicity in the Nepalese media. I requested the Government of Nepal and their official spokesman to use their good offices to set the record straight and dispel false and fabricated rumours. Unfortunately, my suggestion was not taken up by the Nepalese authorities. I then consulted NSA Ajit Doval who suggested that I should personally rebut these reports. Accordingly, I began giving several television interviews, including to the government owned Nepal TV and popular private channel Kantipur TV. In addition, we organized a press conference in the embassy; press releases were also issued in order to set the record straight. Some of the questioning that I faced was very aggressive, even downright rude, but a reasoned and logical response calmed emotions.

One of my colleagues had the brilliant idea of evacuating Indians by road. The roads linking the Kathmandu valley to the Terai border with India were luckily not damaged. Hundreds of Indian trucks laden with supplies were in any case wheezing up the mountain roads. Since most of the Indians in the valley belonged to the states neighbouring Nepal, we decided to request the state governments to send buses to Kathmandu to help ferry our citizens to their home states.

Cabinet Secretary Ajit Seth was taking daily coordination meetings with the participation of Secretaries of the concerned ministries including home, external affairs, National Disaster Management Authority, Border Management as well as Chief Secretaries of the neighbouring states. Consequent to our request, state governments readily agreed to send buses to Kathmandu. My colleagues in the embassy spread the word among the community that buses would leave for the Indian border from a spot near the airport; we identified Tilganga near the temple of Pashupatinath where the Indian government has constructed a beautiful dharamshala for pilgrims. Luckily for us, the embassy had a posse of over sixty sub-inspectors and constables from the Central Industrial Security Force (CISF) as part of our security detail. These were individuals with experience and training of crowd control and management. Pankaj Singh, an officer from the Indian Revenue Service, was put in charge and the entire operation worked with clockwork precision. Several thousand Indians were sent back to India in buses over the course of a few days. It is another matter that most of them returned to Kathmandu some weeks later.

Foreign embassies in Nepal were also turning to India for assistance. Several countries had citizens who had been injured or otherwise needed to be evacuated from difficult and inaccessible locations. We extended full support and were able to rescue many foreign nationals.

Several Indian NGOs also played an important role in providing relief to the Nepalese. Langar teams from Punjab, Haryana and Delhi fed a large number of people in areas such as Bhaktapur, which suffered severe damage. Organizations such as Hindu Swayamsevak Sangh and affiliates of the RSS in India such as Sewa Bharati, Dera Sacha Sauda, Patanjali, Tata Institute of Social Sciences, Tata and Birla companies, Akshay Patra and Oxfam India participated in relief efforts.

Indian NGOs unfortunately face a serious problem in extending their activities to neighbouring countries. Under our financial regulations, money raised in India by Indian NGOs cannot be sent abroad. During the Nepal earthquake, special exemptions were granted by the Government of India permitting some NGOs to transfer funds to Nepal. But this was a one-off exemption. As a result, there are hardly any Indian NGOs that are registered in a country like Nepal. This is in stark contrast to communist China, which has several so-called NGOs that are authorized to work in that country, and hence able to undertake humanitarian and other assistance programmes. Given that India's strength is her democracy and civil society institutions, it is important that NGOs be viewed as part of the people-to-people engagement between the two countries and they should be encouraged to be active especially in neighbouring countries.

India's HADR support to Nepal was successful largely due to the strong relationship between the Indian and Nepalese Armies. Not only were the Chiefs of Staff honorary Generals in each other's armies, but they had a good personal rapport as well. Furthermore, several Nepalese officers had done higher command and other courses in India; the two armies were regularly engaged in conducting joint military exercises such as Suryakiran, held alternately in India and Nepal; HADR, counter-insurgency, counter-terrorism and jungle warfare were some of the areas in which there was close coordination, interoperability and seamless cooperation. The presence of a senior Indian military liaison officer Major (subsequently Lieutenant) General J.S. Sandhu, who was assisted by our outstanding defence adviser, Colonel M.R.S. Mann, facilitated the work of our teams and was in large part responsible for the effective execution of India's largest ever HADR intervention abroad. Following this experience, India has the full capability to be the first responder should natural disasters hit not only South Asia but the wider BIMSTEC region. This would, however, require excellent cooperation between the respective armed forces and underlines the importance of military diplomacy with our neighbours.

An area that needs renewed focus is visibility for our assistance. In Nepal, the government was reluctant to publicly recognize and commend Indian assistance. But the best publicity for us were the hundreds of Indian trucks that criss-crossed Nepal, bringing much needed relief assistance. The Nepalese public saw for themselves the extent of support provided. But we need to give some thought to branding ideas. Chinese tents carried the clear and visible logo—it was visible not only from a distance but from the air as well—China Aid. Our tents and tarpaulins had no visible markings to show that they were from India. Even our NDRF personnel who had rescued several persons from the rubble and retrieved many dead bodies wore jerseys with the NDRF logo but nowhere did it mention India. International press had published photographs of some of our teams, alas, without identifying that they were from India.

A last word on the media. Our press persons need to be briefed about the specific sensitivities of the situation. The earthquake in Nepal and the evacuation of Indians can hardly be portrayed in the same manner as say, evacuation of Indians from Libya, Yemen or Lebanon. Briefings are required in India by the external publicity division and in the country where the disaster has taken place by the ambassador and his media team so that some of the pitfalls faced in Nepal are avoided.

9

Roti–Beti Rishta: The Civilizational Connect

I had been in Kathmandu for about six months when the day of the great festival of Mahashivratri arrived. My Head of Chancery met me the day before the festival and said that all arrangements had been made for my visit to the temple of Pashupatinath on the banks of the Bagmati in Kathmandu, home to a panchamukhi jyotirlinga, conjoined with the Kedarnath jyotirlinga, worshipped by millions of Hindus in Nepal and India. Special buses would ferry Indian embassy officials and families that wished to pay obeisance on this auspicious occasion. Though a newcomer in Nepal, since I knew that it was a country of devout people, I was not keen to visit on a day when huge masses of people would throng the temple. I therefore demurred and said that I would visit on another occasion. Consternation and dismay became visible on the face of my colleague. 'Sir, this will be misunderstood,' he said. 'The Indian ambassador is the only foreign dignitary who pays obeisance at Pashupatinath on Mahashivratri, the night of the Great Lord Shiva, of His cosmic dance of destruction and creation. You cannot not go. The only other dignitaries for whom special arrangements are made for a *darshan* are the President of

Nepal and the ex-king! The godless prime ministers of the leftist variety have no faith and it does not matter to the people of Nepal, but you have to go.' Or words to this effect. I relented and am glad that I did. I was received at Pashupatinath by the secretary of the Pashupati Vikas Kosh, Govind Tandon, an erudite scholar dressed in traditional Nepalese attire.

I expressed my apprehensions to him that people had been waiting for long hours in queues for *darshan* and would object to my jumping the line! But interestingly this was not the case. The people were delighted that the ambassador was praying at Pashupatinath on Mahashivratri! Once inside the temple premises, I was greeted by several Naga *sadhus*, most of whom had travelled from India at the invitation of the Nepalese authorities and from whom they received a traditional *dakshina*! I too distributed some *dakshina* in return for *jhadoo* blessings on the shoulder. I inquired about their well-being and they all said that they were looked after well by the temple authorities. Over a period of time, I got to know the head priest of the temple, Ganesh Bhatt, well; he, as well as the other three junior priests, belonged to a Brahmin lineage from Karnataka. Tradition has it that only the high priests of Pashupatinath, who are Indians, are allowed to touch the holy *shivalinga*! Such is the civilizational connect with India. In 2009, the Maoists, new to government and raring to go, had decided to replace Indian priests with Nepali counterparts, but gave up these new-fangled ideas after protests both within Nepal and from India.

The visit of PM Modi to Pashupatinath on the auspicious first Monday of the month of *Shravan*, i.e., on 4 August 2014, was a much-awaited event in Kathmandu. Large crowds had gathered outside the temple premises to welcome him. Resplendent in a saffron kurta and matching shawl, the PM performed a special puja in the temple. After the puja, the prime minister donated 2500 kg of sandalwood worth Rs 2 crore to the temple. The *chandan* is a special offering to Lord Shiva and is also used as *tilak* for the devotees. An unnecessary controversy was created on whether this was a personal or official offering. How could the government pay for a religious donation to the temple? It was pointed out that a special exception to the export of sandalwood for Pashupatinath had already been made at the time of the previous UPA government; this was to uphold the ancient cultural and religious traditions that bind India and Nepal. Just as the king of Nepal used to donate musk for use by the Jagannath temple in Odisha, India provides chandan to Pashupatinath.

The other important site for Hindu pilgrimage is Janakpur, the capital of erstwhile Mithila ruled by Raja Janak. According to legend, though Sita was born in Sitamarhi, she grew up in Janakpur and performed her *swayamvar*[1] there; Janakpur is the city where her marriage with Lord Ram took place. A beautiful *nau lakha* temple—it is believed that the temple cost Rs 9 lakh to build—was erected in Janakpur in 1910 by the Rani of Tikamgarh in Orchha to commemorate the occasion. It has been a place of pilgrimage for Hindus, especially for those belonging to Mithila and Awadh, where Lord Ram was born. Since the early 2000s, the wedding of Ram and Sita is celebrated on Vivaha Panchami every year when a *baraat* arrives from Ayodhya. The wedding procession follows a prescribed route as does the procession after the marriage. Several *parikramas* or circumambulations are held in the Mithila region commemorating various sites associated with Lord Ram, including the place where the *Dhanush* (bow) used in the swayamvar fell, Dhanushadham. Large number of devotees perform the *parikramas* every year.

Unlike Lumbini, which is a UNESCO World Heritage Site and evokes global interest especially from Buddhist countries and in more recent years from China, Janakpur is largely a neglected provincial town due partly to the fact that it is the political capital of the Terai Madhesh and partly because pilgrims from India are generally poor villagers and ordinary folk who do not have big money to spend. Facilities for stay, including hotels and dharamshalas, are inadequate and not in the best condition. Except for India, no other country has much interest in the development of Janakpur. It is, therefore, incumbent upon the Government of India to assist on a large scale for the development of Janakpur in collaboration with the provincial government, which has its seat in Janakpur. There has been considerable talk about developing a Ramayana Circuit that would eventually link Nepal and India with Sri Lanka, but little progress has been achieved. Similarly, India had promised two Small Development Projects and a grant of Rs 100 crore during the respective visits of the President of India Pranab Mukherjee and PM Modi to Janakpur, but there is little forward movement in project formulation and approval, let alone implementation. A twinning agreement exists between Ayodha and Janakpur, but here again few, if any, activities have taken place. Now that Ayodhya is being developed as a major centre of Hindu pilgrimage, it should be a priority for India to work with Nepal to develop Janakpur along similar lines.

One deeply disturbing Hindu tradition, banned in India, still forms an essential part of the religious rituals of Nepal. Himalayan Hinduism follows the Shiva and Shakti tradition and is greatly influenced by Tantric practices from Eastern India. During the great festival of Dasain, 108 buffaloes and goats are ceremoniously slaughtered by army jawans at Hanuman Dhoka each year. I did not witness the ceremony during my entire tour of office in Nepal. A similar story repeats itself at several Shakti temples throughout the country. Every five years the festival of Gadhi Mai in the Terai attracts thousands of visitors, where hundreds of animals are slaughtered brutally. Most of the animals are brought from India. Most of the visitors to the temple are also from India. It is the most gruesome practice that in the past saw fields covered with the carcasses of dead animals. It also attracted global criticism. The five-year festival fell in 2014 during my tenure in Nepal. Several animal rights groups that also had the backing of Maneka Gandhi, an animal rights activist and politician in India, met me and sought my support to have the sacrifice banned. Since it was a very sensitive religious issue, I did not wish to get involved officially, though I personally found the practice abhorrent. In the event, I only offered advice on the best way for them to pursue their objective, though I am not aware how successful they were. I understand that ritual killing continued at the festival in 2019, perhaps on a reduced scale.

India too is a major place for pilgrimage for most Nepalese. The Char Dham Yatra of Kedar, Badri, Yamunotri and Gangotri is one that all Nepali Hindus wish to perform. Gaya and Kashi are two important places for *pind dan* and the worship of ancestors.

Banaras or Varanasi as it is now known, the eternal city, has a special connection with Nepal. It is not just the temples dedicated to Lord Shiva that link Kashi with Kathmandu, traditionally, Nepalese priestly families have received *diksha* at Vedic institutions in Kashi. A king of Nepal renounced worldly life to retire to a life of meditation in Kashi as Swami Nirgunananda in 1800 and returned to claim the throne of Nepal four years later as King Rana Bahadur Shah.[2] Banaras Hindu University is the alma mater of many distinguished Nepalese personalities, including former prime ministers B.P. Koirala, Manmohan Adhikari and Krishna Prasad Bhattarai. One of the most beautiful *ghats* on the Ganga waterfront is Lalita Ghat, built by King Rana Bahadur Shah of Nepal. A wooden replica of the Pashupatinath Temple is visible from the river just above the *ghat*. The father of Nepalese democracy, B.P. Koirala, spent many years in exile in Varanasi and his children and nephews studied at BHU. In more contemporary times, during PM Modi's visit, a twinning arrangement between Varanasi and Kathmandu was announced and there is now a direct bus service between the two cities. But more needs to be done to invest these sister city agreements with substance. Just as Kashi is famous for its music festivals, the Dhrupad Festival at Tulsi Ghat and the Sankat Mochan Festival at the eponymous temple, similar festivals can be organized at Pashupatinath. Exchanges between Vedic and Sanskrit institutions in both cities, cultural festivals, youth exchanges and study tours could easily be organized under the auspices of the India–Nepal B.P. Koirala Foundation (BPKF), which provides small grants to organizations involved in promoting people-to-people exchanges.

An important deity of the Nath Sampradaya, Gorakhanath, has given his name not only to Gorakhpur but also Gorkha, a district in Nepal which is home to King Prithvinarayan Shah, the founder of the Shah dynasty whose last king was Gyanendra. The mahants of Gorakh Math in Gorakhpur have had a close relationship with the Shah kings. The current Mahant, Yogi Adityanath, has shared a dais with ex-king Gyanendra in Kathmandu and was a vocal advocate for the restoration of the monarchy and Hindu Rashtra in Nepal. His predecessor, Mahant Avaidyanath, was reported to be close to King Birendra. Gorakhnath's guru, Yogi Matsyendranath, has a deep influence in the Kathmandu Valley. Buddhists worship him as an incarnation of Avalokiteshwara, the Lord of Compassion; Hindus, as an incarnation of Lord Shiva. To this day the *Jatra* of *Rato* or red Macchindranath is one of the most important festivals in the Kathmandu valley and is celebrated with great verve and joy every year. One of the most beautiful temples in the old town of Hanuman Dhoka in Kathmandu is the *Seto* or white Macchindranath Temple in Asan, which India is restoring.

The other great religious tradition that connects India with Nepal is Buddhism. Even after it had virtually disappeared from India, Buddhism flourished in Nepal and Tibet where it transformed into the Vajrayana tradition, merging Mahayana with the Hindu Tantric tradition. Indeed, as you travel from Kathmandu northwards to the Tibetan border, you see a unique admixture of Hindu and Buddhist traditions. The practice of *shraddh* by Buddhists, the existence of Buddhist texts such as Prajnaparamita in Sanskrit, not Pali, the fact that Hanuman and Ganesha are prominently represented at Buddhist *Viharas* and Hindus and Buddhists alike worship at the great stupas of Kathmandu stands testimony to the intermingling of the two Indian traditions.

One district that best represents the fusion of the two religious traditions is Mustang. However, travelling there is not for the faint hearted. Very early in the morning you alight on to a small, rickety, at least in appearance, eighteen-seater airplane at Pokhara Airport, fasten your seatbelts, gird your loins, say your prayers and hope for the best. If you are lucky, the mountain pass between the Annapurna and Dhaulagiri ranges is cloud- and wind-free. Beyond ten or so in the morning, as wind speeds increase, it is very unsafe to fly through the pass. Even though it is a twenty-minute flight, the route is one of the most dangerous in the world where the flight loses contact with the control towers in Pokhara and Jomsom for a few minutes. There have been several accidents resulting in fatalities in the past. Ragini Grela, the former Vice Chancellor of the Nepal Academy of the Fine Arts and a member on the Board of the India–Nepal B.P. Koirala Foundation, told me that one of the worst experiences of her life was to fly from Pokhara to Jomsom, the district headquarters of Mustang, for a BPKF meeting. It was turbulent weather, a very bumpy flight and her heart was in her mouth; she clung to the arms of her neighbour throughout the flight. I also recall landing with a sharp thud at Jomsom airport, which has a very small runway; a scary experience. But if you brave the flight, you enter a virtual Shangri La and see the great Nilgiri Peak, sparkling under the rays of the sun. You stretch out your arm and you can almost touch it!

Mustang is home to one of the most important pilgrimage sites for followers of the Vaishnavite tradition, Muktinath, the place for *mukti* or salvation. It is sacred to the Buddhists as the idol is considered to represent Avalokiteshwara, the Buddha of compassion. The shrine is managed by a Buddhist nun who also performs the ritual worship. I do not recall any other temple in the subcontinent that so completely fuses the Hindu and the Buddhist traditions as Muktinath. And if you travel to the Kingdom of Lo on the Tibetan plateau, you will witness perhaps the last remnant of authentic Tibetan cultural and religious traditions.

The community that most represents the fusion of Hindu and Buddhist traditions in Nepal are the Newars, an aesthetically evolved linguistic community that is responsible for much of the beauty of the Kathmandu Valley, the great red brick architecture of the palaces and temples of Hanuman Dhoka, Lalitpur-Patan and Bhaktapur, and the exquisite fine arts, the *paubha* paintings, the woodwork and metal sculpture. They are also famous for their masked dances performed on religious occasions. The great architect Arniko was a Newar. He introduced the pagoda style of architecture, which spread all the way to China and the Far East. Frescoes in many monasteries in Tibet and Bhutan have been painted by Newar artists. The famous Pashupatinath temple, too, is built in the pagoda style. I was introduced to Newar culture by the grand old man of Patan, Buddhiraja Bajracharya, belonging to a family of high priests, keepers of Buddhist temples and *viharas*. He had been mayor of the city for sixteen years and also minister of culture. After retirement, he made it his life's mission to restore and refurbish the Buddhist *viharas* and the famous *bahals* or courtyards of the city. We assisted him in renovating this ancient heritage. According to Bajracharya, the Buddhist connection between Nepal and India dates back to the time of Emperor Ashoka, who sent his daughter Charumati to Nepal. She established a small stupa in Chahbahil and also married a Nepalese prince.

The Newars are the ancient occupants of the Kathmandu Valley ruled by the Malla kings and have been a prosperous community. They were a settled civilization, free from war and conflict, and engaged in trade with Tibet. The Valley was divided into three small kingdoms, Kathmandu, Lalitpur and Bhaktapur, each related to the other through blood and marriage. The kingdoms competed with each other in terms of architecture, fine arts and performing arts. The community was divided into Hindus and Buddhists. Both also worshipped the deities of the other, including Ganesh. Traditionally, the Malla kings had invited priests from Mithila to help with ritual worship and you will find people with the surname Jha who are also Newar. Maithili and Sanskrit were spoken at the Malla court at one time and soldiers from Tirhut, part of their army. They were defeated by Prithvi Narayan Shah in 1769 and subsumed within what came to be known as the Kingdom of Nepal.

Nepal is proud that Prince Siddhartha Gautama, who became the Buddha, was born in Lumbini. A three by one square mile area of land around the Maya Devi Temple has been declared a World Heritage Site by UNESCO. The Lumbini Development Trust is responsible for implementing the architectural design by Kenzo Tange, a Japanese architect. Today, Lumbini is an important place of pilgrimage for Buddhists. It houses beautiful monasteries built by Buddhist countries, each depicting the cultural traditions of the country. The first foreign monastery in Lumbini is, strangely enough, a Vietnamese monastery built by the monk Thay Huyen Dieu in 1993. Also known as the Venerable Dr Lam, he first visited Lumbini in 1969 when it was in ruins. Later, after completing his studies at the Sorbonne in Paris, he came back to Lumbini and built the first foreign monastery on a plot of land given to him by King Birendra.

I got to know Thay Huyen Dieu well when I was ambassador to Vietnam. He is revered in Vietnam as a deeply learned Buddhist monk who has helped a large number of Vietnamese people gain spiritual solace through the Buddhist tradition. Indeed, his second monastery, at Bodh Gaya, regularly receives a steady stream of visitors from home, from the secretary general of the Communist Party and the President and prime ministers of Vietnam to ordinary folk who can afford the pilgrimage to India. His life's work is to spread the message of peace and compassion of the Buddha as a means of resolving conflict. He believes this is the unique message of India and is the answer to the problems that the world is currently facing. In Vietnam, Thay Huyen Dieu is mobbed by ordinary folk wherever he goes. I recall one of his visits to Hanoi, where I was serving as ambassador. My Vietnamese staff requested me to invite the monk to the embassy so that they could receive his blessings. I organized the event at the Nehru Ho Chi Minh Hall in the embassy; we prepared a nice basket of fruits to offer to the monk on behalf of embassy personnel. I was amazed to see the look of devotion on the faces of my colleagues, almost all of whom were communist, when they greeted the monk. Such is the power of the Buddhist tradition in Vietnam today.

Later, as ambassador of India to Nepal, I renewed my acquaintance with Dr Lam and also visited the Vietnamese monastery in Bodh Gaya as well as in Lumbini. The contrast between the two towns is stark. Whereas Lumbini is an oasis of calm and serenity and is being developed according to a master plan, Bodh Gaya is anything but; it is like any small town of India, chaotic, noisy and dusty. There is no separation between the secular and the sacred; small hotels and shops jostle for space with the monasteries and temples. The only peaceful place is the Bodhi Temple where the devout perform the *parikrama* around the sacred Bodhi tree. The problem with both Lumbini and Bodh Gaya is that the population living in and around these towns is not Buddhist, they are Hindus and Muslims with little connection to the Buddhist tradition; they merely seek to benefit from pilgrim tourist dollars. In Bodh Gaya, for instance, there is an uneasy relationship between the hoteliers and the monasteries. Hotels are unhappy that monasteries house foreign pilgrims in their dormitories and steal business from the hotels. The various sites associated with Lord Buddha's penances in and around Bodh Gaya have also not been developed, unlike the sacred grove in Lumbini, Nepal where Prince Siddharth Gautama was born. I had the glorious opportunity of planting a sapling of the sacred Bodhi tree close to the Ashoka Pillar in Lumbini on behalf of the prime minister, who was personally unable to visit Lumbini. If we could only learn from the experience of Lumbini and sincerely implement a master plan for the development of Bodh Gaya and its surroundings, millions of pilgrims who are desirous of walking in the footsteps of the Buddha would be eternally grateful.

While Lumbini has several monasteries belonging to different countries, the absence of an Indian monastery stares you in the face. Why is it that India, home to the most sacred Buddhist sites of Buddha's enlightenment, his first sermon and his Nirvana, does not have a representation at the site where he was born? If the Government of India cannot fund such a project, surely a project can be taken up under the auspices of the Bodhi Society of India. The communist Chinese have a spectacular monastery in Lumbini with a large number of monks. India is notable only by its absence. Indeed, Lumbini has developed into a major tourist attraction for Chinese tourists.

There has also been a lot of talk about developing a Buddhist circuit with seamless travel between the various holy sites in Nepal and India. A public-private partnership model involving development of infrastructure along the routes to the major sites— roads, hotels and other facilities, and partnerships between tour agencies in both countries are needed. Though there is considerable discussion about the use of Buddhism as an element of India's soft power, unless the situation on the ground improves, this will remain just talk. And the Chinese are stealing a march.

Though it is the Hindu and Buddhist links that are most well-known, there is an old connection of the Sikh and Islamic traditions with Nepal. Guru Nanak Dev visited Kathmandu and several other places in Nepal during his third *Udasi*. He is reported to have established a Nanak Math, which still exists, not far from the Indian embassy, on a large tract of land given to him by King Ratna Malla during his 1484–1520 reign. Over a period of time, the land has been illegally sold or otherwise occupied so that the current math is much reduced in size. Unfortunately, within the various Sikh organizations, there have been disputes about who should take over the responsibility for running the math. If some of these issues could get sorted out, the Nanak Math of Kathmandu has the potential to become a major place of pilgrimage for the Sikh community. The Government of Nepal may also be willing to assist if the math is successful in attracting visitors from India.[3]

The same Malla King also gave another parcel of land in central Kathmandu near Durbar Marg to Kashmiri traders. Two prominent mosques, the Kashmiri Takia and the Jame Masjid, are situated there. King Ratna Malla invited Kashmiri Muslims to Kathmandu due to their experience in trade with Tibet. Even today, there are several shops in Thamel, the main tourist drag in Kathmandu, owned by Kashmiri traders though many of them are of more recent vintage. I took Dr Farooq Abdullah, at that time Union Minister for Power, for a walkabout in Thamel in December 2013 during his official visit; as soon as they saw him, several shop owners came out of their shops, greeted him warmly and started conversing in Kashmiri.

Interestingly, both India and Nepal have provided asylum to political exiles belonging to the other country. As long as India was under colonial rule, Nepal became a safe haven for some of the Indian freedom fighters. Begum Hazrat Mahal of Awadh is a prominent personality who went into exile in Nepal. Even though she was a courtesan, she became the favourite Queen of the Nawab of Awadh, Wajid Ali Shah, and was conferred the title of Hazrat Mahal. While Wajid Ali Shah lost his kingdom and was ensconced in luxurious exile in Calcutta, Hazrat Mahal fought alongside the commander-in-chief of the Awadh army against the British during the First War of Independence in 1857. It is only after her defeat that the brave Begum fled with her entourage to Nepal. Jung Bahadur Rana, the ruler of Nepal at the time, had assisted the British in quelling the uprising in Lucknow and returned with considerable bounty, the so-called loot of Lucknow. Despite being in a subservient relationship with the British, Jung Bahadur provided shelter and asylum to Hazrat Mahal, it is rumoured at a huge price in gems and jewellery.

I recall a visit of Akhilesh Yadav, chief minister of Uttar Pradesh, with his family and a large entourage for a wedding in Kathmandu in February 2014. He asked me about the location of Hazrat Mahal's *mazhar* in Kathmandu. Much to my embarrassment, I was unaware of this history. Immediately after the visit, I made enquiries with the Muslim community and found that the grave was lying in a derelict state in a small corner of the Jame Masjid in central Kathmandu near the huge Tundikhel army grounds. I also found out that her death anniversary fell on 7 April. My colleagues and I decided that we should honour her memory. The Jame Masjid reluctantly (Begum Hazrat Mahal was Shia) agreed to organize a small ceremony where we laid a wreath of flowers at the grave, which was spruced up for the occasion. Thereafter, every year my colleagues and I would pay respects to her memory on her death anniversary. This also became an opportunity to develop closer ties with the small Muslim community in Nepal.

Nana Saheb Peshwa is another leader of the First War of Independence who fled to Nepal, though not much information is available about his stay in that country. A few years before the 1857 uprising, Rani Jind Kaur, wife of Maharaja Ranjit Singh, sought refuge in Nepal after the defeat of the Sikhs in the second Anglo–Sikh war of 1849. She lived in Kathmandu for several years before being reunited with her son Duleep Singh in London.

During the Quit India Movement in 1942, Jayaprakash Narayan and Ram Manohar Lohia had been incarcerated in Hanuman Nagar in bordering Nepal since there was inadequate jail space in Bihar. With the help of several of their Nepalese compatriots, a spectacular jail break was organized.

Many Nepalese politicians were deeply influenced by the freedom movement in India launched under Gandhiji's leadership. B.P. Koirala, the father of Nepalese democracy, cut his political teeth in India from the 1930s. He was a one-time member of the Indian National Congress, close to Congress socialists such as Jayaprakash Narayan, and was twice arrested by the British for his political activities in India. His brother G.P. Koirala also participated in the Quit India Movement. It was BPK's conviction that India must be free for Nepal to overthrow the Rana yoke. Much later, after King Mahendra abolished multiparty democracy in 1960, BPK, along with several other Congress stalwarts, went into exile in India. Prime Minister Chandrashekhar had a very close and cordial relationship with several important political leaders of Nepal and played an important role in supporting them in exile. There is thus a long history of the two countries providing shelter to political leaders seeking greater freedoms and democracy.

Indian politicians love to wax eloquent about the *roti beti ka rishta* with Nepal. This relationship of kinship and marriage is prevalent throughout Nepal and not only among communities along the open border between the two countries. The Rana–Shah elite is deeply connected through marriage to the erstwhile Indian royalty. For instance, the erstwhile princely families of Gwalior, Baroda and Kashmir are related to the Ranas of Nepal. Two daughters of King Tribhuvan were married into the Mayurbhanj and Poonch royal families. Similarly, several prominent Rana clansmen in Nepal are married to ladies from India. The tradition continues to this day. Similarly, the Marwari families of Nepal continue to maintain strong links with Rajasthan.

The familial connections are strongest in the border regions. This is as true for the populations living on either side of the Mahakali River in far western Nepal as it is for communities living in the Terai plains, in Mithila and Awadh and indeed in eastern Nepal and the Sikkim–Darjeeling belt. Since the borders remained open even after the Sugauli Treaty and the practice of document-free travel continued unhindered, the drawing of boundaries between the two countries did not significantly alter the pattern of social intercourse over the decades.

Over a period of time, especially with the advent of the Maoist insurgency and the consequent insecurity, and the tumult and turmoil following the Madhesi uprisings and now with COVID-19 restrictions, the cross-border social compact is weakening. Indeed, a senior leader of the ruling Nepalese Communist Party has said that the *roti-beti rishta* is old think[4] and we need to move on from the platitudes of the past. New citizenship rules sought to be introduced by Nepal that make it more difficult for foreign women married to Nepalese men to gain Nepali citizenship will act as a further dampener; so will the desire, particularly of the Nepalese government for stronger regulation of the border on the grounds of security, or measures to document and limit cross-border movement through ID cards and reported harassment by the respective border forces of the two countries, namely, Sashastra Seema Bal (SSB) and the Armed Police Force (APF).

Anju Ranjan, Consul General in Birganj came up with an interesting proposal to organize cross-border meetings all along the Terai in order to smoothen and further facilitate linkages between communities on either side of the border. Unlike in the past when Indian shoppers would visit border *haats* in Nepal to buy foreign goods, today it is the Nepali population that visits the markets of Siliguri, Jogbani, Raxaul, Rupaidiha and Khatima on the Indian side for their purchases of daily necessities, for festivals and celebrations, including marriages. Indeed, the economy of several Indian border towns depends on their Nepali clientele for survival. I attended several such meetings, in Birganj, Janakpur and Nepalganj, where officials from both sides, including Customs, SSB/APF officials, journalists, politicians on occasion, and others would meet on a common platform and would respond to the queries and concerns of ordinary folk.

Travelling to India from the Nepalese Terai, however, is a nightmare. It is like going from a first world country with excellent infrastructure to a third world country. I am referring to the abysmal condition of the roads that link the border towns of Nepalganj, Bhairawaha, Birganj and Biratnagar with Rupaidiha, Sunauli, Raxaul and Jogbani, respectively. I have personally visited each of these border crossings. While Nepal is constructing six- and eight-lane highways on its side, there is generally one narrow, congested lane full of shops on either side that leads into the Indian border towns. Though our national highway system in UP and Bihar is well developed, the link roads from our border towns to the national highway system are pathetic. Sometimes it takes hours to cross the Bhairawaha–Sunauli checkpoint, which is also a designated point for foreign tourists on the Buddhist circuit. The tourist probably receives the shock of his/her life seeing the border condition: teeming crowds, poor sanitation facilities, garbage strewn in no man's land and lack of clean, hygienic places to eat. With the development of the integrated checkposts the situation should improve, but the improvement of the infrastructure should be taken up with speed by the Central and provincial governments.

The Government of India has established a Department of Border Management within the home ministry. The department implements the Border Area Development Programme. For the programme to be truly effective, it should be coordinated with officials on the Nepalese side as well since facilities are used by people on both sides. I recall visiting the famous eye hospital near Nepalganj where most of the clientele was from India. Many of the hospitals and colleges service people from both countries. Another idea that we should seriously consider is to organize cross-border meetings of the provincial governments, now that Nepal has become a federal republic. This would build mutual trust and also address several border related issues, which have a tendency to become major irritants in the relationship if unresolved.

I also vividly recall several other visits to the Terai. A memorable one was to Sarlahi district, to Balra, the constituency of my good friend and Nepali Congress MP Dr Amresh Kumar

Singh. He had a PhD from JNU and I had got to know him well from his time in Delhi. I had gone to his constituency to inaugurate some projects that we had financed under the small projects scheme. He organized a grand welcome for me. The constituency was decorated with welcome arches, and it appeared that the entire population had turned out to receive me. Ordinary villagers would lunge towards me to touch me or extend their hand or simply fold their palms in a namaste. It was an amazing experience. They would make small requests, for a road here, a school somewhere else as if the Indian ambassador could grant all their wishes. The police would be on edge and behave sharply with the crowds, an attitude that was very different from their behaviour in the hills. There they were comfortable; in the Terai they were not.

President Pranab Mukherjee visited Janakpur early November in 2016. The small city of about 2,00,000 people, the third largest in the Terai, was under siege. It was littered with roadblocks. During the passage of the Presidential motorcade through the city, we did not see a solitary soul. It was such a glaring contrast to PM Modi's visit to Kathmandu when thousands of ordinary people lined the streets of the city. Unlike in the hill districts, the security forces in the Terai are extra careful, partly because of the many agitations that have taken place over the last few years.

Bollywood and our media play an important role in bringing the two countries together. Indian film stars and performers are celebrities in Nepal as well. Nepal, too, has provided great artists like Manisha Koirala and Udit Narayan to the Indian film industry. Indian television channels, particularly those that telecast soaps, are very popular. Yoga is popular in both countries. The International Yoga Day in Kathmandu on 21 June 2016 was a memorable occasion. Prime Minister K.P. Oli, his wife Radhika Shakya, as well as deputy prime ministers and other ministers of the Nepalese cabinet participated at a mass yoga event on Durbar Marg, Kathmandu's high street. Similar functions were organized throughout Nepal with the support of Patanjali Yoga that had branches in all districts of the country. The India–Nepal friendship organizations played a supportive role.

Nepal has a unique method of exchanging greetings. On our Independence and Republic Days, various India–Nepal friendship organizations would arrange commemorative events in Kathmandu and other parts of the country. As the programme commences, the anchor for the evening waxes eloquent on India-Nepal ties and then begins to invite dignitaries onto the dais. Thus begins the ceremony of *asan grahan* or assuming seats. One by one, the worthies would climb onto the stage till it appears that almost half the audience is on it. I was always invited first and would constantly worry that the stage would come crashing down. Even after the stage was full, the ceremony would continue. Only now, the compere called out names and then requested the people to remain seated (or standing) wherever they were. About half the duration of the programme was taken up by this ceremony, which was a very serious affair. The speeches would then begin. Invariably, they would start with our relations from Treta Yug, the times of Ram and Sita and ponderously arrive to the present. And as the chief guest I was always the last to speak.

Though I found some of these occasions exasperating, there was genuine affection for India that was reflected in the verbose pronouncements of the dignitaries. Of course, this was an occasion to be seen and heard, the closer you sat to the Indian ambassador, the higher your stock, but it reflected the warmth of the relationship.

The At Home at India House on Republic Day was another important occasion on the Kathmandu social calendar. Almost the entire elite of Kathmandu would be invited to this event; some thousand guests filled the grand lawns of India House. The Nepali Army band would be in attendance; delicacies from the various regions of India would be on offer and everyone would enjoy the lovely afternoon sun. Not being invited to the event was a huge social setback; people tried every trick in the trade to wangle an invite. My colleagues would be inundated with requests that they would handle as best as they could. However, on occasion there were slip ups. I remember someone who bore a grudge against me for a long time for having been left out inadvertently. I recall the event in January 2015. India was not on the best of terms with Oli, given his strident opposition to addressing the demands of the Madhesis and Janjatis for an inclusive constitution. Both he and Bidya Devi Bhandari, then a senior leader of the CPN (UML), arrived at our At Home and I took special care of them; Prime Minister Sushil Koirala also insisted on coming contrary to the advice that he had received from his officials. He had told me that he would come and lived up to his promise.

Despite the ups and downs in the official relationship, the people-to-people relationship remains robust, though it has taken a few knocks. The boundary dispute and the shrill media focus has, for the first time, created a negative attitude in India about the Nepalese. There is a growing perception in India that Nepal is becoming China's cat's paw. Coming as it does at a time when India-China relations are fraught, this does not augur well for the future and is a worrying development. Nepalese politicians should also recognize that the short-term parochial benefits of anti-India nationalism may have long-term ramifications that will negatively impact the overall relationship. Greater regulation of the border in the name of security and a further tightening of citizenship laws will impact negatively on the cross-border relationship and ties of kinship and marriage. Surely an open, friendly border with a peaceful and happy socially interconnected population is a preferable path to mutual security than a regulated, cold, visibly policed border with sullen and suspicious people on the two sides.

10

Enter the Dragon: The Northern Neighbour,[1] the West and the Rest

The year 2016 marked a significant upswing in the Nepal–China relationship. Angered by the imposition of the so-called 'blockade' during September 2015–February 2016 that led to shortages of fuel, gas and other commodities in Nepal, Prime Minister Oli decided to make a huge outreach to China. And China reciprocated in full measure. It signed a slew of long-term agreements ranging from transit arrangements for Nepal's third country trade through Chinese ports to multibillion dollar trans-Himalayan connectivity projects. Is there a renewed convergence of interests between Nepal and China that underpins this cooperation? Is this largely a backlash against India's policy in Nepal, or are other factors at work too?

The Nepal–China relationship has evolved over time. In the early years after Indian independence, the Rana leadership was anxious about the communist takeover of China in 1949 and Tibet the following year. It was worried about the implications for Nepal's own security since the Tibetan buffer had disappeared and Nepal had a direct border with Communist China. Nepal was fearful of the assertion attributed to Chairman Mao that Tibet is the right palm of China and its five fingers are Ladakh, Nepal, Sikkim, Bhutan and NEFA (North East Frontier Association, now the state of Arunachal Pradesh). The fingers had been connected to Tibet in one way or another. In earlier times, Nepal had a robust relationship with Tibet, had engaged in wars and even paid tributes to the Chinese Emperor.[2] The forging of the India–Nepal Friendship Treaty in 1950 should be seen against this background. It placed Nepal squarely within India's security umbrella. Within the Government of India too, there was both a worry about China's activities in the Himalayan region as well as a desire to forge a new relationship with China in the context of Asian solidarity. Sardar Patel had written a famous letter to Pandit Nehru in November 1950, highlighting the Chinese threat along the Himalayan frontier and recommended a series of steps that should be taken by India.[3] The establishment of seventeen checkposts along the Nepal–China border was one of the measures taken with Nepalese consent to step up vigilance along the Himalayas.

However, the Hindi–Chini Bhai–Bhai phase began soon thereafter with the signing of the famous Panchsheel Pact between India and China in 1954, leading up to the Bandung Asian African Solidarity Conference the next year. Nepal, too, established diplomatic relations with China in 1955. Prime Minister B.P. Koirala's visit to China in March 1960 expedited work on a Boundary Agreement and a Treaty of Peace and Friendship between the two countries. The relationship received a further boost after the abolition of multiparty democracy by King Mahendra in 1960. As India was critical of King Mahendra's actions,[4] Nepal turned to China and signed important treaties and agreements, including one demarcating the border and another relating to the construction of the Khasa (Zhangmu)–Kathmandu Arniko Highway through Kodari, connecting Tibet with Nepal.

Despite these overtures, the Nepal–China relationship remained nuanced. Though the India–China relationship was broken following the conflict of 1962 and there was mistrust between India and King Mahendra's regime, India and Nepal entered into an arms assistance agreement with regards to arms imports by Nepal in 1965[5]. Further, Nepal did not seek the withdrawal of Indian forward military checkposts on the Nepal–Tibet border till 1969. Nepal also hosted some of the Khampa rebels in Mustang that were seeking to free Tibet militarily. It is only in 1974 that the Khampas were eventually neutralized by the Royal Nepal Army.[6]

China, as a balancing hedge against India, gained salience for Nepal once again following the merger of Sikkim with India in 1974–75. Nepal responded with its Zone of Peace proposal, a policy of equidistance between its two neighbours, which gained some traction internationally but failed due to the strong opposition by India. Similarly, during the mass protests of Jan Andolan I in 1989 against the Panchayat system, the Palace tried to import anti-aircraft guns from China that led to the border blockade by India and the subsequent collapse of the Panchayat system.

Another occasion when Nepal made a serious outreach to China was following King Gyanendra's political coup in February 2005 when he arrested political leaders and usurped all executive power. In response to India's sharp criticism and suspension of military assistance, King Gyanendra threatened to, and indeed bought military supplies from China. He actively espoused, together with Pakistan, the full membership of China in SAARC even though he was fully aware of India's strong reservations.

While it is true that, in the past, upswings in the Nepal–China relationship coincided with downswings in the Nepal–India relationship, it was a nuanced relationship. Even at the worst of times in the bilateral relationship, Nepal was generally sensitive to Indian security interests. Today, however, it appears to be moving ever closer to China as technology makes the Himalayas more easily passable and a wealthy China is eager to be a strategic partner.

China's approach to the Himalayas in general and Nepal in particular has also evolved over time. Even as normal economic cooperation has continued over the decades—China constructed the Ring Road in Kathmandu in 1977 and the International Convention Centre in Kathmandu that now serves as the Parliament in 1993—even during the worst phase of India–China relations following the 1962 war, China generally conveyed to visiting dignitaries from Nepal that it is in the interest of Nepal to maintain good relations with India. The late Surya Bahadur Thapa told me that Chairman Mao himself had mentioned this to him when he visited China in 1964. At that stage, China's principal interest in Nepal was to ensure that Tibet remained insulated from adverse impulses that could emanate from Nepal. It was worried about the activities of Western countries and international NGOs, particularly with regard to Tibetan refugees in Kathmandu and Pokhara. China was quite content to deal with the king unlike India, which was supporting people's aspirations for political emancipation.

It is only after Nepal became a republic that China too started engaging with a wide cross-section of political opinion in Nepal. Indeed, the protests by Tibetans in Kathmandu, prior to the Beijing Olympics of 2008, were met with deep concern in China and mark the beginning of a new proactive approach in its dealings with Nepal. With the Chinese losing their single and most important point of contact and influence in Nepal, the monarchy, they adapted rapidly to the changing circumstances and started making overtures to all political parties. Naturally, given their own system, it is with the communist parties, namely, the CPN (UML) and subsequently the unified Nepal Communist Party that also included the Maoists, with whom China established the deepest and most organic relationship. Gone were the days when the Chinese were embarrassed about the Nepalese Maoists using the name of their revered Chairman. This did not, however, imply the neglect of the Nepali Congress and the Madhesis, the democratic parties. China facilitated, for leaders and influential members of all political parties, study tours to China and visits to Kailash and Manasarovar, apart from offering a large number of scholarships. A senior leader of the Nepalese Congress told me that he had been gifted a state-of-the-art mobile phone and laptop by the Chinese, but since he was suspicious of malware, he passed them on to his son!

Several geopolitical and other factors have contributed to a qualitative change in the Nepal–China relationship. There is today a deepening convergence of interests. China sees itself as a global power. It has spread its presence all over the globe. The Belt and Road Initiative, a massive infrastructure development programme for the world, harks back to China's golden age, when it was the Middle Kingdom, centre of the world, spreading its munificence with recipient countries paying obeisance. It has echoes of the great Silk Road of antiquity. China would avenge the two centuries of humiliation by the West.

China's rise coincided with its assessment that the West, especially the US, was in terminal decline following the great financial crisis of 2008. With Xi, the dictum, hide your strength, bide your time, was thrown into the dustbin. China had risen. China would be the co-equal of the US, or even surpass it in terms of wealth. Others must accept this fact and fall in line, failing which there would be consequences. China felt that US policies of pivot to Asia had little teeth though they worry about the QUAD, a grouping of India, Australia, Japan and the US; that the US was exhausted through overreach in faraway conflicts in Iraq and Afghanistan, among others. With the advent of the Trump presidency, the US began retreating from global engagement and multilateralism. Trump was alienating foes and friends alike. Trump's mishandling of the COVID-19 pandemic further reinforced this perception. China would step in and fill the vacuum in global leadership. Chinese diplomats began to practise aggressive 'wolf warrior' diplomacy. Of course, with a Biden presidency, things are changing and though the worst unilateralist impulses of the Trump administration are over, the strategic competition between the two countries is likely to endure.

Sensing that this was China's moment, it stepped up its aggressive activities in the South China (and East China) Sea by changing facts on the ground and building military capabilities on several contested islands, reefs and atolls, effectively making the SCS a Chinese lake. Chinese aggression was not confined to the waters alone. All along the Himalayas, China started making inroads into Indian territory; it also started to make claims in Bhutan that it had never raised before. Meanwhile, Nepal too started making new claims in the area of the tri-junction that it had never staked in the past two centuries. And this, at a time when India and China were involved in the most serious border face-off in Ladakh since the 1962 war.

The immediate context for Nepal's current outreach to China was in response to what Nepal projected as an economic blockade by India over differences on issues relating to the Nepalese Constitution. Oli believed that in light of shortages of oil and other supplies, he did not have any option but to get them from China.[7] He would assert that he was a committed friend of India. He rejected his portrayal in Indian media as pro-China. But it was his responsibility to ensure that the people of Nepal did not suffer. Hence his overtures to China. Also, it had been his expectation that the embargo would be lifted as soon as he became PM since he considered himself to be close to India; this did not happen and hence he was left with no alternative but to turn to China. Though there may be an element of truth in his argument, the fact remains that he had played a very divisive role leading up to the adoption of the Constitution and also whipped up anti-Indian nationalism. This perception was confirmed later when he launched a high decibel nationalistic campaign in the run-up to general elections in 2017.

For Nepal today, China does not represent only a balance to India's overarching presence. The Nepalese leadership also sees huge opportunities for mutual benefit with the dramatic rise of China with enormous resources. A new and younger generation is dazzled by the economic success of China and wants to benefit from the opportunities in business, education and tourism. BRI is seen as an important initiative that will bring more rapid development to Nepal. It is viewed as an opportunity, not as a threat, irrespective of how India sees the proposal. My sense is that Nepal would have enthusiastically supported the BRI even if the so-called blockade of 2015 had not happened. This is evident from the fact that despite our extending strong support to the Oli regime during 2017–2019, China's role, presence and influence in Nepal, including in its internal affairs, has only grown. China not only has the intent, but also the deep pockets needed to spread its footprints in Nepal and the wider Himalayan region lying on its south-western periphery.

Since Oli's visit to China in March 2016,[8] there is a qualitative change in the relationship between Nepal and China. A series of major trans-Himalayan projects have been agreed upon. The transit treaty and the connectivity projects are part of this initiative, and they converge with China's BRI. These include road and rail connectivity projects, a cross-border transmission line, a cross-border petroleum pipeline and a cross-border optical fibre network that is already operating commercially. This is in addition to the seven ports—four seaports and three land ports—that have been made available to Nepal for third country transit trade. Nepal has also sought the development of three north-south corridors along the river basins of the Kosi, the Gandak and the Karnali rivers. However, a careful reading of the joint communiques demonstrates that, on many of the high value projects on which Nepal is keen, the Chinese have not made a clear commitment but have agreed to study or consider these projects.

The Trans Himalayan Multi-Dimensional Connectivity Network, including the cross-border Kerung Kathmandu railway, has been included among the overall list of Chinese BRI projects.

On the Chinese side, the railway line is already connected to Shigatse and work on the extension to Kerung is underway. A pre-feasibility study on the basis of a Chinese grant is underway. This was agreed on during Xi's October 2019 visit to Nepal. Xi has spoken about Nepal being land linked instead of land locked.[9] Though the list of projects is impressive and would cost billions of dollars if implemented, it is not certain that they will all fructify. If they do, they have the potential of changing the geopolitics of the region. In any event, they have had a huge psychological impact by giving Nepal an alternative to India in times of emergency.

Unlike the China–Pakistan Economic Corridor (CPEC) or the China–Myanmar Economic Corridor (CMEC), it is difficult to fully comprehend the strategic significance for China of the Trans Himalayan Corridor in Nepal. The Pakistan and Myanmar corridors both provide an alternative to the Malacca Straits for Chinese oil and other supplies as well as exports. Myanmar is also rich in natural resources. Nepal neither provides a strategic route to China and its most valuable resource is water, which flows downwards into the plains. Nepal is also a very small market for China, both in terms of exports and imports. If the train link is established, it may bring in Chinese goods and tourists, but what will it take back? There is not too much that Nepal can sell to China. The only possible importance of the corridor to China could be access to the huge market of India, especially of UP and Bihar. Only if India is on board will the Trans Himalayan railway project from Tibet to Kathmandu, Pokhara and on to Lumbini in the Terai become economically viable.

Apart from the technical difficulties and environmental issues, these are big-ticket projects costing billions of US dollars. Financing them is a huge issue, with Nepal seeking grants and China thus far willing to provide loans. Nepal is aware of some countries getting sucked into a debt trap. Furthermore, both in terms of logistics costs and time taken, the ports of Kolkata and Vizagapatam are far more efficient for Nepal's third country trade as compared to Tianjin and other Chinese ports on the eastern seaboard that are several thousand kilometres away compared to Kolkata, which is less than a thousand kilometres. Nevertheless, given the inefficiency of Kolkata port, one cannot automatically rule out the possibility that Tianjin may become viable. But for the present, the bulk of China's trade with Nepal follows the sea route from Shanghai to Kolkata. But we should note that China has started supplying cargo by rail to Europe! Further, in the changing geopolitical environment, it is possible that China is seeking to ensure its influence, even if it is at great cost, particularly in its neighbourhood. How the US–China relationship will pan out in the Biden era, whether it will be competitive, cooperative or conflictual, or a combination of the three, whether the world would again be divided into competing blocs and/or spheres of influence, would also impact Chinese policy.

Though the Trans Himalayan Multi-Dimensional Connectivity Network is the crown jewel of Nepal–China cooperation, there has been a rapid enhancement and deepening of engagement in several other areas as well. President Xi's visit, the first by a Chinese President in over two decades, elevated the relationship to a strategic level, implying thereby a sustained and comprehensive partnership in all aspects of the relationship both at government and party levels.

Defence cooperation has received a boost with the first-ever visit of a Chinese defence minister to Nepal in March 2017 and the beginning of joint military exercises. China has stepped up cooperation with Nepal's paramilitary armed police force by building a training academy. There is close cooperation between Nepalese and Chinese security organizations with regard to the activities of Tibetan refugees. The ingress of refugees is down to single digits. Several new restrictions have been placed on refugees; for instance, they are denied permission to celebrate the birthday of the Dalai Lama or hold public demonstrations. Since 1989, no ID cards are issued by the Nepalese authorities to Tibetan refugees or to children of refugees born in Nepal, effectively making them stateless, although there was an understanding with UNHCR that they would be allowed to travel to India. There are rumours that those seeking to flee Tibet may even be pushed back by the Nepalese security forces. That the Nepalese constantly reiterate their commitment to the One China policy is clear from all Nepal–China joint statements. But the extent to which they bend over backwards to accommodate China's concerns about Tibet is clear from the following incident that happened during my tenure in Kathmandu. News arrived in Kathmandu that H.H. the Shamar Rinpoche had passed away in Germany in 2014. His body was to be brought to Nepal, where he would be cremated by his followers. The Home Ministry, led at the time by Bam Dev Gautam of the CPN (UML), initially denied permission for fear of upsetting the Chinese. The BBC reported that the change of mind was because the Rinpoche 'contributed so much to Buddhism' according to the government.[10]

Economic engagement is growing apace. China today is the largest source of FDI into Nepal. Sectors include hydropower, infrastructure, cement, hospitality and tourism industry, aviation and telecommunications, among other areas. If you visited Kathmandu in 2019 as the author did, you would see a city plastered with billboards of Hongshi Shivam cement, a joint venture that has recently made a foray into this key sector. Two large airport projects in Pokhara and Bhairawaha and the 1200 MW Budhi Gandaki hydro-power project are being executed by Chinese companies. The total investment in these projects runs into hundreds of millions of dollars. Himalaya Airlines is a new Tibet–Nepal joint venture with participation by the Tibet government and a Nepalese company, Yeti Group. It is competing with the national carrier, Nepal Airlines Corporation (NAC), for lucrative international routes. The NAC is a loss-making venture and stays afloat merely because of the ground handling charges that it receives at Tribhuvan International Airport, Kathmandu.

In a recent decision, the contract for ground handling was given to Himalaya Airlines, prompting protests from NAC.

Unlike India, which has won big ticket projects on the basis of international competitive bidding, several large projects have been handed over to the Chinese on a government-to-government basis through negotiations. Two projects that stand out are the 1200 MW Budhi Gandaki hydro project and the Pokhara International Airport. The Budhi Gandaki Project is the largest hydro project to be executed in Nepal, the other two being Upper Karnali and Arun III that are being constructed by Indian companies. It will have the highest dam, 225 metres, in Nepal and cost upwards of US$2.5 billion. The project has an interesting history.[11] During the last days of his government in May 2017, PM Prachanda, of the NCP (Maoist Centre), handed over the project to China Gezhouba Group Corp (CGGC) on an EPC basis with financing under BRI. The next government under Sher Bahadur Deuba (Nepali Congress) cancelled the project on grounds of irregularities, due to lack of global tendering. It was decided that Nepal would develop the project by itself. Following Oli's CPN (UML) victory in the general elections, the government gave the project back to CGGC in September 2018. Former PM Baburam Bhattarai has publicly made allegations of corruption against leaders of both the then ruling Nepal Communist Party and the opposition Nepali Congress in regard to this project.[12]

The case of the Pokhara International Airport is also indicative of the manner in which Chinese companies operate in Nepal. Against an estimated budget of US$165 million, the lowest bid received was for US$305 million from among the three Chinese companies that bid for the project. The lowest bidder, China CAMC Engineering Company, thereafter agreed to do the project in the earlier budgeted amount. However, the final agreement signed by Nepal was for an amount of US$216 million, some US$51 million more than the estimated cost.[13] The project is funded on the basis of a soft loan from China—the first 25 per cent is interest free with the balance available at an interest rate of 2 per cent.[14] Interestingly, Indian lines of credit are available to Nepal at a cheaper coupon rate of 1 per cent. Former PM Baburam Bhattarai has alleged corruption involving all political parties in such infrastructure projects. The Pokhara Airport project, interestingly, had been clinched by a Nepali Congress finance minister who had been a strong opponent of the project, but made an about turn following a visit to China.

The Chinese are also undertaking huge investments in Jhapa, the home district of PM Oli.[15] A large industrial park is coming up in Damak, the PM's constituency, with an investment of US$536 million. The project is being undertaken by a company from Lhasa. They are building the world's largest statue of the Buddha in Damak. In addition, they have committed to building a dam and embankments on all the rivers flowing through Jhapa.

Tourism and hospitality industry is another destination of choice for small Chinese investors. After India, China is now the largest source of inbound tourism for Nepal. The preferred destinations are Kathmandu, Pokhara and Lumbini. If you walk through the lanes of Thamel, formerly a hippie hangout and today one of the most touristed parts of Kathmandu, you will be struck by the number of Chinese restaurants, hole-in-the-wall eateries and small shops that have come up during the last few years. Billboards welcome visitors using Chinese characters. You can taste the most authentic Szechuan cuisine in some of the Chinese restaurants in Kathmandu.

The same situation is repeated in Pokhara. Cafes and restaurants in this beautiful lake town have special menus in Chinese characters to cater to visitors from across the Himalayas. Nepal is one destination that the Chinese encourage their citizens to visit. There are sixty flights between Kathmandu and Chinese cities every week.

Nepal also complains that India is paranoid about Nepal's cooperation with China even as India's own cooperation with

China has grown by leaps and bounds, with bilateral trade in the neighbourhood of US$90 billion.[16] They argue, and with some justification, that Chinese companies are active in infrastructure construction in India, and so why could Nepal not seek similar investment? Furthermore, according to them, why should India object to investments by India–Chinese joint ventures operating in India; indeed, they would like to see projects undertaken by India and China jointly in Nepal.

The other issue that fascinates the Nepalese is trilateral cooperation between the three countries. They see Nepal as a bridge between the two fast-growing large economies and wish to provide a further avenue through Nepal for India–China cooperation. Prachanda has also spoken about trilateral cooperation.[17] China is also keen on China–India plus cooperation in South Asia along the model of Afghanistan. Of course, some of this is wishful thinking, particularly in the context of India–China relations, which are in a trough currently, with the stand-off between the two armies in Ladakh. Having said that, the economic and financial viability of Nepal as a bridge is open to question, particularly since the linkage between India and China through the Bangladesh, China, India and Myanmar (BCIM) corridor through our north-east, Bangladesh, Myanmar and then to Yunnan, may be more efficient and cheaper than the difficult trans-Himalayan route.

China is active in exploiting the soft power of Buddhism. If you go down to the Terai, to Lumbini, the birthplace of the Buddha, you will see that the largest Buddhist monastery constructed in the UNESCO world heritage site is by Communist China. It regularly sends large delegations to conferences on Buddhism organized by the Nepalese authorities that proclaim that Nepal is not only the birthplace of the Buddha but is the fountain of Buddhism. I recall participating in one such event. Several important dignitaries were present in a conference hall listening to an important Chinese Buddhist monk, Yin Shun, vice president of the Buddhist Association of China, who was delivering his address in Mandarin.

There was no translation, but every so often the hall would break into loud applause from the Chinese participants, which the Nepalese would also join. In 2011, PM Prachanda had signed a US$3 billion project with a Chinese foundation, the Asia Pacific Exchange and Cooperation Foundation, for the development of Lumbini, but not much has been heard about it since.[18]

Today, Mandarin is taught in Nepalese schools and Confucius and China Study Centres have been established. Kathmandu and Tribhuvan universities, the two most prestigious centres for higher learning in Nepal, are hosts to Confucious centres. In a reply to a Parliament question in March 2015, MOS V.K. Singh said that there were twenty-six China Study Centres in Nepal, including in the Terai, aimed at strengthening cultural and educational interaction between Nepal and China.[19] A large number of Nepalese students study in Chinese universities and there is a steady exchange of delegations and study visits between the two countries.

The Chinese are now actively engaged in Nepal's internal politics. They played an important role in the merger of the CPN (UML) and the Maoists following the 2017 elections. A senior Maoist leader mentioned to me that the Chinese ambassador was active in resolving hurdles and roadblocks when the merger talks were underway between the two parties. More recently, in April and May 2020, when Oli was under severe attack within his party for his autocratic behaviour and mishandling of the COVID-19 pandemic and its economic fallout, the Chinese ambassador was visibly engaged in shuttle diplomacy between the key leaders of the NCP, following a high-profile telephone conversation between President Bidya Devi Bhandari and President Xi Jinping. Though Oli survived, the problems within the party did not disappear. Even as they recurred and the party appeared to be heading to a split, the Chinese were active in ensuring that the communist force remained united. It is evident that the Chinese have taken a decision that a unified communist force in Nepal is in their strategic interest. When the Chinese were asked about their involvement in the internal affairs of Nepal, and especially the role of the ambassador, the response was that they wanted the NCP to remain united.[20]

The years 2019–20 also witnessed growing party-to-party engagement between the Communist Party of China (CCP) and the erstwhile Nepalese Communist Party (NCP). Prior to President Xi's visit to Nepal in 2019, a comprehensive MOU was signed between the two parties. Apart from exchanges and sharing of experiences, the CCP was engaged in training NCP cadres on subjects such as Xi Jinping Thought, how to strengthen the party domestically and what the relationship between the party and government should be.[21] It appeared that the CCP was keen to mould the NCP in its own image. Now that the Supreme Court in its decision in March 2021 has annulled the merger of the CPN (UML) and NCP (Maoist Centre) into the NCP and restored the pre-merger status, it remains to be seen how the relationship of the CCP will develop with the two Nepalese communist parties.

One thing is clear. China has decided to invest more time and money in its relationship with Nepal. And it is now intervening in internal political affairs. What is more, the Chinese are doing this openly. Chinese diplomats are not only active but also visible. They are also adept at the use of social media to push their agenda among the wider public. Following the March 2021 decision of the Supreme Court of Nepal, Chinese efforts to unify and consolidate communist parties has suffered a setback. But the Chinese are long-term players; they will likely continue to work for what they view as a strategic objective in Nepal.

Another important initiative of the Chinese has been the July 2020 meeting of China, Nepal, Afghanistan and Pakistan, ostensibly to discuss COVID-19 related issues, but a key outcome was to explore synergies between CPEC and the Trans Himalayan Network.[22] This was followed up by a subsequent meeting at the vice minister level and expanded to include Bangladesh and Sri Lanka.[23] All South Asian members of this series of meetings are participants in the BRI. In all, four such meetings at minister/

vice minister level have been held. Neither India nor Bhutan was invited/participated. These meetings have led to the establishment of a China–South Asian Countries Poverty Alleviation and Cooperative Development Centre in Chongqing in July 2021. Further, the meaning of 'synergies' is unclear. Does China want to model the Trans Himalayan Network on the basis of CPEC? Or is it potentially offering Nepal the use the CPEC infrastructure as an alternative supply route? Is it a Himalayan string of pearls to encircle India from the North, just as China is doing in the maritime domain? Given the ongoing conflict along the contested Himalayan border with China, any collaboration between China and other SAARC members in this region is naturally of interest to India.

Some have argued in India that Oli has raised the boundary question with India at the behest of China. Our army chief's statement in May 2020 at a webinar organized by the Manohar Parikar IDSA seemed to suggest this.[24] My own sense is that Oli focused on the map issue with India as a means to divert attention from the internal political problems that he was facing rather than due to instigation by China. But this in no way implies that the Chinese will not seek to benefit from the impasse this had created in the India–Nepal relationship.

There have been media reports[25] stating that China has recently funded a study by one of the China Study Groups in Nepal on the question of Nepalese Gorkhas joining the Indian Army. The motivations for this are unclear. A related aspect is also the treatment meted out to Gorkha soldiers of the Indian Army taken prisoner during the India–China War of 1962. In an interesting article in the *Nepal Record* on 8 December 2014, General Sam Cowan refers to the differential treatment by China of Indian POWs and Indian Army Gorkha POWs and the communist brainwashing that the POWs were subjected to. Cowan states that the Chinese treated the Gorkha POWs better than the Indian POWs and the Chinese tried to indoctrinate the Gorkhas against their Indian officers and told them that the Chinese and Nepalese were 'brothers'. He also mentions the fact that the Chinese wanted to return the Gorkha POWs directly to Nepal, which the latter declined.[26]

Another interesting incident in late 2020 reveals how concerned the Nepalese are about Chinese sensitivities. Media reports emanating from Nepal have suggested Chinese encroachment of Nepalese territory in several border districts, including Gorkha and Humla. A local district official of Humla also visited the border areas and gave a statement to the press about the Chinese land grab and the fact that they had constructed several buildings on Nepalese land and also removed border pillars. The Nepalese government immediately denied that any such incident had occurred. A show-cause notice was issued to the hapless district official. Thereafter, a sitting MP from the district visited the area and confirmed Chinese encroachment![27]

Today, with a fraught India–China relationship, the China card is an effective instrument that Nepal leverages vis-à-vis India. This, however, need not always be the case. During my tenure in Nepal, I had established a good working relationship with the Chinese ambassador. We hosted regular meetings of key officers of both embassies over lunch. The purpose was to share views and exchange opinions about Nepal. Both India and China, as neighbouring countries, want political stability in Nepal. Both countries supported the electoral process for CA II and were keen that a new constitution be adopted. Neither country wanted third countries and international NGOs to step up activities that could have negative implications. There is thus a limited convergence of views between India and China, something that could be built upon. Though it is difficult to visualize today, we should not rule out a possible joint India–China project in Nepal along the lines of a similar project in Afghanistan.[28] On our respective economic projects in Nepal, the Chinese were as frustrated as us at the slow, inefficient pace at which they progressed. Chinese ambassador Wu Chuntai once recalled his experience, similar to ours, about how projects when completed, were sometimes left to decay without due maintenance and adequate care;[29] thereafter, the Nepalese would again seek assistance to have the project repaired and/or restarted. Indeed, a mechanism similar to the one established with India was set up between Nepal and China to expedite project implementation.[30] I also recall an instance when I hosted Ambassador Wu Chuntai for lunch at Hotel Soaltee. News of this meeting spread rapidly causing considerable consternation in Nepal; it appeared in the press with people speculating about what the two countries were up to. To a large extent, Nepal's leverage with India depends on the continued uneasy relationship between India and China.

Western countries have promoted their own agendas in Nepal. For the US, Nepal's strategic location between two large Asian rivals is an important element in the significance it attaches to this country. The US also closely monitors the issue of Tibetan refugees and is concerned at the growing restrictions placed on them by the Nepalese government.

The US, like India, was also deeply concerned about the Maoist insurgency and for many years had included them on the list of global terrorist organizations. India worked closely with both the US and UK in the context of the peace process that eventually brought the Maoists into the democratic mainstream following the famous twelve-point agreement of November 2005.

More recently, a key issue for the US during the constitution drafting process was that Nepal should be a secular state. This position was supported by other Western countries as well and a large number of international NGOs. Those in Nepal that were opposed to a secular state and were in favour of Nepal becoming a Hindu state, were increasingly concerned at the proselytization activities of Christian evangelical groups from Western countries as well as South Korea, particularly among the Janjatis who have converted in significant numbers to Christianity. This is evident from the number of churches that have mushroomed in Nepal, not only in Kathmandu but in the hill areas where communities such as the Tamangs have converted en masse. The South Korean Unification Church is believed to have deep links with the Nepal Family Party whose programmes were graced by Prime Minister Oli and other dignitaries.[31] Proselytization activities are also being undertaken in the Terai.

A major US initiative is the US$500 million grant under the Millennium Challenge Corporation for building electricity transmission lines and improving the road network in Nepal. The project had got bogged down in the politics of the then Nepalese Communist Party. Important leaders, including former prime minister Jhalanath Khanal, argue that the project is part of the US Indo–Pacific alliance; that it is against the BRI initiative of China and is generally anti-China.[32] Even though the project will bring enormous benefit to Nepal by strengthening the electrical grid connectivity with India and help the people living in far-flung and remote mountain areas through better maintenance of rural roads, the project has not been approved by Parliament.

The United Kingdom and the European Union are also important partners and provide significant development assistance to Nepal. The EU had allocated a sum of Euro 360 million for the period 2014–20 and is working in sectors such as education, reconstruction and rural economy, in addition to election support and the peace process. The UK too is a major donor with a planned budget spend of 82 million pounds during 2019–20 in sectors such as health, post-earthquake reconstruction, security and justice. In the past, the UK had worked closely with the Janjatis and assisted the Nepal Federation of Indigenous Nationalities (NEFIN) that brought together a large number of Janjati organizations by funding a 'Janjati Empowerment Project' to 'increase participation of Janjatis in socio-economic and political processes at all levels'.[33]

Meanwhile, Pakistan's involvement in Nepal has ebbed and flowed over the years. In the past, the large Pakistani embassy in Kathmandu was very active, with a strong ISI component. In reply to a Lok Sabha question on 1 March 2000,[34] the then external affairs minister Jaswant Singh said, 'The Government of India have discussed from time to time with the Government of Nepal our concerns about the ISI misusing the Nepalese territory and the open India–Nepal border for activities inimical to India's interest. Reports received by the government indicate increasing evidence of ISI using Nepal as a staging post for terrorist activities directed against India. The Nepalese government have been sensitised on this issue. The Government of Nepal have assured that their territory would not be used for activities inimical to India's interest . . .' The hijack of IC 814 in December 1999 from Kathmandu to Kandahar is still fresh in memory. Several important terrorist operatives such as Yasin Bhatkal and Tunda, have been arrested along the India–Nepal border. Pakistani agencies have also been funnelling fake Indian currency through the open India–Nepal border.[35] Criminal gangs are engaged in smuggling activities, kidnapping, extortion and human trafficking. India needs to remain vigilant, including through strengthened cooperation between the respective intelligence, police and border guarding forces of India and Nepal.

More recently, Pakistan has tried to benefit from the downturn in the India–Nepal relationship. Pakistan PM Shahid Khaqan Abbasi visited Kathmandu early March 2018 to congratulate PM Oli on his electoral win; both Pakistan and Nepal favour China's membership of SAARC and are enthusiastic participants in the Chinese-promoted Belt and Road Initiative. It is possible that Pakistan and China could team up together in Nepal, a development that India would need to constantly monitor.

As the role and influence of countries such as China and Pakistan, on the one hand, and the US, the UK and the European Union on the other, grows in Nepal, India will need to fashion an approach that ensures that our core interests are protected. Some measures that India could consider adopting are discussed in the epilogue.

Epilogue

Uncertain Future: The Way Forward

Tumultuous changes continue to impact global society. Technology and the information revolution have made the world flat, to use Thomas Friedman's phrase: human behaviour, how we think, what we do and how we interact with each other has been transformed. The world is at your doorstep, with the click of a mouse. Free movement of goods, services, capital and to a limited extent human resources have enabled hundreds of millions of people to escape poverty. But there is a pushback against globalization. As inequalities increase, and rapid technological change and automation make many skill sets obsolete, as production moves to places that are most cost effective and efficient, there is growing unemployment and even greater discontent, especially in many developed countries. New walls are being erected in place of old ones that had broken down. My country first is the new slogan. Under Trump, the US retreated from global commitments; with Biden 'America is back' in the multilateral arena. With Brexit, sovereignty is reasserting itself forcefully in Europe. India has stayed away from RCEP[1] and has fashioned new policies of Make in India and Atmanirbhar (self-reliant) Bharat. President Xi

Jinping has spoken about the Chinese dream for the rejuvenation of the nation and a desire to avenge the humiliations of the past. Nationalism has asserted itself. Old frameworks and structures are becoming obsolete and ineffective. The certainties of the past have given way to a state of fluidity and flux. The clear and present danger of climate change and the harrowing experience of the COVID-19 pandemic will shape the emerging world order.

Contours of a fresh global compact are still hazy, though new groupings and alignments are in the air. This is the age of multi-alignment; there is no contradiction between membership of the SCO[2] and the QUAD[3] at the same time. Learned debates take place on whether the new world order will be a bipolar one with multipolarity or a multipolar one with elements of bipolarity. Will the world again be divided into opposing camps? Those that dominated the old world are loathe to let go their power; new actors are clamouring for their place at the table. No country can remain unaffected. It is only a matter of time that China will overtake the US as the country with the highest GDP in the world. India too, we hope, will advance rapidly. The US–China contestation for influence, of systems, cultures and values will affect the world at large. The India–China relationship will affect our region and indeed the wider world.

It is amid these uncertainties that we have to navigate India–Nepal ties. What is the future that we wish to see in our relationship with Nepal, say, over the next twenty years? How do we relate the concept of *Sabka Saath, Sabka Vikas, Sabka Vishwas* (development for all with full participation and trust) with *Samriddha Nepal Sukhi Nepali* (prosperous Nepal, happy people)? Nepal has changed; it is a youthful country with new aspirations. It is no longer content to be a part of the Indian security umbrella or have a 'special relationship'. It has more options today and wants out from what it perceives to be a claustrophobic embrace with India. Nepal wants a relationship as between friends, not an unequal relationship that it feels is thrust upon it by historical treaties and geography. At the same time, it would like to retain the privileges of national treatment for its citizens in India inherited from the same treaties. Culture, religion and ties of family and kinship, factors that are stressed by India in the overall relationship, are seen as of secondary importance by the Nepal leadership, particularly among the communists.

China is no longer viewed as a mere counterbalance to India. Nepal sees huge opportunities for economic benefit from its engagement with China. Like our other neighbours, it is attracted to the 'no strings' support. It enthusiastically participates in the BRI, despite being aware of the pitfalls of a debt trap and unmindful of Indian concerns. Indeed, for some, China is the only economic game in town. Elites in some developing countries, including Nepal, have been won over. Leaders appear unconcerned about the long-term implications of their deals with China, reflecting John Maynard Keynes's dictum, 'In the long run we are all dead.' It is only in June 2021 that the G7 countries at their summit in the United Kingdom have proposed a programme known as Build Back Better World or B3W for infrastructure development in developing countries to rival BRI. However, few details are available in the public domain so far.

There is a growing divergence between India and Nepal about mutual security. India sees China as a major threat, most visibly demonstrated by the ongoing crisis in Ladakh; Nepal sees China largely as an opportunity that must be seized. China is increasingly going to be the third factor in all of India's relationships with her neighbours. Unless India resolves the border issue with China (and Pakistan), we will continue to be obstructed from fulfilling our own aspirations for leadership, from becoming a *'Vishwaguru'*.

Relations between asymmetric neighbours are never easy; both sides need to demonstrate sensitivity to the aspirations and interests of the other. India must respect Nepal's desire for greater political space and an independent foreign policy, just as we strive for greater strategic autonomy as part of our own foreign policy goals. India should not view every Nepalese agreement with China as adversely impacting Indian security, especially when we ourselves have substantial cooperation with China. Nepal, on the other hand, must ensure that nothing that it does affects India's security interests, particularly since the two countries share an open, friendly border.

Any close, even intimate relationship such as the one between India and Nepal, is prone to misunderstandings and differences; there is a tendency for complacency to set into the relationship. The relationship needs to be nurtured constantly through ever greater engagement at all levels.

So, has the time come for a new compact, a reset in the ties between India and her neighbours, particularly between India and Nepal? What would be the key features? At a political level, the 1950 treaty could be amended along the lines of the revised Bhutan Treaty. As it is, the mutual security clauses of the treaty are inoperative.

The old foundations for our relationship with Nepal, though important, are no longer sufficient. We have to lay deeper foundations by providing an overarching economic vision for the relationship both bilaterally and at the sub-regional and regional levels. Since SAARC has fallen victim to the hostility between India and Pakistan, we should focus on sub-regional cooperation, particularly between BBIN (Bangladesh, Bhutan, India and Nepal) countries and in the BIMSTEC[4] region. What are the economic dimensions of such a compact? How do we create a buy-in among all neighbours for the idea of a common, integrated economic space, without let or barriers, where each partner benefits from the progress of the other, and where each member has the opportunity to exploit its comparative advantages to the full? Regional supply chains need to be developed for the domestic markets as well as for export. As the biggest country, India has to create conditions by which our neighbours, including Nepal, benefit from the Indian growth story and develop a vested interest in India's rapid progress. We have already laid the legal framework in terms of the many agreements on trade, transit, taxation and investment both at bilateral and regional levels. We have developed a grand strategy for greater connectivity at a bilateral level, more broadly within the region and between regions. A slew of cross-border rail and road connectivity projects, oil and gas pipelines, electricity transmission lines, even inland waterways will enhance and deepen engagement.

Implementation is key. We cannot use the template that we use to implement domestic projects. Global standards and quality, more pragmatic and efficient systems, and rules and procedures must be employed to improve project delivery. No longer can we afford to hear our neighbours complain that India promises but it is China that delivers. Important strides have been made in India's development partnership with Nepal. The oil pipeline from Motihari to Amlekhganj was completed in record time. The ICP at Raxaul–Birganj is functional; work on the Jogbani–Biratnagar ICP is underway. Two more ICPs, one at the Nepalganj–Rupaidiha border and another at Sunauli–Bhairawaha, will complete the basic infrastructure for hassle-free movement of trade between the two countries as well as third country trade for Nepal. Of the five cross-border railway links, the Jaynagar–Janakpur–Kurtha line is operational. Once these are completed, Nepal will have complete access to the entire Indian railway system from its border towns. Similarly, preparatory work on the Raxaul–Kathmandu rail link has begun. Implementation of ICPs and cross-border rail links must be speeded up; they should be implemented as prestige projects and fast-tracked with special rules and procedures, as in the case of the Delhi Metro Project. With the opening of the Varanasi-Kolkata section of the Ganga for riverine transport, new opportunities have opened up for Nepal as well. Following a bilateral motor vehicles agreement, several cities of India, including Delhi, Varanasi, Lucknow and others, are connected to various parts of Nepal, from Kathmandu to Pokhara, Mahendranagar, etc.

Hydropower projects and the development of sub-regional electricity grids should be expedited. Water is the most valuable resource that Nepal possesses. Helping Nepal harness its water resources is a win-win for both countries. Several hydro-power projects with varied modalities are underway, including Pancheshwar, Upper Karnali and Arun III. Together these three projects envisage an investment of several billion dollars. While Upper Karnali and Arun III are being implemented by the private and public sectors respectively, Pancheshwar is a bilateral project between the two governments. It should be our highest priority to ensure that all pending issues preventing finalization of the Joint DPR for the Pancheshwar project are resolved politically so that financial closure can be achieved soon. This project has the potential of dramatically improving the quality of the India-Nepal relationship.

We should give up the shibboleths of the past with an unhealthy and eventually self-defeating focus on just the bilateral approach. In addition to bilateral projects, we have to strengthen trilateral cooperation and quadrilateral projects. We need a coordinated approach for the integrated development of basins of transnational rivers, such as the Ganga and the Brahmaputra, with the participation of all stakeholders. Involving Bangladesh in the Kosi High Dam Project in Nepal will make it politically more acceptable for Nepal. The sale of Nepalese power to a Bangladeshi or Myanmar off-taker will benefit the entire region. India should view such possibilities more strategically.

Tourism and the development of various circuits, including the Buddhist and Hindu circuits, will significantly boost bilateral cooperation and strengthen people-to-people ties. Bringing Nepal within the ambit of the Indian LTC[5] scheme for government servants would provide a huge impetus to a sector that is critical for Nepal both in terms of contribution to GDP as well as employment. It would also deepen the people-to-people interaction.

Similarly, development of high value commercial agriculture, medicinal herbs and plants and niche crops, as well as horticulture, together with the development of cold supply chains and an assured market in India, would bring enormous benefit. Already, Indian companies are active in this sector in Nepal and the scale should be expanded.

The great earthquake of April 2015 demonstrated the crying need for Indian NGOs that could assist with the rebuilding activities in neighbouring countries. Our restrictive policies for transfer of funds from India, as well as the fact that we do not encourage Indian NGOs to operate abroad, needs review. The Small Development Project scheme is vital to reach out to the general public throughout Nepal. It has now been revived. We must vigorously implement and expand the scheme.

The left and communist parties of Nepal should deeply introspect whether sustained anti-India nationalism is in the long-term interest of their country. We should work for strengthening the more moderate voices. India must be seen to be objective and fair, with the best interests of both countries at heart. Our interaction should be transparent and open; we must speak not only to the government, but to the people of Nepal. We should openly and vigorously convey the logic of our policy and actions so that people understand where we are coming from. Irritants in the relationship should not be allowed to become cankerous sores; or as planks for deeper anti-India nationalism.

There should be consistency in our policy and predictability. Our own public should also be made aware of why we are pursuing a certain course of action. We should set clear and achievable goals, short term and long term, and not allow ourselves to be swayed by temporary impediments in achieving them. A peaceful, stable, prosperous, democratic Nepal is in India's own interests. Our policy should be fashioned accordingly.

What of the relationship between the peoples of the two countries? There is a growing perception, more so in Nepal than in India, that the open border is a liability from the security perspective; that greater regulation is required in the easy and document-free movement of people across borders; that there is need for a stronger and more visible presence and patrolling by border-guarding forces on the two sides. Nepal is worried about migration from India into the Terai; India too is worried about the misuse of the open border by terrorists, smugglers and third-country actors. The answer to these problems does not lie in further controls and border regulations. These have been tried in the past and have failed; for instance, ID cards for cross-border movement were found to be impracticable following a pilot project that was launched in the early 2000s. We need a smart border with less visible security presence; to prevent misuse, we need greater cooperation between border guarding forces and intelligence and police services on the two sides.

Border guarding forces, such as the Sashastra Seema Bal (SSB), need to be trained to ensure that they facilitate hassle-free crossings. This is a friendly, open border. It is not like our borders with Bangladesh or Pakistan. I have personally witnessed passengers of the Modi bus taking a few hours to cross the border in Sunauli. Every passenger is asked to disembark, and the entire baggage of all passengers is checked. This is not necessary. This reminds me of the airport checks some years ago when clearing immigration and customs was a nightmare. Our land border crossings should be made as smooth as at our airports. This will not only help people living in border areas but also third country travellers, especially those on the Buddhist and Ramayana circuits.

Mutual security is best ensured by happy and prosperous people living in harmony on both sides of the border. We should begin to coordinate our border development projects with Nepal. Facilities on one side should also cater to the requirements of people on the other side. Academic institutions, such as medical and engineering colleges, hospitals and vocational institutions have a catchment area which includes both sides of the border.

Cross-border meetings of the respective provincial governments should be encouraged.

Border infrastructure is pathetic. Development of our border outposts and towns such as Jogbani, Raxaul, Sunauli, Rupaidiha and Tanakpur should be national projects. They should be declared smart cities and jointly upgraded by the Central and state governments. Roads leading up from these border towns to the national highways network on the Indian side should be elevated to national highway status.

Our societies are animated by the dreams, desires and aspirations of our youth. Programmes need to be devised to engage this section of society. Sports festivals, vigorous exchange programmes between universities and youth wings of political parties are some instrumentalities that could be considered. We can also develop joint university courses along the lines of the Erasmus programme in the European Union where students of one University can receive credits for undertaking a semester in an institution in another EU country. Nepalese students should not be charged exorbitant fees in US dollars at our educational institutions.

Cricket is all the rage in Nepal. India is well placed to help. Bollywood is a big social influencer and a symbol of India's pluralism and soft power. Both conventional and social media play a critical role in moulding mutual perceptions. Our news channels, however, have sometimes complicated the relationship. Heightened nationalism in both countries and the race for TRPs by our electronic media has meant that rigour and maturity in news analysis has been sacrificed for verbal wars and high decibel *tamasha*. The portrayal in 2020 of Nepal in a similar light as Pakistan or China, has deeply offended the Nepalese who in turn temporarily banned some Indian news channels. Such portrayal also creates a wedge between the two peoples. There is need for more informed coverage in both countries. The relative lack of academicians, experts and think tanks specializing in neighbourhood studies needs to be addressed. The Nepal Centre at BHU is dormant; there is no India Studies Centre in Nepal. There should be more frequent conversations between strategic thinkers and academics of the two countries. A beginning has been made during COVID-19 times and this needs to be sustained.

There was a time when a close personal friendship existed between political leaders of the two countries. Today, there is little interaction. Parliamentary and legislative exchanges are necessary. These will engender mutual trust and understanding, dilute the anti-India sentiment in Nepal and create a more positive atmosphere in the relationship.

The army-to-army relationship is a strong pillar of overall bilateral relations. This was demonstrated most visibly in the aftermath of the great earthquake of 2015. Cooperation between the two sides was seamless and exemplary largely because of the close and cordial relationship between the two armies and the then army chiefs, General Gaurav S.J.B. Rana and General Dalbir Singh Suhag, both of whom are also honorary generals in each other's armies, a tradition that continues to this day.

Apart from stepping up cooperation through exchange of visits, training and conduct of joint military exercises and supply of military material, to the extent possible, the relationship should be kept insulated from the negativity that sometimes characterizes the political relationship between the two countries. The tradition of close and frequent engagement between serving and retired service chiefs of the two countries must continue. So should the cooperation between intelligence and police services. These connections need to be strengthened. Pending projects, such as the Police Academy, need to be implemented without further delay.

China will remain for the foreseeable future, an important factor, the third player in the relationship. Fluctuations in our relationship with China will impact our relationships with neighbours. The temptation to use and the efficacy of the China card will be inversely proportional to the state of the India–China relationship. Though our relationship with China has elements of cooperation, competition and confrontation, the challenge is to ensure that it does not become conflictual. Of course, this depends, to a large extent on China's own calculations and actions. Neighbours are closely watching the border stand-offs between India and China.

Even as we deal bilaterally with China, we have to strengthen cooperation with like-minded countries, whether in the QUAD or in ASEAN. In our neighbourhood, we should work with other partners to pursue projects that will fulfil our vision of South Asia as a common integrated economic space. Jointly implemented hydro projects, development of connectivity infrastructure and development of regional supply chains should be open to partnerships from like-minded countries.

India's comparative advantage over China is her soft power. China is not loved; it is feared. China is influential because it is rich, but its autocratic system does not attract anyone. China simply does not have the kind of cultural connect that we have with Nepal and other countries in our region. India does not have the deep pockets to prevent Chinese ingress into our neighbourhood. Our USP is our democracy, celebration of our diversity and our culture that we should use smartly. We need a people-centric policy, to engage deeply all sections of society in Nepal. We need more engagement not less; our ambassador must be a visible and public figure, perceived to be someone who has the best interests of both countries at heart. He or she must win over the trust of the Nepalese public. Communication and social media efforts of the embassy should be stepped up.

For any Indian diplomat, Nepal represents one of the finest assignments, complex and challenging, enriching and rewarding all at once. Being our closest, it is perhaps the most difficult relationship with a lot of historical baggage, perceived grievances and prejudice on both sides. Nourished by the same mountains and rivers, our civilizations are inextricably intertwined. Nevertheless, any relationship as intimate as between our two countries throws up serious problems from time to time, problems that require to be handled with maturity and calm. There is no option but for the two countries to grow together in harmony with each other. Nature and geography have so ordained, and this will remain a fact of life in the foreseeable future.

Our neighbours are carefully watching developments in our own society. India's global image has suffered as the country was hit hard by the COVID-19 pandemic. From a first responder in times of natural disasters India became a recipient of international aid. Neighbours are contrasting the experience of China, where the virus originated, and India during the pandemic. The goodwill earned through the Vaccine Maitri initiative has been squandered as India was unable to follow up on supplies given the dire requirements at home. China has stepped in to help our neighbours. As economic growth suffers and not only due to the pandemic, doubts have arisen in the minds of some neighbours about India's capacity to assist. Hopefully, this is a transitory phase and India will bounce back soon with robust double-digit growth.

The impact of domestic policies on relations with our neighbours should also not be underestimated. Neighbours look up to our democracy and rule of law, our celebration of diversity and ability to take all sections of society along, our pluralism. India is seen as benign, not just a country but a civilization, a melting pot of cultures, religions, ethnicities where every person can revel in his or her individualistic identity and remain a proud Indian, where your parochial identity(s) is not in conflict with your national identity. We have an ancient tradition of *Vasudhaiva Kutumbakam*, the world is a family. We are and should remain a shining example to our neighbours, several of whom are struggling in their efforts to manage diversity and diverse aspirations within their respective societies. Gurudev Rabindranath Tagore established Visva Bharati, a place where the world is in communion with India. The motto of this university is: *Yatra viswam bhavatya eka nidam*, where the world makes its nest. India should be the magnet that attracts our neighbours, a role model worthy of emulation, a country that leads by example.

Notes

Chapter 1: Why Don't They Like Us? Identity, Nationalism and Mutual Perceptions

1   ET Bureau, 'India announces $1 billion aid for rebuilding Nepal', *Economic Times*, 26 June 2015.

2   Soutik Biswas, 'Why is Indian media facing a backlash in Nepal?', BBC News, 4 May 2015.

3   Chandan Nandy, 'Toxic Relief: India Supplies Foul Cooking Oil, Rice to Nepal', Quint, 28 May 2015.

4   Official Spokesman's Response to Media Queries, 9 August 2020, https://mofa.gov.np

5   Anil Giri, 'Amid Soured India-Nepal Ties, Oli is Threatening Relations Between Peoples of Two Countries, Leaders and Experts Say', *Kathmandu Post*, 14 July 2020.

6   THT online, 'Nepal's PM K P Sharma Oli "claims" real Ayodhya is in Nepal', *Himalayan Times*, 13 July 2020.

7   Karan Manral, 'Yoga originated in Nepal: K P Sharma Oli's Latest Startling Claim', *Hindustan Times*, 22 June 2021.

8   Madhur Sharma, 'Language Strife Raises its Head in Nepal: Lawmaker Demands National Status for Hindi', *Swarajya*, 7 January 2019.

9   Avtar Singh Bhasin, *Nepal–India Nepal–China Relations: Documents 1947–June 2005*, Prime Minister Nehru's Speech in the Rajya Sabha, 20 December 1960 (New Delhi: Geetika Publishers, 2005)

10   Amish Raj Mulmi, 'In Kathmandu's Support for BRI, an Old Story of India Losing Ground in Nepal', TheWire.in, 25 July 2017.

11   Maharajakrishna Rasgotra, *A Life in Diplomacy* (New Delhi: Penguin Books, 2019), Chapter 20.

12   https://www.indembkathmandu.gov.in/page/about-defence/

13   Press Trust of India, 'Indian Blockade More Inhuman Than War: Nepal PM', *Economic Times*, 6 November 2015; Special Correspondent, 'Nepali Prime Minister K P Oli was Once Called "Man of India". Why Has He Turned Such a Bitter Critic?', Scroll.in, 18 July 2016.

14   Siddharth Shekhar, 'PM K P Oli Plays "Nationalism" Card, Accuses India of Conspiring with Nepal Political Forces to Topple His Govt', Times Now, 29 June 2020.

15   Singh Durbar, 'Press Statement on News Reports About Nepal–China Boundary', Ministry of Foreign Affairs, Kathmandu, 25 June 2020.

16   Pashupati Shumsher J.B. Rana, *Contemporary Nepal, The Evolution of Nepalese Nationalism* (New Delhi: Vikas Publishing House, 1998).

Chapter 2: Violent Change: The Maoist Insurgency

1   Deepak Thapa, ed., *Understanding the Maoist Movement of Nepal*, Martin Chautari, 2003.

2   https://mea.gov.in/bilateral-documents.htm?dtl/7532/India++Nepal+Joint+Press+Statement

3   Michael Hutt, 'The Royal Palace Massacre, Conspiracy Theories and Nepali Street Literature', Eprints.soas.ac.uk

4   For a detailed account from a Nepalese perspective of this period see Sudheer Sharma's *The Nepal Nexus* (New Delhi: Penguin Viking, 2019).

5   Statement of Official Spokesperson of MEA, 1 February 2005, mea.gov.in

6   Rita Manchanda, 'Talks and Fears', *Frontline*, 11 April 2003

7   Prashant Jha, *Battles of the New Republic*, Aleph Book Company, 2014, pp. 61–62. See also Hisila Yami, *Hisila: From Revolutionary to First Lady*, Penguin Books, 2021, p. 87.

8   Teresa Whitfield,' Nepal's Masala Peacemaking' in *Nepal in Transition* by David Malone, Sebastian von Einsiedel, Suman Pradhan (New Delhi: Cambridge University Press, 2012).

9   Hisila Yami, *Hisila: From Revolutionary to First Lady*, Penguin Books, 2021, page 102. She states that their (Maoist) relationship was with the people and not the state.

10   S.D. Muni, 'Bringing the Maoists Down from the Hills: India's Role', *Nepal in Transition* by Malone, et al., p. 167.

11   Shyam Saran, *How India Sees the World* (New Delhi: Juggernaut, 2017), p. 160, has an interesting account of Shyam Saran's conversation with the then RNA Chief General Pyar Jung Thapa on the need for the army to avoid a violent confrontation with the massive crowds. Saran had travelled with Dr Karan Singh, the prime minister's special envoy, to urge the king to 'yield to the democratic forces and retain only a ceremonial role'.

Chapter 3: People's Aspirations: The New Constitution

1   Pramod K. Kantha, 'Understanding Nepal's Madhesi movement and its future trajectory', *Himalayan Journal of Development and Democracy*, vol. 5, no. 1, 2010.

2   For a Nepali account of this period, see Sudheer Sharma, *The Nepal Nexus* (New Delhi: Penguin Viking, 2019).

3   For details see brief on India Nepal Relations at mea.gov.in

4   Nepalese Constituent Assembly election, November 2013 in electionguide.org

5   John Whelpton, 'Nine Years On: The 1999 Election and Nepalese Politics Since the 1990 Janandolan', Himalaya.socanth.cam. ac.uk

6   A summary is available at mea.gov.in

7   PM Modi's speech at National Trauma Centre Nepal on 25 November 2014 is available at pmindia.gov.in

8   'Nepal SC Stays Federalism Deal Reached by Political Parties', TheWire.in, June 20 2015.

9   Though the interim Constitution had referred to 'an autonomous Madhesh Pradesh', during the negotiations, the Madhesi parties were willing to accept two provinces covering the twenty districts.

10 Human Rights Watch, 'Like we are not Nepali; Protest and Police crackdown on the Terai region of Nepal', 16 October 2015.

11 Ibid.

12 'President's Letter to CA Chairman that Drew Flak Made Public', THT online, 14 September 2015.

13 Author's personal recollection.

14 'Oli le punah gijyaye madhesi lai, manav sanglo na bhayee makhe sanglo bhay ko tippani', Hulakinews.com, 4 October 2015.

15 'Oli le naya tukka: rukhbat dui teen wata aamp jharda kin aatinne!', onlinekhabar.com

16 'Oli le sodhe – UP ra Bihar pani chahiyo? Madhesi dal bhanchhan – humiliate gariyo', pahilopost.com, 7 January 2015. See also 'Ekantipur Report: Oli refuses to apologise to Madhesis', *Kathmandu Post*, 8 January 2015.

17 Shubhajit Roy, 'Make Seven Changes to Your Constitution India tells Nepal', *Indian Express*, 13 July 2015.

18 Bhim Bhurtel, 'India Has No Right to Pretend It Is an Inclusive Democracy', 18 September 2018, *Asia Times* quoting senior Maoist leader Narayan Kaji Shreshta.

Chapter 4: The Post-Constitution Fallout

1   'Oli le sodhe – UP ra Bihar pani chahiyo? Madhesi dal bhanchhan – humiliate gariyo', Pahilopost.com, 7 January 2015.

2   'UN, Nepal Blockade Puts Millions of Children at Risk', BBC News, 30 November 2015.

3   Ross Adkin, 'Anti-India Protests Erupt in Nepal as Fuel Rationing Bites', Reuters, 28 September 2015.

4   'Govt recalls Nepal's Ambassador to India, Upadhyay', *Kathmandu Post*, 6 May 2016.

5   I recall a meeting that I had briefly attended, at the house of businessman Binod Chowdhry with participation by several important Nepalese personalities, which was addressed by Sri Sri Ravi Shankar, where he spoke in favour of Nepal being a Hindu state.

6   Prashant Jha, 'Nepal secularism has a pronounced Hindu tilt', *Hindustan Times*, 16 September 2015.

7   Harinder Baweja, 'ISI Consolidates Hold in Nepal through Politicians, Businessmen After Hijack of IC 814', *India Today*, 12 June 2000.

8   'Statements Not Enough: Deuba', *Himalayan Times*, 11 May 2020; Kamal Dev Bhattarai, 'Nepal Proposes Talks on Kalapani, Awaits India's Response', TheWire.in, 6 December 2019.

9   PTI, 'Nepal's Supreme Court Reinstates Dissolved House of Representatives', *Economic Times*, 23 February 2021.

10 In a judgment in March 2021, the Nepalese Supreme Court decided to take away the name Nepalese Communist Party from the ruling party on the grounds that it had been allocated earlier to another party. Accordingly, the current NCP stood 'dismissed'. The two parties that had merged would also stand revived. Yubaraj Ghimire, 'Nepal Top Court Quashes 2018 Formation of Ruling Nepal Communist Party', *Indian Express*, 8 March 2021.

11 https://www.constituteproject.org/constitution/Nepal_2015.pdf, pp. 45–46.

12 Tika R. Pradhan, 'Supreme Court Orders Government Not to Enforce Citizenship Ordinance', *Kathmandu Post*, 11 June 2021.

13 'Supreme Court Relieves Oli's 20 Ministers of Jobs', Online Khabar (English), 22 June 2021.

14 On the occasion of International Yoga Day, 21 June 2021, Oli asserted that yoga was discovered in Nepal and not in India, which did not exist at the time.

15 Shyam Saran, 'India Must Engage with Nepal – without Intervening', *Indian Express*, 29 May 2021. The grand welcome accorded to ex-king Gyanendra and his wife at the Kumbh Mela in Haridwar in April 2021 has perhaps contributed to these conspiracy theories.

16 Tika R. Pradhan, 'Oli's Aversion to Secularism and Federalism Becoming Apparent', *Kathmandu Post*, 5 July 2021.

17 *Kathmandu Post*, 12 June 2021.

Chapter 5: Disputed Boundary: Kalapani, Lipulekh and Limpiyadhura

1   Some sources in the public domain mention the total area as 400 sq. km. I am also grateful to Shekhar Pathak and Lalit Pant for their excellent paper, Kalapani aur Lipulekh: Ek Padtal published by Pahad, Talla Danda, Nainital, Uttarakhand in July 2020.

2   Official spokesperson's response to media query on 20 May 2020, Ministry of External Affairs, www.mea.gov.in

3   Special Correspondent, 'Nepal Protests New Political Map of India', *The Hindu*, 7 November 2019.

4   Official spokesperson's response to media queries on inauguration of road on 8 May in Pithoragarh district, Uttarakhand, 9 May 2020, in www.mea.gov.in

5   Mayank Singh, 'Nepal Might Have Raised Lipulekh Issue at China's Behest, Hints Army Chief', *New Indian Express*, 15 May 2020.

6   WION Web Team, 'Our Army Will Fight If Necessary: Nepal's Defence Minister on Indian Army Chief's Remark', 27 May 2020.

7   Kallol Bhattacharjee, 'Adityanath's Comments on Nepal Inappropriate: Oli', *The Hindu*, 10 June 2020.

8   Full text available in Avtar Singh Bhasin (ed.), *Nepal-India, Nepal-China Relations, Documents 1947-June 2005* Geetika Publishers, New Delhi, 2005, vol. I, doc. no. 1, Enclosure II, pp. 16–18, Section I.

9   Reasons for not attaching a map are detailed in Sam Cowan's article 'The Gorkha War and its Aftermath', *Record Nepal*, 14 November 2020.

10 Nrip Singh, former chief secretary of Uttarakhand, article in *Garhwal Post*, 27 August 2020.

11 Swami Pranavanda, *Kailash and Manasarovar*, June 1949.

12 Charles A. Sherring, *Western Tibet and the British Borderlands*, originally published in London, 1906, reprinted by Asian Educational Services, New Delhi, 1993, p. 50.

13 Swami Pranavananda, *Kailas Manasarovar*, June 1949.

14 Efforts are currently underway to construct a road from Darchula (Nepal) to the Tinkar Pass. This would provide an alternative to Lipulekh Pass for the Nepalese who wish to access Tibet. See Navin Bhatt, 'Chin tak naya sadak marg bana raha Nepal, Kathmandu ka badega samarik mahatva, dragon ko hoga phayda', Livehindustan. com.

15 A.S. Bhasin (ed.), *Nepal-India, Nepal-China Relations, Documents 1947-June 2005*, vol. IV, Appendix-IV, pp. 2024–35.

16 ibid., Doc No. 1, Enclosure IV, pp. 21–22, Section I.

17 This is another riverine boundary segment between India and Nepal along the Narayani Gandak River on an east–west axis. Since the river has changed course, territory that was on the Nepalese side at one time has now shifted to the Indian side. In view of the land being very fertile, villagers from both sides are keen to use it for cultivation, thereby creating law and order issues from time to time.

18 mea.gov.in

19 Some sources mention the area as 60 sq. km.

20 Sam Cowan, 'The Gorkha War and its Aftermath', *Record Nepal*, 14 November 2020,

21 J.L. Cox, 'Papers Respecting the Nepal War from the Papers Regarding the Administration of Marquis of Hastings in India, Printed in Conformity to the Resolution of the Court of Proprietors of East-India Stock of the 3rd March 1824', quoted in Cowan, Art, 14 November 2020, p. 57.

22 Dwarika Dhungel, Jagat Bhusal and Narendra Khanal, 'North Western Boundary of Nepal', *Journal of International Affairs*, vol. 3, pp. 1–41, 2020, Department of International Relations and Diplomacy, Tribhuvan University, Kathmandu, Nepal pp. 25–26.

23 https://pahar.in/wpfb-file/1927-Skeleton-Map-Of-Nepal-By-SOI-jpg

24 See also Harka Gurung, *Maps of Nepal* publisher (White Orchid Books), which has more details on this map.

25 Some articles in the public domain suggest that the territorial claim has increased from 60 to 400 sq. km.

26 In a letter from the secretary to the governor general, I. Addam, dated 5 September 1815, to G.W. Traill, commissioner to Kumaon, it is clearly stated in paragraph 2 that 'The Governor General entirely approves your having declined to transfer to the Chountra Bum Sah the two villages of Kuntee. and Nabee in Pergunah Byans . . .' A.S. Bhasin (ed.), *Nepal–India, Nepal–China Relations, Documents 1947–June 2005*, vol. IV, Appendix-IV, pp. 2024–35.

27 Sudheer Sharma, 'Kalapani: Kin la kasari Bharat le Seema Micheko Cha, Mulyankan', Issue of Sawan 2055 (Nepali calendar).

28 Though Shreshta lists eighteen posts, the foreign minister of Nepal had listed seventeen Indian military checkposts in his statement to the Rashtriya Panchayat on 25 July 1969. Budhi Narayan Shreshta, *Border Management of Nepal*, Bhumichitra Co. Pvt Ltd, P.O. Box 6769, Kathmandu, Nepal. See also Sam Cowan's article in Nepal Record.

29 Cowan, Nepal Record 14 December 2015.

30 Sudheer Sharma, 'Kalapani: Kin la kasari Bharat le Seema Micheko Cha, Mulyankan', Issue of Sawan 2055 (Nepali calendar).

31 Told to the author by Nrip S. Napalchyal, former chief secretary of Uttarakhand, who belongs to Byans Patti.

32 Shyam Saran, 'Thinking Through the Nepal Policy', *The Hindu*, 24 August 2020; also see A.S. Bhasin, *Nepal India Documents*, vol. I. Foreign minister's statement on a private member's bill in the Rashtriya Panchayat, 25 July 1969, p. 547, for a listing of the seventeen military checkposts.

33 Paper by Pathak and Pant, July 2020.

34 A.S. Bhasin (ed.), *Nepal–India, Nepal–China Relations, Documents 1947–June 2005*, vol. V., pp. 3494–99.

Chapter 6: Historical Treaties: Is It Time for Revision?

1 For full text and accompanying letters, see Bhasin (ed), vol. I, Section II, pp. 94.

2 Ibid.

3 Pandit Nehru's speech in Parliament, 6 December 1950.

4   For full text, see P.N. Chopra (chief editor), *The Collected Works of Sardar Vallabhbhai Patel*, vol. XV (1 January 1950–15 December 1950), Konark Publishers Ltd., 1999, p. 275.

5   Interview by Prime Minister Kirti Nidhi Bista, *Rising Nepal*, 24 June 1969, Bhasin (ed.) *Nepal-India, Nepal-China Relations*, p. 522.

6   'Ayo Gorkhali!', 'The Gorkhas are upon you!' is the battle cry of one of the world's famous hands of fighting men: Nepal's 'happy warriors', *New York Times*, 18 October 1964.

7   Sanjay Sharma and Deepak Thapa, 'Taken for Granted, Nepalese Migration to India', Centre for Study of Labour and Mobility, Working Paper III, Kathmandu, 2013, pp. 31–32.

8   Sharma and Thapa, pp. 33–37.

9   Himalayan News Service, 'UK Did Not Accept Proposal, says Prime Minister', *Himalayan Times*, 17 June 2019.

10   The British refer to them as 'Gurkhas', whereas India refers to them as 'Gorkhas'.

Chapter 7: The Economic Partnership: We Can Grow Together

1   Press Trust of India, 'Nepal Recalls Envoy after she called Qatar "Open Jail"', *Indian Express*, 26 September 2013.

2   Devendra Raj Pandey, 'The Legacy of Nepal's Failed Development', in Sebastian von Einsiedel, David M. Malone and Suman Pradhan (ed.), *Nepal in Transition: From People's War to Fragile Peace*, Cambridge University Press, New Delhi, 2012.

3   Constantino Xavier and Riya Sinha, 'When Land Comes in the Way: India's Connectivity Infrastructure in Nepal', Brookings India, 12 August 2020.

4   For an interesting account of the Kosi negotiations, see Sandeep Bhardwaj, 'Political Economy of Indo-Nepal Hydro-Cooperation, Centre for Policy Research'.

5   J. Oza, 'Resisting for the River: Local Struggle Against the Proposed Saptkoshi River Dam', SIT Digital Collections, Spring 2014.

6   For the full text see www.mowr.gov.in, the website of the Ministry of Water Resources, India.

7   Website of the Indian embassy in Kathmandu, www.indembkathmandu.gov.in

8   India tourism statistics 2019, Research Division, Ministry of Tourism, Government of India.

9   TNN, 'Manipal Group of Companies Ready to Pull Out of Nepal', *Times of India*, 16 September 2011.

Chapter 8: Humanitarian Assistance and Disaster Relief

1   Some details are available in: i) 'Four Big Steps in India's Nepal Earthquake Rescue Effort', *Economic Times*, 27 April 2015; ii) Saneet Chakradeo, 'Neighbourhood First Responder: India's Humanitarian Assistance and Disaster Relief', Policy Brief, Brookings India, Sambandh Regional Connectivity Initiative, August 2020; iii) Media briefings by foreign secretary and others on 26 and 29 April 2015 at mea.gov.in; iv) Rajya Sabha Question No. 380, 23 July 2015.

Chapter 9: *Roti–Beti Rishta*: The Civilizational Connect

1   Practice in ancient India where a lady chose her husband.

2   Amish Raj Mulmi, 'Swami Nirgunananda: The Monk Who Would Have Given His Kingdom Away', TheWire.in, 1 July 2017.

3   For a more detailed account of the Sikh connection in Nepal, see 'Sikh Heritage of Nepal', 2019, www.indembkathmandu.gov.in

4   Siddhant Sibbal, '"Roti beti ka rishta" is Old Rhetoric, Says Deputy Chief of the Foreign Affairs Department of the Ruling Party in Nepal', WION News, 22 June 2020.

Chapter 10: Enter the Dragon: The Northern Neighbour, the West and the Rest

1   For a detailed account from a Nepalese perspective, see Amish Raj Mulmi, *All Roads lead North: Nepal's Turn to China*, Context, 2021.

2   Ibid.

3   P.N. Chopra (chief editor), *The Collected Works of Sardar Vallabhbhai Patel*, vol. XV (1 January–15 December 1950), p. 275.

4   Avtar Singh Bhasin (ed.), *Nepal-India, Nepal-China Relations, Documents, 1947–June 2005*, vol. I, p. 94.

5   Sangeeta Thapliyal, 'Contesting Mutual Security: India Nepal Relations', Observer Research Foundation Commentaries, 26 June 2003.

6   An interesting account can be found in Gen Sam Cowan's article 'A Secret Nepal File and the Battle for Information', Nepal Record, 11 September 2017.

7   Author's personal recollection.

8   Joint press statement following PM Oli's visit to China, March 2016, www.mofa.gov.np

9   Gopal Sharma, 'Nepal Pushes to End Dependency on India with China Rail, Tunnel Deals', Reuters, 13 October 2019.

10 'Tibetan Monk Shamar Rinpoche Cremated in Nepal', BBC News, 31 July 2014.

11 'Budhi Gandaki Again Awarded to China Gezhouba without Free Competition', Setopati, 18 Falgun 2077 (Nepal Samvat), en.setopati.com

12 'Bhattarai's Recent Embezzlement Allegations Against Top-Rung Leaders Need to be Examined', Record, Nepal, 13 October 2020, recordnepal.com

13 Sangam Parsain, 'Cost of Pokhara Airport Project Unrealistic: Mahat', *Kathmandu Post*, 8 March 2014; Lal Prasad Sharma, 'Construction of New International Airport in Pokhara On Track Despite Lockdown', *Kathmandu Post*, 14 June 2020.

14 Himalayan News Service, 'Exim Bank makes Pokhara Airport's Loan Effective', *Himalayan Times*, 11 June 2017.

15 Yubaraj Biswas, 'Chinese Investment Pouring in Jhapa', July 28, 2018, myrepublica.nagariknetwork.com

16 https://www.eoibeijing.gov.in/economic-and-trade-relation.php

17 Anil Giri, 'Nepal PM proposes trilateral partnership with China and India', *Hindustan Times*, 16 October 2016.

18 Ananth Krishnan, Prashant Jha, 'Chinese Foundation Plans $3 Billion Project in Nepal', *The Hindu*, 17 July 2011.

19 Question No. 1515, 'Chinese Study Centres along Border', Lok Sabha, 4 March 2015, https://mea.gov.in/lok-sabha.htm?dtl/24876/Q_NO1515_CHINESE_STUDY_CENTRES_ALONG_BORDER

20   Since then, politics has taken a different turn, with the Supreme Court annulling the merger of the CPN (UML) and NCP (Maoist Centre) into the NCP in a judgment on 6 March 2021 and restoring status quo ante prior to the merger.

21   Anup Kaphle, 'A Blueprint for Consolidating Power: China Exports Xi Jinping Thought to Nepal', *Kathmandu Post*, 24 September 2019.

22   See state councillor and foreign minister Wang Yi's comment on Fmprc.gov.cn, 27 July 2020.

23   Press Trust of India, 'China holds COVID-19 Vice-Ministerial Meeting with Pakistan, Bangladesh, Nepal and Sri Lanka', *Times of India*, 12 November 2020.

24   Pradip R. Sagar, 'Nepal Objecting to India's Roadwork at "Someone Else's Behest": Army Chief', *Week*, 15 May 2020.

25   Times Now, '"Why are Gurkhas joining the Indian Army?": China Wants Nepal NGO to Audit', *Economic Times*, 12 August 2020.

26   Sam Cowan, 'Prisoners of War', Record, 8 December 2014; see also, Prashant Jha, 'Post 1962, China Treated Gorkha POWs Better, Indoctrinated Them: Research', *Hindustan Times*, 1 December 2014.

27   'Chinese Encroachment in Humla? China Denies It, So Does MOFA', Himalayan News Service, 24 September 2020.

28   Geeta Mohan, 'India, China begin First Joint Afghan Project', *India Today*, 16 October 2018.

29   Author's personal recollection.

30   'China, Nepal Agree to Complete Ongoing Bilateral Projects in a Timely Manner', Xinhua, 4 December 2018.

31   Seulki Lee, 'Korean Movement Gains Political Foothold in Nepal', *Nepali Times*, 1–7 April 2016; Yubaraj Ghimire, 'Nepal PM KP Oli Criticised for Accepting Church Award', *Indian Express*, 3 December 2018.

32   Binod Ghimire, 'Why the MCC Compact Courted Controversy in Nepal', *Kathmandu Post*, 9 January 2020.

33   Susan Hangen, 'Creating a "New Nepal": The Ethnic Dimension, Policy Studies', 34, East West Centre, Washington, 2007, p. 43, https://www.files.ethz.ch/isn/45633/ps034.pdf

34 Ramchandra Paswan, Raviprakash Verma, 'Unstarred Question No:1097 Answered on:01.03.2000 ISI's Anti-India Activities from Nepal', https://eparlib.nic.in/handle/123456789/440903?view_type=browse

35 V.K. Shashikumar, 'Pakistan's Export of Fake Currency via Nepal', Indian Defence Review, vol. 23, 4 October–December 2008.

Epilogue: Uncertain Future: The Way Forward

1 Regional Comprehensive Economic Partnership between ASEAN countries, China, Japan, South Korea, Australia and New Zealand. India participated in the negotiations but eventually decided not to join.

2 The Shanghai Cooperation Organization comprises several Central Asian countries, Russia, China as well as India and Pakistan.

3 The QUAD, comprising US, Japan, Australia and India met at summit level for the first time in March 2021.

4 Bay of Bengal Initiative for Multi-Sectoral Technical and Economic Cooperation. Members include Bangladesh, Bhutan, Nepal, India, Sri Lanka, Myanmar and Thailand.

5 Under the Leave Travel Concession scheme of the Government of India, government servants are entitled to flight/train tickets for the entire family to travel on holiday within the country once in four years.